CONCUSSION INC.

THE END OF FOOTBALL AS WE KNOW IT

IRVIN MUCHNICK

ECW PRESS

Copyright © Irvin Muchnick, 2015

Published by ECW Press
2120 Queen Street East, Suite 200, Toronto, Ontario, Canada M4E 1E2
416-694-3348 / info@ecwpress.com

Library and Archives Canada Cataloguing in Publication

Muchnick, Irvin, author
Concussion Inc. : the end of football as we know it / Irvin Muchnick.

ISBN 978-1-77041-138-8
also issued as: 978-1-77090-650-1 (PDF); 978-1-77090-651-8 (ePub)

1. Football injuries—United States. 2. Brain—Concussion—United
States. 3. Football—Moral and ethical aspects—United States. I. Title.

RC1220.F6M82 2015   617.1'027   C2014-902582-3
C2014-902583-1

MIX
Paper from
responsible sources
FSC
www.fsc.org   FSC® C016245

Editor for the press: Michael Holmes
Cover design: David Gee
Cover images: brain © angelhell/iStockphoto; helmet © lishenjun/iStockphoto

Printed and bound in Canada by Friesens   5   4   3   2   1

TO JIM LEESON, 1930–2010
Reporter, Associated Press.
Director, Race Relations Information Center.
Mentor.
Friend.

CONTENTS

INTRODUCTION

In the summer of 2011, I changed the name of my blog from *Wrestling Babylon* to *Concussion Inc.* This reflected the latest tweak of an oeuvre whose continuous thread is: *if pro wrestling is as fake as everyone says, then what are we supposed to make of the rest of the world, which never ceases to imitate it?* Epistemological angels have danced on the heads of thinner pins.

Wrestling Babylon was also the title of my too-long-marinating collection of articles for mostly mainstream publications about behind--the-scenes maneuvering and scandal in an industry that graduated in the 1980s from territorial mafia to international brand, thanks to the emergence of cable TV; a burst of rampant, made-in-America deregulation; and late-empire cultural devolution. The latter was the stuff of Edward Gibbon. Turns out that global hegemony isn't as easy on the old collective psyche as it looks.

A few people, some of them wearing thick eyeglasses, took my thesis as seriously as I did. Vince McMahon watched (or directed) his wife, Linda, in two wildly expensive and unsuccessful runs for a United States Senate seat from Connecticut. For presidential aspirants, a skit on *Raw* became as obligatory as televised debates. And one of the most quoted gurus on the newly risen issue of traumatic brain injury in sports — as well as one of the most successful profiteers therefrom — was the medical director of WWE.

In short, *Concussion Inc.* was the right cliché at the right time. You've heard of Fast Food Nation, Steroid Nation, Murder Inc.? (Plus, perhaps, the Green Day rock album and Broadway operetta *American Idiot*?) Concussion Inc. became a nod to the notion first formulated in *Horse Feathers* by Groucho Marx, who longed for the Huxley College football team to finally get a school it could be proud of. Not since the surgeon general's report on the dangers of cigarette smoking in 1964 had American corporatocracy found a public health crisis so worthy of its capacity to equivocate, rationalize, delay, and deny.

As I confessed in the revised introduction to my second book, *Chris & Nancy: The True Story of the Benoit Murder-Suicide and Pro Wrestling's Cocktail of Death*, I gave too much weight to drug abuse and too little to concussion syndrome, in the immediate postmortem of that tragedy. By the time Chris Benoit committed his heinous crimes in 2007, Dr. Bennet Omalu, a Nigerian-born forensic pathologist who had the fatal flaw of being beholden to no old boys' network, already had begun finding accumulations of tau protein in his brain autopsies of prematurely dead Pittsburgh Steelers. Omalu labeled as "chronic traumatic encephalopathy," or CTE, the associated phenomenon of depression, loss of impulse control, and dementia, which was consistent with similar findings of early neurocognitive decline in boxers going back to the 1920s.

Omalu's Benoit study, released three months after the horrific incident in Georgia in 2007, was the first under the auspices of the Sports Legacy Institute. That group was started by Chris Nowinski, proud holder of the American elite trifecta: Harvard education, WWE superstardom, traumatic brain-injury author-activist.

From there, things only got better — or worse, depending on your perspective — in the person of Dr. Joseph Maroon, a neurosurgeon whose patient list spanned all the way from the Saudi royal family to wrestling legend Bruno Sammartino. Maroon was an aging anti-aging huckster whose University of Pittsburgh Medical Center colleagues, at minimum, were linked to the steroid and human growth hormone use of the six-time Super Bowl champion Pittsburgh Steelers — a team *paid by* its doctors for the right to advertise themselves as its official sports-medicine practitioners.

Maroon lied about the back story of Steeler Terry Long's suicide. Maroon lied about his and WWE's access to Omalu's Chris Benoit brain study. Maroon and his co-physician entrepreneurs in the Steel City (where health care was the main post-industrial employment growth center) played fast and loose with facts on the efficacy and standards of their ImPACT "concussion management system," which one state's laws after another's gradually foisted on public high school football programs in order to appear to be doing something . . . anything . . . to counteract the systematic braining of young American males. Maroon fudged his relationship with a helmet manufacturers' borderline-fraudulent study — the latest in the serial scientific book-cooking in which he engaged for more than a decade as a member of the National Football League's head-injury advisory committee.

Joe Maroon was the white coat who put the *Inc.* in *Concussion Inc.*

As my rebranded blog took off, many readers tried to cast me as some sort of concussion cop, but that was never my purpose. Wisely or not, I even somewhat resisted the temptation to expand my scope into sports other than football, and especially into female athletes (even though there is credible evidence that comparatively innocuous actions like soccer heading are also quite dangerous, and that girls and women are more susceptible to concussions than boys and men). All along, I wanted to stick to two basic points:

- Like boxing — and unlike soccer, cheerleading, and overly vigorous tooth-flossing — football is uniquely and even intentionally a blood sport. Traumatic brain injury is not incidental but central. Further, the NFL is a $10-billion-a-year industry with a footprint on our culture that long ago passed beyond "out of control." On the 1 to 11 scale of the guitarist's amp in *This Is Spinal Tap*, football is a 12.
- Purported corrective measures should be viewed with deep suspicion. The alignment of the money forces makes it far likelier that "solutions" are self-serving cottage industries rather than of genuine public health net benefit.

By no means do I claim to be on the ground floor of any of these insights. Robert Lipsyte, whose keyboard I can't even carry, was on to the trap of what he dubbed "SportsWorld" decades ago. Matt Chaney, a little-known author in Missouri, has exhaustively documented the cycles of death and hocus-pocus safety measures in American football; his research gives much of the credit for this persistent national delusion to the successive rise of, first, rotogravure Sunday newspaper magazines, then radio and television. By comparison, your humble blogger was and is a sociological bottom feeder — a mere investigative reporter/social critic with perspectives not found much elsewhere.

No, ground floor was Chris Nowinski. Ground floor was Alan Schwarz of the *New York Times*. Compelled, like a ball-hawking free safety, to the infliction of equal-opportunity offense, I've alternated praise and criticism of those two worthies: praise of their prescience and basic accuracy; criticism of the Nowinski group's ill-advised decision to accept a $1 million NFL grant and of Schwarz's naive reporting of developments flowing from the NFL's new and responsible age of "concussion awareness." (In the fall of 2013, Nowinski reprised the whole process with his old employer, WWE — trading a seven-figure research grant commitment for a Sports Legacy Institute award for corporate responsibility. The honor is known, inappropriately enough, as the "Impact" award.)

With respect to Nowinski in particular, I do appreciate that he has a more intense relationship with the football industry than I do, that he is more emotionally invested in the goal of "saving the sport from itself" than I'll ever be, and that he works on the front lines — with professional players and with the star-struck kids and parents for whom the pros are the most wobbly of role models.

In the end, the *Concussion Inc.* blog has been whatever it is. Sensing saturation, I largely moved on to the under-covered scandals of sexual abuse in American club swimming — a subject my collaborator Tim Joyce and I find we have all too much to ourselves. And hey, if I wake up on a Sunday morning determined to wax rhapsodic about Norah Jones's "Chasing Pirates" or the St. Louis Cardinals' fire-balling relief pitcher, Trevor Rosenthal (whom I've dubbed "the Ashkenazi Express" on Twitter, much to the cringe-inducement of my kids) . . . well, what is the management of ConcussionInc.Net LLP supposed to do about it? Threaten to pay me less than nothing? (Readers of this book should know that neither Norah nor Trevor will be found otherwise herein.)

I hope the format of this book gets across, at the very least, my disinterest in journalistic convention. I organized the content of my daily noodlings into topics. Sometimes I kept original columns intact. Sometimes I cheated, by adapting and rearranging verbiage from multiple posts, in the hope of clarifying what is a retrospective reading experience with an open ending. Continuity or reader conning? You tell me.

No jokes, please, about whether the result is evidence of the author's own early onset dementia. If this modest volume contributes to the documentation of our strange times — when bread and circuses rule, and societal mental health is an afterthought — I'll be a little happier and a little less dependent on Obamacare.

Irvin Muchnick
Berkeley, California

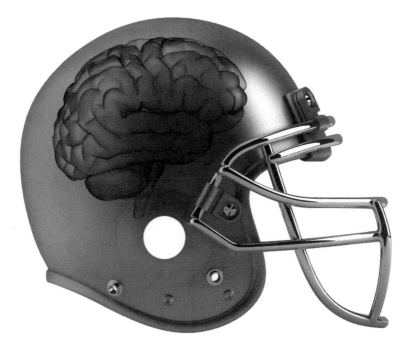

THE UNITED STATES OF FOOTBALL

Sean Pamphilon, a one-time ESPN production assistant who has risen
to the ranks of elite sports documentary filmmakers, has produced the
very best movie on the football concussion crisis, *The United States
of Football*. Though not accessible everywhere, it has about as wide a
release as is possible for any nonfiction film not directed by Michael
Moore.

Whatever you do, go see *USOF*.

As someone who's not paid well enough to hide his natural can-
tankerousness, I'll be discussing below my disappointment that
Pamphilon made the movie he could readily get lots of people to pay

to watch, rather than the one I would have made were I as brilliant at this medium as he is. Read on for one person's critique, but at the same time, pay no attention to the grump behind the screen.

I also am proud to call Sean a friend, so let's get the narcissistic part of this review out of the way first.

For reasons that must have cost his poor parents thousands of dollars in fees to child psychologists, Pamphilon was bound and determined to include my voice in *USOF*. In order to fulfill that promise, he had to go out of his way to interview me at the end of a trip to the Bay Area to visit a dying relative. All kidding aside, I am grateful and humbled to be juxtaposed in this work with assorted journalistic betters in two spots.

One clip has me sourly pointing out that the National Football League's underwriting of federal research on traumatic brain injury is equivalent to the Tobacco Institute's drafting of a report by the surgeon general.

In the other one, I verbally bodyslam Dr. Joe "ImPACT" Maroon of the University of Pittsburgh Medical Center, the Pittsburgh Steelers, the NFL coterie of book-cooking scientific researchers, and, of course, World Wrestling Entertainment.

(Not for the first time, I'm struck by how the real WWE reveals more about the way the world works than the fake NFL does. *USOF* also has on camera Pittsburgh radio commentator Mark Madden, who boasts wrestling industry broadcast roots — along with, obviously, Chris Nowinski, the Harvard football player turned WWE performer whose investigations into his own bout with concussions permanently changed the national narrative of this issue.)

If there's too much Muchnick for everyone else's taste, there's too much Bob Costas for mine. This is not directly a knock on Costas (also an acquaintance verging on friend) — for only a fool could fail to acknowledge that he is the best we have, maybe even a little too sharp for sports. The setup in which Costas asks the unanswerable question — "What can

a football official responsibly tell a parent about the safety of football?"
— is perfect.

Costas with a pitchfork, however, becomes a mere rhetorical Houdini, a little too fuzzy for full-blown social criticism. Pamphilon isn't Ken Burns (thankfully), and this film doesn't need the imprimatur and homilies of the most recognized face in network sports. When Costas rips ESPN for its now-defunct violence-pandering football segment "You Got Jacked Up!" I feel the same as when he pontificates about the failure of CBS's Masters coverage to probe the controversy over the racist Augusta National Golf Club. Personally, what I want to see is whether Costas, who hobnobs with swimming's biggest stars and anchors NBC's Olympics package, will ever use his platform for a word or three about the national disgrace that is USA Swimming's generation-long widespread youth sexual abuse and cover-up, now the subject of Congressional and FBI investigations.

(Yes, your reviewer is a free-range curmudgeon. Again, the bosses at ConcussionInc.Net LLP don't pay me well enough to be otherwise.)

Though "You Got Jacked Up!" was indefensible, *USOF* is, if anything, too restrained in its depiction of football porn. The movie presents only one monster hit featured on that segment, with associated cackles and guffaws by Chris Berman, Tom Jackson, and the other ESPN frat boys. I believe an extended montage would have reinforced the point more powerfully than the clucking Costas and other talking heads.

In the same vein, Pamphilon's hour-and-40-minute feature should have had more than a polite once-over-lightly on all the big hits orchestrated across the "United States of football" every single day, by vicariously bloodthirsty peewee coaches whose orders are dutifully and routinely carried out, pipsqueak on pipsqueak. This is what I mean about Pamphilon not making the same film I would have ordered off the shelf.

Then again, that wasn't this director's vision. His is a frankly

NFL-centric story, with a *Band of Brothers* frame, and it was exe-cuted sincerely and beautifully. There's no doubting the bond between Pamphilon and retired player Kyle Turley, whose life's second act as a musician provides the soundtrack, even as his activism against the NFL's default on traumatic brain injuries lurches toward a complex moral.

Always fighting, on the field and off, Turley is inspiring and tragic. But for my money, the male star of the movie is Sean Morey, the special-teams kamikaze whose frightening post-career loss of impulse control, accompanied by ritual denial, plays out in real time on the screen in painful, emotionally naked scenes with his wife. Successive footage shows Morey pushing the NFL Players Association toward honest research of concussion syndrome and fair play for its victims; censoring himself under pressure from the powers that be at a Super Bowl week press conference; and ultimately quitting in disgust the very committee he had co-founded to bring transparency and justice to this ongoing problem.

This is heartbreaking stuff, yet it's equaled and surpassed in scenes involving the two female stars of the film: Eleanor Perfetto and Sylvia Mackey, the "living widows" of, respectively, chronic traumatic encephalopathy–impaired Ralph Wenzel and Hall of Famer John Mackey. (Both women became actual widows during the shooting of the movie.) Here's where Pamphilon's camera is indeed unsparing, as he shows us legends in wheelchairs far too young, drooling, heads at grotesque angles, unable to feed themselves. Clearly, he made the cin-ematic decision that this particular brand of pornography was more important to exploit than the by now overly familiar video of 100 G-force collisions. And he may well be right about that.

As America cruises through yet another season of football carnage — death, catastrophic injury, silent and inexorable erosion of the gross national cognitive product, all in the name of mass entertainment at the supposed national hearth — what matters most is not whether filmmakers as talented and passionate as Pamphilon make my movies or their own. No, let me correct that: it is essential that they make only their own. Phenomena like the systematic braining of boys and the systematic raping of girls — both byproducts of our obsessive and pro-fessionalized sports culture — take hold and persist precisely because we're spectators, consumers, looking over our shoulders at what other people are saying, rather than using our own eyes and ears and other senses, and thinking and speaking for ourselves.

Let a hundred *USOF*s bloom. Then let's roll up our sleeves and do something about what this sport is doing to us, and what we are doing to ourselves.

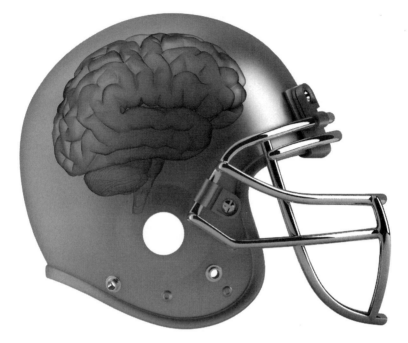

SANTA CLARA SYMPOSIUM
ON SPORTS LAW AND ETHICS

And now for a heartwarming anecdote from last weekend's Pro
Football Hall of Fame festivities that you probably don't know: the
executive director of the National Football League Players Association,
DeMaurice Smith, crashed the dinner in Canton, Ohio, which is traditionally reserved for Hall of Famers and new inductees, and started
to speak. According to NFL legend Joe DeLamielleure, blogging for
Dave Pear's Independent Football Veterans, around a dozen guys
walked out in the middle of Smith's remarks.

The NFLPA chief "had no idea that this audience consisted

mostly of pre-1993 players," said DeLamielleure, who estimated that the Hall of Famers in attendance included around 40 guys who receive monthly pension checks of exactly $176 from the $9-billion-a-year NFL. Confronted by the retirees, Smith said the "legacy fund" negotiated in the new collective bargaining agreement (CBA) would increase them to between $1,000 and $1,500 a month.

But here's the thing, football fans: a lot of NFL veterans, for good reason, don't trust the NFLPA to negotiate on their behalf and honorably administer the new centimillion-dollar legacy fund.

After a group of the richiest-rich NFLers filed their antitrust lawsuit in Minnesota, *Brady v. NFL*, which helped end the lockout, Judge Susan Nelson of U.S. District Court allowed a class of disabled retiree plaintiffs to join the lawsuit. That contingent, led by Carl Eller, didn't obstruct the consummation of the CBA and the resumption of the 2011 season. But the Eller class action does demand a seat at the table as the devil in the details of the legacy fund gets hashed out.

Another set of facts with which few in the general public are familiar is the sickeningly corrupt history of the NFLPA under DeMaurice Smith's predecessor, the late Gene Upshaw.

According to dissident retirees, the "union" not only abandoned their interests in a morally and financially sound pension and disability system, but also blatantly ripped off the athletic and celebrity personae of ex-players for royalties from the Madden video game and other licensed merchandise. These measures contributed to feathering a bloated and overpaid NFLPA bureaucracy and enriched Upshaw in particular (along with "super agents" with NFLPA ties, such as Tom Condon) to the tune of impossible millions.

A new book, *The Unbroken Line: The Untold Story of Gridiron Greats and Their Struggle to Save Professional Football* — co-authored by former Dallas Cowboys tight end Billy Joe DuPree and his lawyer, Spencer Kopf — traces the narrative to the end-game negotiations of the 1982 players' strike. Today the key fault line in the fight to design equitable pension and disability plans is between active players (who tend to defer to their agents and the NFLPA) and those who retired before 1993.

When he accepted the NFLPA post following Upshaw's 2008 death from cancer, "De" Smith pledged "due diligence" of the organization's controversial past practices. But dissidents say he has kept the Upshaw office team intact.

What makes all this even more intriguing and grotesque is that Smith is a former aide, and by some accounts best friend, of U.S. attorney general Eric Holder. That gives fresh perspective to explanations for why President Barack Obama, a hopeless March Madness addict, crusades on superficial fan issues, such as abolition of college football's Bowl Championship Series, while saying nothing about the Big Sports public health issue of concussions.

I don't think for a minute that Obama is the problem in contemporary America. But I know he's not the solution. There was a time in our country when we elected presidents, but in the mauve days of late empire, the only thing we're doing is appointing Jocksniffers in Chief.

8 SEPTEMBER 2011 --------------------------

Today I attended the second annual Sports Law Symposium at Santa Clara University Law School. I wanted to see the advertised panel on concussions, including the keynote speech by DeMaurice Smith, executive director of the National Football League Players Association.

Dissident NFL retirees, who don't like the union's performance in safeguarding their health and interests, say Smith no-showed his scheduled appearance at last year's Santa Clara symposium.[1]

I enjoyed the opportunity to meet symposium panelist John Hogan, the Atlanta attorney who has done valuable work representing retired players (plus others from all walks of life) on disability issues. The symposium's proceedings book includes a comprehensive and lucid paper by Hogan entitled "Concussions, Brain Injury, and NFL Disability." I highly recommend the article, available at the Dave Pear post listed below.

Regarding De Smith, I was disappointed when the organizers of the event canceled the public question-and-answer portion of the concussion session, explaining that the symposium was behind schedule. This had the unfortunate effect of giving it the feel of a rubber chicken circuit rather than a colloquy.

Smith prefaced his keynote speech with some lame jokes about his Baptist preacher forebears and asked indulgence to deviate from the concussion prompt and address the issue in the total context of "justice and fairness" for athletes. That actually was not a bad frame at all for the discussion, and it led to the panel's most interesting moments when the special guest, football great Jim Brown, gently pressed Smith on the NFLPA's second- and third-class treatment of retirees. Appropriately, Smith countered by citing improvements in this area in the new collective bargaining agreement. Some of these, such as the redistribution of hundreds of millions of new "legacy fund" dollars, remain vague in the details, but they will certainly be improvements, even if still inadequate.

My own No. 1 purpose in attending this event was to confront Smith about a cause I have been championing, essentially all by myself, for months: the idea that the joint NFL-NFLPA disability review board must reopen all claims rejected during the board tenure of the late Dave Duerson. Decisions during that period were fundamentally tainted by the participation of a player advocate who not only had publicly downplayed the link between football and mental disability in Congressional testimony, but also wound up committing suicide — whereupon he was found to have had chronic traumatic encephalopathy himself.

With the announcement that the concussion panel was skipping the public microphone, I joined a gaggle of audience members who pressed Smith at the podium for one-on-one dialogue. (Just ahead of me was Delvin Williams, the 56-year-old former NFL running back. Williams and Smith seemed to be discussing a private matter.)

By the time I got Smith's ear, he was being hustled out the door to his next appointment. Unburdened of the need to give my Duerson question a lot of background for the benefit of a general audience, I said, "Mr. Smith, picking up from your theme of justice and fairness, can you please tell me whether you think Duerson-reviewed claims should get a second look? Please don't answer in legalisms — the confidentiality of the review board process, or not knowing exactly how Duerson voted in individual cases or whether his votes made a difference. Isn't this Fairness 101?"

Smith regurgitated the question but didn't answer it before we separated.

7 SEPTEMBER 2012 ----------------------

Yesterday, for the second straight year, I observed the Santa Clara University Law School's annual Sports Law Symposium — the third. The event provided loads of good foundational information on topical issues in sports world dysfunction. To my pleasant surprise, the university's Institute of Sports Law and Ethics has not skimped on the second half of its titular mission.

Last year I panned the conference for allowing one of the keynote speakers, National Football League Players Association boss DeMaurice Smith, to stray from the prompt, then duck out a side door before he could be confronted with public questions. These included my own on why the NFL retirement plan board won't reopen rejected mental disability benefits claims which had been reviewed by board member Dave Duerson.

This year's Santa Clara confab was much more substantive, with fewer Kiwanis Club flourishes. I didn't mind a couple of the eye-glazing presentations on such technical arcana as the state of right-of-publicity law; after all, this was a continuing education event aimed at professional practitioners.

I still feel the symposium falls short on public colloquy, largely because of time constraints. That problem can be solved by trimming the panels, which are overloaded with the usual suspects. For example, Linda Robertson, a *Miami Herald* sports columnist, could hardly have been blander or more redundant.

The keynoter was Joe Nocera, the *New York Times* op-ed columnist who lately has become civil rights historian Taylor Branch's baby brother in trumpeting equitable compensation for athletes in the college "revenue" sports of football and men's basketball. As readers here know, I am sympathetic, having penned a piece on the subject for the *Los Angeles Times Magazine* in 2003. But I also have become skeptical of the *reductio ad absurdum* of this solution. (Dan Wetzel of *Yahoo Sports* now calls for paying the pipsqueaks of the Little League Baseball World Series.) More importantly, I believe the labor-management model here distracts from the root pathologies of our national athletics system, which can be found in open amateur programs for ponderously professionalized niche, or *wannabe revenue*, sports.

That said, I appreciate the currency of this topic, especially when, as in Santa Clara, it becomes a bridge to an examination of child rapist Jerry Sandusky's Paternoville and loss of institutional control — and soul.

And my old friend Ramogi Huma, head of the precursor union National College Players Association, was exceptionally strong in his presentation. The old warhorse Harry Edwards, whose 40-plus years of scholarship and advocacy sometimes come off like a greatest-hits package, brought his "A" game to Santa Clara and nailed the Penn State scenario as the logical end point of the sports arms race. Sonny Vaccaro, the repentant old sneaker company marketing specialist, delivered a jeremiad.

Though disappointed that sex abuse was not probed in greater depth, I applaud the Santa Clara organizers for giving a reception-speaker slot to Katherine Starr of Safe4Athletes. We will all be hearing a lot more from Katherine in the years to come as she builds her program.

13 SEPTEMBER 2013 -----------------------

For the third year of its four-year history, I thank the organizers for giving me a seat in the audience of the University of Santa Clara's Sports Law Symposium. The lunch buffet and the program compendium of background articles were great. The depth of two-way conversation fell short, though in entirely expected ways, given that three of the four major sponsors are local major league sports franchises (San Francisco 49ers, Oakland Athletics, San Jose Sharks).

I enjoyed the opportunity to network with friends and colleagues, some of whom I had the pleasure of meeting in person for the first time. So as not to compromise their own more lubricious relationships with the hosts, I'll name none of them.

The notable exception to my general criticisms below is Tom Farrey of ESPN and the Aspen Institute's Sports & Society Program. In the panel he moderated, "Could Concussion Liability Reshape Youth Sports?" Farrey did his best to propel a substantive dialogue on the fraught future of public high school football. Unfortunately, despite his efforts to get out of the Kiwanis Club comfort zone, his co-panelists gave him nothing to work with. More on that shortly.

The winner of this year's Linda Robertson Award — named for the Miami sports columnist who last year was flown thousands of miles to the Bay Area for the purpose of saying absolutely nothing of intellectual heft — is Shawn Stuckey, the former National Football League linebacker who is now a Minnesota-based litigator for ex-players' claims.

On the Farrey panel, Stuckey first said high schools had little to worry about from the NFL's recent $765 million settlement with retirees, as the law is well established that the schools don't have much custodial responsibility for the welfare of participants in extracurricular activities. Later, Stuckey said schools are liable if they don't provide safe, up-to-date equipment. From there, he zigged and zagged like Barry Sanders in tanbark, with standard riffs on the NFL's bottom-line avarice.

For all our sympathy for the plight of disabled pros who have been screwed by the NFL, Stuckey's performance is a reminder that this population does not supply our most articulate or trustworthy arguments in the area of public policy.

As is the case every year, the main problem with the Santa Clara symposium is the preponderance of usual-suspect speakers, plus poor time management. These combine to kill audience feedback time. I don't fetishize open mic per se, but an event advertised as offering continuing education for legal practitioners and freewheeling debate should not be allowed to fritter the day away with filibusters and mutual back-scratching. How about fewer redundant panelists and more hard-hitting Q&A?

Alan Schwarz of the *New York Times* was one of the keynote speakers, and I don't begrudge Schwarz his victory lap as the granddaddy of mainstream concussion crisis coverage. Also, Schwarz was witty, informative, and well prepared with a solid multimedia presentation. I was fascinated by audio clips of two of Schwarz's earliest (2007) interviews with key figures. In one, the late National Football League Players Association president Gene Upshaw disclaimed a link between football and early cognitive decline — even as Schwarz politely pointed out that an NFLPA-funded study by the University of North Carolina said otherwise. In the other clip, NFL commissioner Roger Goodell had the nerve to blow off the concussion problem by mentioning a head injury his brother once sustained in a swimming pool.

The other keynoter, Hall of Fame defensive back Ronnie Lott, reprised his decades-old sensitive assassin shtick. I count myself among the minority who are thoroughly weary of this routine, which comes complete with weepy and inapt parallels between his blood sport and the traumatic brain injuries and wanton death of military exercises. In other words, the entertainment of football and wars to protect our sovereignty and freedom are equivalent, and we're supposed to be OK with that, even sentimental about it. Pat Tillman, the football player turned post 9/11 army volunteer who got killed by friendly fire in Afghanistan, apparently is fungible enough to be exploited by every conceivable agenda.

Lott recalled the 1989 paralysis of his 49ers secondary mate Jeff Fuller. I recall it, too: I was at Stanford Stadium that day reporting my cover story on Joe Montana for the *New York Times Magazine*. That was the day the media relations staff herded us down to the field with four minutes left because of changed post-game interview logistics (the game had been shifted from Candlestick Park after the big earthquake). Standing on the sidelines, I had close-ups of half a dozen car wrecks per play . . . all during garbage time of a game whose result had long ago been decided. For me, it was the day the football music died. I was 35 years old and ready to define adulthood for myself.

In the course of clichéd encomiums to the late coach Bill Walsh, Lott bragged that the 49ers offensive linemen "were real good at" crack-back blocks: sadistic blind-side shots behind the opponents' knees. Of course, Lott would do it all again, at the stroke of a stroke. But of course, he would do so *repentantly* — this time he'd practice "safe football." It's so important to save football from itself — for it is only by means of this precise outlet for mitigating phenomena such as "childhood obesity" (have you looked at a "run-stuffing" defensive tackle lately?) that America's boyly boys can be transformed into manly men. Some of us feel otherwise, that the process can be achieved in multiple ways — for instance, by teaching boys (and girls) to use their heads, including to think.

Lott concluded his stem-winder with a wish list for all youth football players, including and especially in the ghetto from whence he came: brand-new helmets and pads every year, a sideline athletic trainer, baseline neurocognitive tests starting the day they were weaned from mama's breast, and a municipal ambulance service on standby to cart off quickly every kid whose brain matter gets mooshed or spinal cord cracked. The Santa Clara Sports Law Symposium offered no platform for the point of view that the proponents of "concussion awareness" and "safe football" don't even bother to put forth back-of-the-envelope projections of what this would cost our society and whether it would be worth it.

The lunchtime presenters were Jack Clark, the legendary Cal rugby coach, and Jim Thompson, the cloying CEO of an organization called the Positive Coaching Alliance. These two gentlemen flashed the infamous video of jackass Rutgers basketball coach Mike Rice's verbal and physical abuse in practice. The publicity from the *Saturday Night Live* Melissa McCarthy spoof of the footage would get both Rice and Rutgers athletic director Tim Pernetti fired. Clark and Thompson shook their heads and earnestly agreed that this is *not* positive coaching.

From the buffet line, I was recognized and allowed to ramble for a minute about a contemporaneous and much worse coach outrage: the widespread sexual and physical abuse of swimmers at the University of Utah by coach Greg Winslow. The difference was that nobody cared and Utah athletic director Chris Hill, after covering up for Winslow for years, wasn't canned. (An "independent review" of the cover-up, commissioned by the university trustees, concluded that Winslow should have been fired a year earlier, for being a boozer.)

I might as well have been speaking in Serbo-Croatian. Thompson thanked me and moved right along to such questions as whether girls start crying more quickly than boys when coaches yell at them.

In a subsequent email, Thompson told me, "I had not heard about the [Winslow] case. We most often focus on high school and youth sports so I don't keep up with college sports in general."

That doesn't explain the session's theme of Mike Rice, a college coach. Nor does it explain why the Positive Coaching Alliance seems to have zero knowledge, much less a position, on the Catholic Church–level problem of sexual abuse of far too many of the 400,000 youth by far too many of the 12,000 coaches in USA Swimming.

Admirably, Tom Farrey's panel tried to lock on the question of how much it would take for public high schools to get out of the football business.

My first criticism here is a quibble. Though Farrey correctly used the recent NFL settlement as his hook, his cite of the fast-following Dougherty family $2.8 million wrongful-death settlement with their high school in Montclair, New Jersey, missed an opportunity to talk about not just liability costs, but also the dubious effectiveness of preventive measures. The Dougherty case includes facts about the school district's incipient use of the ImPACT concussion management system, developed by the ever-reputable medical director of the WWE, Dr. Joe Maroon.

More Dougherty-style lawsuits are sure to follow. Baseline testing is a key component of the pie-in-the-sky state-by-state concussion awareness mandates, the so-called Lystedt Laws, which NFL lobbyists love because they shift the football industry's public health tab completely onto the back of the public sector. If ImPACT and all the other nice-sounding measures don't do the job anyway, then what are we talking about here, besides continuing mass delusion?

The other basic flaw of Farrey's panel is that he talked about the cost side for schools only in terms of lawsuit exposure, insurance premiums, and equipment. But Farrey did press panelist Mike Pilawski, the athletic director of Saint Francis High School in Mountain View, to disclose the total "nut" for the football program. Pilawski finally said around $80,000 — an obviously low-ball number, as it didn't account for insurance, facilities maintenance, and other line items not charged to the athletic department budget. Moreover, Pilawski acknowledged that as a private school, Saint Francis has a lot more flexibility to subsidize football than a public institution does.

Perhaps next year the Santa Clara conference can give us a public high school athletic director, tasked with providing real and transparent answers to these questions. And in order to give that presentation time, maybe the organizers can scale back on the blathering of the Positive Coaching Alliance.

---

1   See Dave Pear's blog, davepear.com/blog/2011/09/second-annual-santa-clara-law-sports-law-symposium/.

DAVE DUERSON AND OTHER DISCONTENTS

The gruesome decades-long underground American saga that is the football concussion crisis has never gotten in our faces quite like the story of the suicide last week of one-time National Football League man of the year Dave Duerson.

How many levels are there to the news that Duerson, at age 50, put a gun to himself but not before texting his family that he wanted his brain donated for research on the brain-trauma syndrome now known as chronic traumatic encephalopathy? Let us count them. It begins with the fact that he shot himself in the chest — perhaps with supreme confidence that by avoiding his head and leaving intact his postmortem brain tissue, he would be confirmed as (approximately) the 21st diagnosed case of CTE among former football players.

Duerson is the latest casualty of a sport that has evolved, via training technology and industrial design, into a form of gladiatorialism whose future human and economic viability is questionable. The *New Yorker* and the *New York Times* have started assessing this cultural phenomenon with their own brands of competence and Ivy League restraint. From the closeted gutter of pro wrestling, where all the same venalities play out with less pretense, I'm here to tell "the rest of the story" — such as how the same corrupt doctors who work for the NFL also shill for World Wrestling Entertainment, and how it's all part of the same stock exchange of ethics for profits and jock-sniffing privileges.

I would not be hasty to label Duerson a "victim"; for most of his 50 years, he was personally driven to make particular professional choices. But the thing that fans, parents, people still haven't wrapped their minds around is the magnitude of the toll on the Dave Duersons at the amateur level, and below the age of consent, via a nationally unhealthy system of dangled glory and riches.

And with Duerson, there's a wrinkle that takes journalistic and governmental investigations of this public health issue into its murkiest waters yet.

Duerson was not just a leader of the record-setting — and skull-crunching — defense of the 1986 Super Bowl champion Chicago Bears. He was also a member of the six-person NFL committee that reviewed the claims of retired players under the league's disability plan and the so-called 88 Plan, a special fund to defray the costs for families in caring for players diagnosed with dementia.

Don't look for this last point to be prominent in Duerson retrospectives. We can count on quotes from fellow ex-NFLers about how scary it all is, and we can count on further details on Duerson's bankruptcy and collapsed personal life, but we're not likely to get into the 88 Plan files he was helping process.

When news of Duerson's death broke, but before the suicide details emerged, the NFL was first out of the gate with a statement of condolence. It's in keeping with a strategy of triangulation that has been its hallmark ever since it became apparent that research articles in clinical medical journals such as *Neurosurgery* — literature largely written by NFL-paid doctors, including the Pittsburgh Steelers' Joseph Maroon, who is also medical director for WWE — consciously lowballed the evidence on CTE for many years. The *Neurosurgery* reverse-hype also deftly promoted for-profit diagnostic stopgaps, such as Maroon's ImPACT concussion management system and the Riddell helmet company's "Revolution" model. The latter is now the focus of a Federal Trade Commission investigation undertaken at the request of Senator Tom Udall.

The league recently launched a website, NFLHealthandSafety .com,[1] with exquisite timing and calculated transparency. The site touts the NFL's $20 million in funded research, without examining exactly what that $20 million has bought.

The site's media center also links to important stories in the news. As this article was being published, the top one was "Debate arises concerning use of helmets in girls' lacrosse" (*New York Times*, February 17). Well, let's see how NFLHealthandSafety.com covers Dave Duerson's suicide. Let's see, for example, if it links to this story.

23 FEBRUARY 2011 ----------------------
One of the coldest aspects of the Dave Duerson suicide is its recursive irony: Duerson served on the National Football League committee that helped process disability claims of families of retired players, including the "88 Plan," which defrays the medical bills of victims of dementia.

Even if Duerson's golden life and career had not deteriorated to the point where he was himself one of the disabled, and even if he hadn't plummeted into the financial bankruptcy so common among sufferers of chronic traumatic encephalopathy (the devastating disease for which his brain will now be tested), becoming intimately involved in the paperwork of the heartbreaking cases of his ex-colleagues must have been profoundly depressing.

The scenario reminds me of the constant stream of funerals and memorial shows for dead fellow wrestlers Chris Benoit found himself attending five or so years ago, until he himself snapped.

History — if not, in the nearer future, our courts of law — will have much to say about the NFL's response to evidence that its product was killing its talent and, by its enormous commercial and cultural influence, spreading brain trauma through the American sports superstructure like a weed.

Dr. Bennet Omalu named the disease CTE but he didn't invent the problem of epidemic head injury. That was for others before him to reveal — or ignore.

Information on the 88 Plan itself is at NFLPlayerCare.com. Earmarked for ex-players with dementia, the plan was inspired by the case of Hall of Fame tight end John Mackey, who is now in his late sixties but has had severe cognitive problems, culminating in dementia, probably for a decade or more. The "88" refers to Mackey's uniform number with the Baltimore Colts; in the original concept, dementia benefits were to be capped at $85,000 per claimant, but in honor of Mackey it was upped to $88,000. The program started in September 2007.

As Alan Schwarz reported in the *New York Times*, Dave Duerson had a "testy exchange" with former UCLA and Minnesota Vikings offensive lineman Brent Boyd at a 2007 Congressional hearing. Boyd said his clinical depression was the result of cumulative football hits. Duerson disagreed.

That is a very interesting addition to the Duerson narrative in multiple respects. When the work of the NFL disability committee began,

Duerson could have been a voice who, either generally speaking or in particular cases, was overly sympathetic to the league's company line in his interpretation of claims, and that, in turn, could have led to guilt and exacerbated his depression as his own symptoms accelerated. Again, the instruction of the Chris Benoit experience: near the end of his life, Benoit, who had always defended the wrestling industry's hyper-macho credo, found himself resignedly agreeing with disgruntled colleagues who unloaded with him about their unconscionable working conditions.

Brent Boyd is on the board of directors of a former players' advocacy group called Dignity After Football (DignityAfterFootball.org). I am trying to reach Boyd for comment.

24 FEBRUARY 2011 ---------------------

The Dave Duerson suicide has ricocheted through the media as a wake-up call on the American sports concussion crisis. But one of Duerson's chief adversaries over the years — retired Minnesota Vikings offensive lineman Brent Boyd, himself a concussion victim and head of an advocacy group for disabled ex-players — has a different perspective.

In a lengthy telephone interview on Wednesday night, Boyd portrayed Duerson as a management lackey — full of bluster about the player disability claims he helped adjudicate on an NFL committee, generally hostile to players' interests, and out of control at a 2007 Congressional hearing that explored these issues.

Boyd began our conversation by extending sympathy to Duerson's family. "No matter what my differences were with Dave, this is a terrible tragedy, and family comes first. My heart goes out to his loved ones," Boyd said.

But Boyd held little back in his criticism of Duerson's post-career NFL work. Specifically, Boyd added much detail to a *New York Times* story this week, which reported:

Duerson . . . joined the six-man volunteer panel that considered retired players' claims under the NFL's disability plan, in addition to the 88 Plan, a fund that has assisted more than 150 families caring for retired players with dementia since its inception in 2007. Duerson read applications, testimonies, and detailed doctors' reports for hundreds of players with multiple injuries, including those to the brain that in some cases left players requiring full-time care. He had to vote on whether these people received financial assistance.

In 2007, two Congressional committees held hearings into whether the disability board was unfairly denying benefits. Duerson testified before the Senate Commerce Committee alongside Brent Boyd, a former Minnesota Vikings lineman whose depression and cognitive impairment had been ruled unrelated to his playing career, therefore warranting significantly lower benefits. It is unknown how Duerson voted on Boyd's case. He did get into a heated exchange when Boyd, then 50, asserted that his condition — and that of other players with dementia — was caused by football.[2]

Boyd's NFL disability claims date all the way back to 2000; his litigation of the league's denials of his claims is now at the Fourth Circuit Court of Appeals.

With respect to Duerson's role, Boyd said, "The *Times* said it is not known how Duerson voted on the committee in my case, but the answer is pretty obvious. At the Senate Commerce Committee hearing and at the NFL committee meetings, he repeatedly denied the evidence of my medical condition and accused me of being a faker who was trying to grab benefits to which he wasn't entitled."

And that wasn't all. At the Congressional hearing room during an intermission, according to Boyd, Duerson initiated a verbal confrontation with older retired players Sam Huff and Bernie Parrish. Huff, a Hall of Fame linebacker with the New York Giants and the Washington Redskins, and Parrish, an accomplished defensive back with the Cleveland Browns, were pioneers in the development of the NFL Players Association in the 1960s. Both became outspoken critics of the union under the leadership of its long-time president, Gene Upshaw, who died in 2008.

Boyd: "Duerson was spewing profanities at Huff and Parrish. He said, 'What the fuck do you know about the players union?' He was acting like he wanted to fight them physically. That wasn't too smart with respect to Huff especially. He looks like he could still play."

Boyd said Duerson landed a spot on the NFL disability committee after his company Duerson Foods — at one point a major supplier to McDonald's — went into receivership in 2006. Duerson was appointed by Upshaw. (The committee consists of three owner representatives and three named by the union.)

Duerson "liked to talk and talk about what an expert he was on ERISA [the Employment Retirement Income Securities Act, which governs employee benefit plans]," Boyd said. "But he was constantly misquoting and misrepresenting the law. He didn't know what he was talking about."

Boyd, a Southern California native, now lives and struggles with his health and finances in Reno, Nevada. He played for the Vikings from 1980 to 1986. In his Congressional testimony and elsewhere, Boyd has spoken movingly about his bouts with headaches, depression, and chronic fatigue. On several occasions he has been homeless. Like Duerson has been, Boyd fears that he will be determined after his death to have had the degenerative brain disorder chronic traumatic encephalopathy.

Boyd founded the first ex-players' advocacy group, Dignity After Football. The tasks of fundraising and website management became overwhelming. Ultimately, he abandoned efforts to register the organization as a 501(c)(3) charity.

"We aren't well equipped to handle and distribute money," Boyd said, "and ultimately we have come to realize that the task of educating the NFL alumni community is largely complete. The retired players out there understand what has happened to them and what their situation is. Our big job now is to get something done by mobilizing fans and league sponsors."

Boyd also serves on the board of Chris Nowinski's Sports Legacy Institute (SLI). Like many other players with NFL medical claims, Boyd worries that the group's work might be compromised by its research affiliate, Boston University, accepting a $1 million NFL grant. "When SLI honored [NFL commissioner] Roger Goodell with its Impact award, that really ticked me off," Boyd told me. "Money can buy anything."

On Dave Duerson, Boyd summed up, "He spent years denying the concussion claims of other players. Then when the same symptoms started closing in on him, he killed himself. What does that tell you?"

25 FEBRUARY 2011 -------------------------------

Writer Rob Trucks interviewed Dave Duerson, three months before he committed suicide, as part of an oral-history project on life challenges at age 50. Deadspin.com, the provocative sports news site, published an excerpt this week. It's a valuable and timely document that everyone should read.[3]

I have a number of problems with this piece, starting with the title "You Have to Accept My Pain." It took some desperate cutting and pasting to make that line the headline of the article. Far down in the interview, we finally get to the P-word:

I do hold myself to a higher standard. I do. But the flip of that is, every one of us has things in their life they regret. For instance, I'm a Trekkie. And it wasn't the series so much as the movies, the Star Trek movies. I remember a scene from one of the latter ones with William Shatner. This guy, Spock's cousin or his brother, he could hug you and take away your pain. And he says, "Come join with me, and let me take away your pain." And Dr. McCoy and everybody else is like, "Jim, you've got to do this. It's wonderful." And Captain Kirk tells him, "I need my pain, because it defines who I am." And so in that regard when people come up to me and they tell me, "Man, I wish I were you," I tell them in the same breath that in order to be me, you have to accept my pain.

The first reaction to this loopy snippet is "Huh?"

The other is that Duerson's "pain" turns out to be defined as second-hand kitsch. That's of a piece with the interview as a whole, which is narcissistic — painfully so. The locutor not only can't seem to take responsibility for something as simple as being a *Star Trek* fan. He also can't take responsibility for having wanted to be a football player, or for his arrest for domestic violence, or for watching late-night TV. We pay no honor to the real accomplishments of Duerson's life — his NFL career and his once-prosperous food-supply business, which employed hundreds — by pretending otherwise. A good guess is that brain damage from thousands of athletic blows had taken their toll.

As a reader with four kids himself, let me just say that it is profoundly disturbing for this man either to have had all along, or to have developed, an active fantasy life based on dying at 42. Death wishes are not admirable things, whether issued from jihadism or from the "Die Young, Stay Pretty" wing of rock and roll.

In addition, as someone who joined my sister in burying our father and mother, respectively seven and six years ago, I find dreadfully self-pitying the way Duerson dwelled on the deaths of parents in his middle age and their old age. That is the circle of life. Now, *parents burying their children*, as is happening with a generation of totally pointless casualties in sports and sports entertainment — that's a different story.

Duerson called his 2005 arrest for beating his wife, which cost him his position as a trustee at his alma mater, Notre Dame, a loss of control "for three seconds." I don't know about that. The county prosecutor in Indiana filed two counts of battery and two of domestic battery. The police report said Duerson struck his wife and then shoved her out the door of a motel room so hard that she banged against a wall.

Most of the Twitter chatter has centered on Duerson's remembrance that Buddy Ryan, his defensive coordinator with the Chicago Bears, told him, "I don't like smart niggers." (Ryan denies it.)

In a similar motif, I got an email yesterday from a journalist who read my interview with Brent Boyd and said that Boyd's depiction of Duerson diverged from the journalist's own, which is that of a forceful union guy who clashed not only with Ryan but also with then head coach of the Bears, Mike Ditka. Decades later, Ditka is a vocal critic of what the NFL Players Association has failed to do for disabled ex-players, and the journalist says this is a chapter in a long-running narrative with racial overtones.

My own view is that race is not terribly pertinent to concussion syndrome, except perhaps to the extent African Americans are wildly oversubscribed to the entire sports dream machine. This includes, by the way, the current president of the United States, who upon taking office proclaimed his No. 1 sports priority to be the institution of a college football championship tournament to replace the current Bowl Championship Series. Some of the reasons for the racialization of athletics indeed touch on the great open wound of our national experience. But Dave Duerson's occupational hardships with redneck coaches aren't very illuminating on the subject of brain trauma in gladiator divertissement. He did fine for himself until about five years ago when finances, family affairs, and cognitive function all turned sour.

Recognizing that the Deadspin article is only an excerpt, I emailed author Trucks two days ago, asking if the full transcript and/or audio of his conversation with Duerson would be made available. Trucks did not respond.

25 FEBRUARY 2011 ----------------------

In covering Dave Duerson's suicide pointedly, I mean no disrespect to the memory of someone who, according to many people who knew him, was a good guy. I never met the man myself. But my research on the murder-suicide of wrestler Chris Benoit and its offshoots has turned me into a lay Ph.D. candidate on the ugly personality changes, loss of emotional control, and sheer cognitive deterioration that are hallmarks of chronic traumatic encephalopathy — from which Duerson, like Benoit and so many others, may be proved to have suffered.

So I have specific reasons for resisting the mawkish sentimentality of much of the Duerson media coverage. That coverage reflects the culture we inhabit. It is also perfectly appropriate for family and friends to be eager to keep his legacy positive. For my money, however, such a legacy must be tied to outcomes.

One such outcome is an adjustment of the record created by Duerson's work for the NFL retirement and disability board. I checked with Brian McCarthy, the National Football League's communication director, and he told me that since the February 2007 inception of the 88 Plan, the joint labor-management disability claims committee has received 170 applications. All but 19 have been approved. Eight applications are pending. Eleven have been rejected.

I am not sure how many of the 11 rejections came during Duerson's tenure on the committee; I assume all or almost all. (An NFL Players Association spokesman did not respond to inquiries.) Out of respect for his sacrifice and in acknowledgment of what, in retrospect, was his diminished competence, these 11 files should be reopened and reconsidered at once.

The same should be done for all non–88 Plan claims on which Duerson deliberated. I believe these would include the claims of ex– Minnesota Viking lineman Brent Boyd. (Boyd's file began in 2000, pre–88 Plan, and may never have referred to that part of the disability benefits program; he claimed football-related mental illness, but I don't believe that included dementia.)

The NFL and NFLPA can litigate to death the question of Duerson's disqualification. Or they can take the high road in at least this narrowly defined area, in return for considerable public good will. On the field, they've instituted replay review for the sake of getting the call right. Today, off the field, the lives of disabled NFL veterans and their families require nothing less.

28 FEBRUARY 2011 ------------------------

One truth revealed by the maudlin first round of reaction to the news that Duerson probably had severe brain damage from football concussions — something postmortem study will have to confirm — is that NFL players union contract negotiations do not, in the familiar idiom, simply pit greedy billionaires against greedy millionaires. Rather, they pit *billionaires who know what they're doing against millionaires who don't have a clue.*

That's the only logical conclusion I can draw from the fact that Duerson, while losing his Goliath post–NFL career food distribution business, plunging into personal bankruptcy, seeing his house seized by a bank, and getting arrested for beating his wife — all telltale signs of chronic traumatic encephalopathy — was being appointed by the

Players Association as one of the trustees of a league fund, jointly administered by management and union, to compensate retired players with disability claims.

Who needed a fox guarding the chicken coop when there was a hypermacho-enabling union more focused on the division of the NFL's $9 billion revenue pie than on whether its members worked under conditions that would give them a reasonable expectation of living and functioning past age 50?

No doubt Duerson had the best of intentions for his fellow athletes when he insisted, both on the NFL retirement board and in Senate commerce committee testimony, that ex–Minnesota Viking lineman Brent Boyd's mental illness in his forties wasn't proven to be football related. Duerson pointed out that his own father had Alzheimer's disease in his late seventies or eighties, yet had never played football!

But sincere or not, we now know more than just that Duerson's argument was nuts. He was, too. Cognitively impaired. Of diminished capacity. Lacking responsible judgment. All from the very phenomenon about which he was instrumental in making administrative-legal rulings — a role for which, in retrospect, he was clearly incompetent.

That's why I say enough with the media's Duerson pity party. If his friends and loved ones take comfort that his donated brain will contribute to public awareness of CTE, then by all means give them their soft landing.

But the powers that be in the NFL and the NFLPA? Not so fast. Duerson was no hero. There were already dozens of confirmed cases of CTE, and undoubtedly hundreds of other unreported or ill-reported cases, by the time Duerson put a gun to his chest.

If we're really intent on honoring Dave Duerson, then let's put some substance on his legacy. I have a three-point plan. We can call it the Double D Three-Point Stance.

Reopen all rejected disability claims by retired players. Even as I write this, I'm sure lawyers are preparing new litigation arguing that the evidence of Duerson's incompetence should invalidate the disability claim rejections. Instead of fighting a legal war of attrition over the inevitable, the league and the union should concede the morally obvious and order immediate "replay review" of these rejections.

Double the 88 Plan's outreach and benefits. The plan — named for Hall of Fame tight end John Mackey, who wore uniform No. 88 — grants up to $88,000 a year in reimbursement for the medical expenses of dementia victims. At Duerson's funeral on Saturday in Chicago, his son Brock said the family would be setting up a foundation to aid players with mental illness. But hey, let's cut out the middleman here. To date, the 88 Plan has distributed around $7 million. In the NFL and the NFLPA's contract talks, let them take off the table enough crumbs from their $9 billion food fight to double the size of the disability fund endowment and benefits.

Give fans and sponsors ownership of player care. This is the hardest one for me to talk about in specifics at this point. But nothing will get the league and the players union to take meaningful action until fans pull their heads out of their hero-worshipping butts and start taking responsibility for the human and societal costs of their entertainment. One possible idea: there is much promising research on the efficacy of Omega-3 supplements in reversing or at least slowing brain damage. Fan groups could raise money for distributing free supplies to NFL alumni and pressure beer companies, which tag "drink responsibly" bromides onto their wall-to-wall football telecast commercials, to pitch in, too.

While I was filing this piece, obsessed fans were already turning the page on Duerson and refocusing on the disgusting meat rack that is the NFL pre-draft combine coverage. (Where is Jesse Jackson when you really need him for an observation on how the big-time sports system is just like an antebellum plantation?)

As millions pondered Cam Newton's flexing pecs and stopwatch reading in the 40-yard dash, a report out of Canada said that former

NFL and Canadian Football League defensive back Ricky Bell died 10 days ago at age 36. Both Bell's girlfriend and his mother in South Carolina declined to comment on the cause of death.

2 MAY 2011 -----------------------------

At a just-concluded press conference in Boston attended by Dave Duerson's ex-wife and their four children, doctors affiliated with Boston University and Chris Nowinski's Sports Legacy Institute announced that the postmortem study of the brain of Duerson, who committed suicide in February, confirms that he had chronic traumatic encephalopathy. He is one of dozens of recently deceased athletes, at least 13 of whom were National Football League players, shown to have had CTE.

I asked the following question:

> Mr. Duerson served as a trustee on the NFL commit-
> tee that reviews disability claims of retired players. A
> league spokesman told me that a total of 11 claims to
> the Mackey 88 Plan for dementia-related acute-care
> expenses have been rejected. There is some addition-
> al number of line-of-duty and disability benefits that
> have been rejected, and many of those also involve
> brain injuries — a subject that certainly weighed heav-
> ily on Mr. Duerson. In light of this new information
> confirming that he was himself of diminished mental
> capacity when he participated in these NFL Player
> Care deliberations, do you agree that there is a moral,
> if not also a legal, obligation to reopen the files of these
> rejected claims?

Everyone should view Nowinski's video on his CTE work, "Game Changers,"[4] but there is a danger that the NFL's activism in finding a cure for CTE and promoting sports safety reforms is way too little and way too late. That is why I asked the question.

Robert Stern, co-director of the center, replied that his organization was not in the business of telling the NFL how to distribute disability benefits. He also said that the Duerson CTE finding could not be extrapolated to determine just when and how, or even whether, this player and fallen business tycoon came to incur "diminished mental capacity."

Though fair enough as far as the response went, this reticence to use the Duerson cautionary tale for more aggressive generic comment on the political landscape ahead may point to the limitations of the Sports Legacy Institute's new million-dollar partnership with the NFL. In a related vein, I believe the question is not whether youth football coaches should be cutting back on contact in practices; it is whether youth football should exist at all.

Further unfortunate fallout from the public progress on concussion reform is the schism between the Boston group and the West Virginia Brain Injury Research Institute headed by Drs. Julian Bailes and Bennet Omalu. The latter, now chief medical examiner of San Joaquin County, California, is the researcher who took the NFL head-on while more established voices — often doctors with league connections and other commercial conflicts of interest — were still equivocating in journal articles.

A hint of the Boston–West Virginia turf war was evident yesterday after Boston University's Dr. Robert Cantu correctly linked CTE to the phenomenon of "punch-drunk syndrome" in boxers, which was first isolated in 1928. Cantu went on to suggest, incorrectly, that CTE became widely recognized in the '60s and '70s. In fact, the pathology was neither named nor defined before Omalu came along in 2002. If there was widespread awareness of the scale of concussion syndrome in the immediate aftermath of football players such as Al Toon getting blasted into early retirement in the 1990s, then the NFL made sure it was a well-kept secret.[5]

In any case, the point isn't who gets credit for the discovery of CTE so much as who will pay the bill for the current generation of sports-generated broken lives. This exercise runs deeper than the NFL's bottom line. Half-baked prospective solutions driven by an image-conscious, money-hungry corporation will not significantly arrest the CTE pandemic. And as writer Matt Chaney has noted, it is non-professionals and their families — along with the nation as a whole — who bear the brunt of the NFL lobby's current campaign to shift responsibility to state legislatures by mandating new practices for cash-strapped school and other amateur athletic programs.

A better idea: make commissioner Roger Goodell and his 32 owners cough up some realistic restitution for the brain-injury mill from which they profit so obscenely. A mere $20 million in research grants and $7 million in aid to retired players with dementia won't cut it. That is the background of my question at the Duerson press conference.

5 MAY 2011 ------------------------------

Alan Schwarz of the *New York Times* has taken the Dave Duerson story exactly where it needs to go: toward no-holds-barred examination of the NFL disability benefits system, which Duerson himself, with cruel irony, had helped administer and defend.

> Another question beginning to circle among retired players whose claims were denied during Duerson's tenure is whether they can refile given his admitted impairment. Board votes are not disclosed to applicants or to the public.

John Hogan, a lawyer for dozens of players in disability matters, said that he might request an audit by the United States Department of Labor to see how Duerson voted on claims.

"He had to exercise a high degree of care, skill, prudence, and diligence — the CTE findings, coupled with his suicide, certainly raise the question of whether he was capable of properly fulfilling those duties as is required in such an important undertaking," Hogan said. "It therefore calls into question the possibility that some or all of the decisions he made when passing on disability claims are suspect, and perhaps invalid."[6]

I welcome Hogan's assumption of a more aggressive stance than he articulated to me in the immediate aftermath of Duerson's February suicide. Back then, while not hesitating to brand the entire NFL disability apparatus illegitimate, with or without the Duerson factor, Hogan had added that probing Duerson's specific cases on the compensation board would be a tough road to hoe because of confidentiality laws and the possibility that he had actually cast his own votes in favor of retired players whose claims were rejected.

NFL lawyer Douglas Ell reinforces this point to the *Times*: "He knew of no case where 'if Dave's vote were disregarded, the outcome would have been different.'"

I think the league's position is wrong. The disability committee is not tainted because of *Duerson's individual votes*, but because of his *overall participation*. As one of the three NFL Players Association appointees, Duerson carried an expectation to deliberate and advocate on behalf of a constituency in need. To use a very loose analogy, if a lawyer is found to have provided inadequate representation to an accused criminal, the process is understood to be flawed and a rehearing required. Wargaming the final verdicts of the disability panel to determine whether they would have turned out the same anyway does not remove their procedural cloud.

At Monday's press conference in Boston, officials at the Center for the Study of Chronic Traumatic Encephalopathy (a partnership of Boston University and the Sports Legacy Institute, recently infused with a $1 million NFL grant) declined to go there. But even if the best-known faces of concussion reform are getting unhelpfully cautious in their rhetoric, the sports commentariat and the federal government have the means to take the Duerson narrative all the way home.

11 MAY 2011 ----------------------------

A couple of different readers, with a couple of different viewpoints, have told me that my coverage of the announcement of Dave Duerson's chronic traumatic encephalopathy maligned Boston University's Dr. Robert Cantu by stating that he had vaguely backdated the definition and naming of the disease in a way that disrespects the work of Dr. Bennet Omalu.

On this point, I think the critics are right and I was wrong, so let me correct the record here.

After that, I'll proceed to explain why I believe exposure of my error only deepens the suspicions that the sports medical establishment fell down on the job and that the National Football League was none too eager to see that a better job be done.

What Cantu said in Boston a week ago Monday was that CTE was identified in boxers as "punch-drunk syndrome" in the 1920s, and "since the '60s and especially the '70s it has been known as chronic traumatic encephalopathy, with multiple case reports in the world's clinical and neuropathological literature."[7]

That is accurate. Nor is there any reason to dispute this fuller chronology from the Sports Legacy Institute:

The term "chronic traumatic encephalopathy" appears in the medical literature as early as 1969 and is now the preferred term. Through 2009, there were only 49 cases described in all medical literature since 1928, 39 of whom were boxers. Many thought this was a disease exclusive to boxers, although cases have been identified in a battered wife, an epileptic, two mentally challenged individuals with head-banging behavior, and an Australian circus performer who was also involved in what the medical report authors referred to as "dwarf-throwing."[8]

CTE remained under the radar when a Pittsburgh medical examiner named Bennet Omalu identified CTE in two former Pittsburgh Steelers who died in his jurisdiction in 2002 and 2005. He published his findings, drawing the attention of SLI co-founder Chris Nowinski, who worked with families to deliver three more cases that Dr. Omalu and others diagnosed with CTE, including SLI's first case, former WWE wrestler Chris Benoit.

What happened?

In my several lengthy conversations with Dr. Omalu, he has taken credit for the term CTE; on one occasion, Omalu even reminded me that he had been the sole, and not merely a major contributory, coiner of it. To the extent that I ran with Omalu's assertion, bad on me. If I've somehow misinterpreted what Omalu has been telling me (but I don't think I have), then double bad on me. (Omalu declined comment in an email this morning.)

Now that that piece is out of the way — again, apologies to Cantu, Chris Nowinski's SLI, and the Center for the Study of CTE for the implication that they were deflecting due credit to Omalu by fudging history — what does all this mean for the story of the national head-injury crisis in sports?

The answer is that it is, if anything, even less flattering to the powers that be. Bennet Omalu didn't discover CTE or even attach the most widely recognized handle to it. *He was just the first to identify CTE in football players.*

CTE was wending its way through the medical literature throughout the 1970s in association not just with boxers, but with battered women and circus performers as well. Meanwhile, as concussions took a skyrocketing toll on football players over the next 30 years, no one made the connection.

Remember Travis Williams, "The Road Runner," a speedy running back who set kickoff return records as a rookie for the 1967 Super Bowl champion Green Bay Packers? He was finished way too early, battled depression, wound up penniless in a homeless shelter in Richmond, California, and died at 45. Of course, we can't know if Williams had CTE, but his story is just one of dozens or scores or hundreds of similar ones prior to that day in 2002 when Omalu happened upon Mike Webster's brain.

All of which leads to another broad observation, about the folly of "peer-reviewed scientific literature." This phrase, preferably uttered in hushed tones and on bended knee, is the talisman of the same priesthood that has failed a sports-mad nation in disseminating needed public health information. Peer review, in my opinion, is a pastiche of standards, honored as much in the breach as in the observance when convenient, and it comes embedded with its own set of social, professional, and commercial biases.

12 MAY 2011 ---

Yesterday I apologized for incorrectly suggesting that Dr. Robert Cantu had airbrushed the history of chronic traumatic encephalopathy research in his remarks last week at the Dave Duerson brain study press conference.

Today I offer an extended P.S. on the nuances of that research and its political landmines. The story of CTE involves maimed and prematurely dead athletes, of course. But it also includes egos, grants, media coverage . . . *careers*. The behind-the-scenes rivalry between the Boston research group, led by the Sports Legacy Institute's Chris Nowinski and Boston University Medical Center's Cantu, and the West Virginia research group, led by Drs. Julian Bailes and Bennet Omalu, is a glimpse into that world. The stakes are high for the parties — and for the rest of us.

Let's stipulate that any controversy over the origins of the naming of this brain disease is a sideshow in comparison with the substance of what Omalu brought to the table — unfortunately, it was the autopsy table — over the past decade. I would summarize it thus:

- For many years, there was an understanding that boxers suffered various symptoms resembling Parkinson's disease, accompanied by dementia.
- There was also an escalating appreciation that people in all walks of life who suffered major traumatic brain injury could develop a disease that resembled Alzheimer's.
- Beginning with Mike Webster in 2002 and continuing through to the Nowinski group's initial and breakthrough finding on pro wrestler Chris Benoit in 2007, Omalu put what we now call CTE on the map. Omalu determined that minor blows to the head, over time, with or without documentation — notably in football, hockey, lacrosse, and wrestling — could result in a disease distinct from Alzheimer's.

Omalu has defined CTE as a *disease entity*. He also has confirmed that what we used to think of as Parkinson's or Alzheimer's or their offshoots are not these diseases in victims of CTE, which has distinct pathognomonic diagnostic features.

Nomenclature aside, there was no media attention given to CTE until after the publication of the Mike Webster paper in 2005.

About that nomenclature:

- There is evidence that "punch-drunk syndrome" in boxers, or dementia pugilistica, was also being called "traumatic encephalopathy" as early as the 1930s.
- A 1996 paper in *Pathology*, "Dementia Pugilistica in an Alcoholic Achondroplastic Dwarf," by David J. Williams and Anthony E.G. Tannenberg, says that dementia pugilistica is "otherwise known as chronic progressive post-traumatic encephalopathy of boxing." Not exactly the same as CTE — though so close that I probably would have felt compelled yesterday to clarify and apologize to the Boston folks even if they hadn't also shared with me . . .
- A 1966 paper from *Proceedings of the Royal Society of Medicine*, "Mental Sequelae of Head Injury," by Henry Miller, has a subsection headed "Chronic Traumatic Encephalopathy." Though Miller did not seem to go anywhere with this term in the body of the article, nor give it the abbreviation CTE, the exact sequence of the three words clinched at least the minimal point that great minds prior to Omalu had thought at least somewhat alike. And it confirmed that I'd stubbed my toe in my May 3 story on Duerson.

13 MAY 2011 ------------------------------

At this moment the national sports concussion fight, like many others, is bogged down in a fetish over "peer-reviewed scientific literature." I argue that a lot of the vaunted peer-review process is pompous bunk, a ritual by elites to demonstrate their eliteness while giving aid and comfort to the status quo.

Peer review is a bit like another academic institution: tenure in higher education. The concept is that it promotes intellectual freedom. But in all too many cases, those who have it don't need it, and those who need it don't have it.

In 2007, Chris Nowinski started his Sports Legacy Institute in Boston and got the brain of dead pro wrestler Chris Benoit for Dr. Bennet Omalu to study. When the Boston group announced that Benoit (who, at age 40, had murdered his wife and their seven-year-old son before killing himself) had chronic traumatic encephalopathy, World Wrestling Entertainment derided the finding as "not published in a peer-reviewed journal." Then, when Omalu published a paper about it in a peer-reviewed journal, it was "only" the *Journal of Forensic Nursing*, not one of the high-end publications like *Neurosurgery*. Of course, the reason was that Omalu, for a time and for all intents and purposes, had been blackballed by *Neurosurgery*, which was in the National Football League's pocket. Earlier this year Omalu did resume publishing in *Neurosurgery*; I'm waiting for the next pointless excuse from the naysayers.

Some of us who admire Nowinski's work with SLI and want to see its mission succeed worry that he is falling into the peer-review trap. We also worry that the NFL's $1 million grant to SLI's sister Center for the Study of CTE at Boston University will become part of a larger pattern of delay and dilution.

The Boston group has said that it is moving away from announcements to journalistic outlets and toward releasing findings only after they are published in peer-reviewed scientific journals. They made an exception 11 days ago with the Dave Duerson press conference because, Dr. Robert Cantu explained, they always bow to the wishes of the family.

But even assuming that the policy is plausible, I believe the wishes of the family are the wrong exception. As a result of Nowinski and company's own logic and energy, sports concussions are a major societal issue. Instead of carrying on about peer review and then making exceptions anyway, when convenient, I would rather hear the response to a call from Omalu, in his forthcoming *Neurosurgery* article, for new protocols allowing automatic CTE study of postmortem brains of certain populations, such as athletes in contact sports.

Please don't tell me I'm being simplistic. I'm being *simple.* Obviously, there's a role for editorial gatekeepers — in academia, journalism, and elsewhere. The point is that we don't need to study 500 more dead football players' brains before coming to common-sense conclusions about important actions and political solutions. Take it from an old college dropout: peer-review rhetoric is mumbo-jumbo.

23 MAY 2011 -----------------------------

We now know that hockey player Derek Boogaard's recent mysterious death at age 28 was caused by a fatal mix of alcohol and the painkiller oxycodone. After Boogaard died, his family donated his brain to the chronic traumatic encephalopathy research group in Boston, led by Dr. Robert Cantu and spearheaded by Chris Nowinski. The Boogaard tragedy followed close on the heels of the Boston group's announcement that Dave Duerson had CTE when he committed suicide.

A cluster of recent sports suicides highlights the American concussion crisis, of course. But it also raises another tough question: after years of being asleep at the switch on the scope and magnitude of industrial brain injuries in our couch-potato entertainment, are the sports establishment and media now contributing to a feeding frenzy that is actually *causing* additional deaths rather than preventing them?

Viewed in the round, the CTE story is starting to look a little bit like the rape story — an outrage for which awareness and reporting levels inevitably influence public understanding. The root issue should drive consensus, but the methods are delicate. In raising all this in my own indelicate way, I am not indicting Nowinski, who has done the yeoman's work of putting the whole subject in play in the first place.

In a piece last September, "Why a 2011 NFL Strike or Lockout Would Be the Best Thing for America," I predicted that this year would be one of reckoning for concussions. Naturally, a yahoo reader (with a small "y") immediately wrote to call me "an idiot." I'm not sure he realized that even as his billet deux rocketed through the ether, police in Denver were discovering the suicide of a young Broncos player named Kenny McKinley. Did McKinley have CTE?

In February, while the sports pages were filled with stories about what a great guy Dave Duerson was — even though he was on record in Congressional testimony, and as a member of a player-management compensation board, as downplaying the connections of retired players' mental disability claims — a former NFL player named Ricky Bell died, with little attention, in South Carolina at 36. His family refused to comment on how. Did Bell have CTE?

My theory is that CTE news is scaring athletes, as well it should. And that some of them could be getting scared to death. Or at least, with the onset of their own horrible multiple-concussion syndrome symptoms, finding themselves wondering if it's better to end it all than to live an additional 10 or 20 years — with the prospect of winding up homeless and self-destructive like Mike Webster, or homicidal like Chris Benoit.

If there's a lesson here, it's that the federal government has to get on with the task of cleaning up this mess. Investigating the sharp angles of football helmet hype doesn't even begin to cut it. There's a long and sorry history here of research conducted and research subtly censored, and the trail is paved in NFL gold.

Another lesson emerging from the Duerson suicide is that the dog-and-pony show of brain-study-finding news conferences may have passed its peak of usefulness. At this point, we need appeals for more brains to study a lot less than we need more action.

I'll give the last word of this round to Michael Benoit, the father of

Chris Benoit. Mike and I have had our ups and downs, but I've never doubted his integrity.

"What are my thoughts?" Benoit said to me. "My thoughts are that the CTE doctors and advocates need their behinds kicked. Everyone loves to be in front of the cameras talking about the latest case of CTE, but no one is talking about the people who are currently suffering. The research world is an old boys' club. How many more brains do we need to prove that concussions can cause CTE?

"Here's what I say: if you are an athlete in a contact sport, take three to five grams of high-grade Omega-3 oils daily. If you get concussed, it will provide protection for your brain and greatly reduce your recovery time. If you are already showing symptoms of CTE, take five to 10 grams of Omega-3 oils daily. It will help your brain by reducing inflammation, and it is a mood enhancer and may help people who are suicidal."

1 JUNE 2011 ----------------------------

On the subject of what is being done on behalf of the untold number of former athletes who are walking around with serious brain injuries (though many are capable of doing little else), I caught up with Brent Boyd.

Following the suicide of Dave Duerson, I told the full story of the confrontation between Boyd and Duerson in a Congressional hearing room in 2007, and of the latter's less-than-helpful service on the NFL disability benefits board. Boyd, founder of the advocacy group Dignity After Football, also is on the advisory board of Chris Nowinski's Sports Legacy Institute. However, Boyd is highly critical of the Boston chronic traumatic encephalopathy research team's acceptance of a $1 million NFL grant to support the Center for the Study of CTE at Boston University. Boyd and others believe that this skews research and compromises advocacy.

Last year Robert Stern, Nowinski's co-director at the center, co-authored a study of an innovative imaging technique to determine if CTE is detectable in living people, a key component of the search for cures. (At the moment the disease can be identified only in post-mortem brain tissue.) The findings from this round of "virtual biopsies" suggested that all five athletes who participated — three football players, one boxer, and one wrestler — have CTE.[9]

Brent Boyd, 54, whose six-year NFL career ended in 1986, was one of the football players who underwent a virtual biopsy. As a result, he considers himself one of "the only yet identified living persons to walk the earth knowing they have deadly CTE."

Boyd also thinks he was "a guinea pig" who was treated brusquely and received no counseling or support in the wake of the finding. "It was like, 'Here's lunch money, you have significant CTE, and here are your return flight tickets. Thanks for coming!'" The ordeal "has left me sleepless for months," Boyd said. "What am I supposed to do with this information?"

Chris Nowinski is out of the country. This morning I spoke with Dr. Robert Cantu, the leader of the Boston CTE research team. Cantu emphasized that he was not involved in the "virtual biopsy" study, which was presented last December in Chicago at the annual conference of the Radiological Society of North America.

"We can have an index of suspicion that certain individuals have CTE, and given Brent's history of brain trauma, the level of suspicion is very high," Cantu said. "But we still don't yet have blood markers or any other way of identifying CTE with certainty, except through finding tau protein in the brain tissue of dead people."

Cantu added that as a physician, which many CTE researchers are not, he regards himself as having doctor-patient relationships and being sensitive to the need for treating research subjects with dignity and humanity.

Cantu also acknowledged that counseling and support are missing pieces of concussion reform work: "It would be ideal for SLI to have a personal advocacy wing. That is not as easy to pull off as it may sound. On almost a daily basis, SLI gets contacted by people offering help in these areas, but before accepting that help, we must determine their level of qualifications for assisting those with brain trauma with their cognitive and other life problems. Without a doubt, building that network is a very important task as research and advocacy move forward."

9 JUNE 2011 -----------------------------

On May 24, Judge J. Frederick Motz of U.S. District Court in Maryland ruled against former Minnesota Vikings offensive lineman Brent Boyd in the latest round of his long-running administrative and legal fight with the Bert Bell/Pete Rozelle NFL Player Retirement Plan.[10]

This is a miscarriage of justice, turning not on a serious substantive dispute about Boyd's football-caused mental illness so much as on procedural technicalities about whether his reapplications of previously denied claims established "changed circumstances." This is another chapter of shame for both the National Football League and the NFL Players Association.

This does not need to be the last chapter of the Brent Boyd story. Unfortunately, though, Brent told me yesterday that his attorney, Mark DeBofsky of the Chicago firm Daley DeBofsky & Bryant, does not have the resources to pursue an appeal on a contingency basis (that is, without payment of ongoing fees rather than the hope of recovering them as part of a settlement or judgment). But that does not mean that a fund cannot be set up on Boyd's behalf to help sustain the work of his legal team, or that other representation cannot be persuaded to join the effort on a contingency or pro bono basis.

10 JUNE 2011 ----------------------------------

To the best of my knowledge, not a single media outlet except this blog has reported on the May 24 ruling in Baltimore by U.S. District Court Judge J. Frederick Motz, who threw out retired Minnesota Viking lineman Brent Boyd's case against the Bert Bell/Pete Rozelle NFL Player Retirement Plan.

Boyd's attorney, Mark DeBofsky, told me, "We felt we had presented sufficient evidence of changed circumstances and that despite the court's finding of no conflict of interest, the numbers suggest otherwise. Given the paltry number of claims paid by the NFL disability and retirement plan for head injuries, it appears the plan is biased against such claims out of fear of an avalanche of brain trauma disability claims."

Cut through the cowardly judge's legalese and split hairs, and it comes down to this: the court decided that the retirement plan "did not abuse its discretion" in rejecting Boyd's reapplications and administrative appeals. There was no showing of "changed circumstances" — even though we have tons more basic information on the legitimacy of Boyd's claim of traumatic brain injury from football than was known at the time of the original filing some 11 years ago, and even though one of the three Players Association members of the disability claims board was Dave Duerson, who himself had chronic traumatic encephalopathy when he committed suicide in February.

What extraordinary judicial incuriosity.

Boyd attorney DeBofsky told me that during litigation, "We had requested discovery that would essentially have been an audit of the plan and benefits paid for head injuries, but the judge denied our request."

Judge Motz's rulings on discovery and on the merits were both farces. They must not stand.

On May 24 — the very day Judge J. Frederick Motz of U.S. District Court in Maryland dismissed former player Brent Boyd's appeal of the National Football League retirement plan's rejection of his mental disability claim — Mike Lopresti of *USA Today* wrote a touching column headlined "Struggle continues for widow of Dave Duerson."[11]

In the piece, Alicia Duerson called her former husband's February suicide "the tip of the iceberg" of the NFL's traumatic brain-injury problem. Lopresti recounted the former star defensive back's domestic violence arrest, personal bankruptcy, and postmortem finding of chronic traumatic encephalopathy. He was a big man with a shrinking brain; Alicia Duerson said, "His brain had started dying 10 years ago."

There's one small thing *USA Today* didn't discuss, and Alicia Duerson apparently is not incorporating into the talking points of her CTE public awareness tour: the fact that Dave Duerson served on the review board, consisting of representatives from both the league and the NFL Players Association, which has stonewalled other retired players' claims for head-injury benefits. In 2007, he even argued the retirement plan's position on Capitol Hill and, during a break at a Congressional hearing, exploded in abuse at Brent Boyd and old players union leaders Sam Huff and Bernie Parrish.

And without that crucial connection, Dave Duerson's suicide becomes just one more sob story.

In his travesty of a decision, Judge Motz held that Boyd's attorneys did not prove "changed circumstances," "abuse of discretion," or "conflict of interest." The Bert Bell/Pete Rozelle NFL Player Retirement Plan successfully sold the argument that introducing into evidence a decade's worth of new published findings on CTE, along with the reason for Duerson's own death by self-inflicted gunshot, was simply a desperation ploy by a rejected disability claimant to get "a second bite of the apple."

Oh, I see. The Duerson suicide was not a "changed circumstance" for the dozens, scores, or hundreds of retired players still living with depression, still unable to function or support their families or live normal lives, still getting no relief from the $9-billion-a-year NFL. It was only a "changed circumstance" for Alicia Duerson.

Outrageous.

14 JUNE 2011 --------------------------

In the story of the late Dave Duerson's loud altercation with Sam Huff and Bernie Parrish in a Congressional committee hearing room in 2007, I have characterized both Huff and Parrish as historic builders of the National Football League Players Association who became disenchanted with the NFLPA's advocacy on behalf of disabled retired players.

In an email to me, Dave Meggyesy objected to what he called "revisionist history" with respect to Huff. "Sam Huff was not a union supporter or a union leader. He was and is a management guy," Meggyesy wrote. "Sam claims union affiliation and sentiment through his father, mine workers I believe. This apple fell far from the tree. The Marriott hotel chain is and has been non-union; Sam has been a spokesman for them for years."

I respect Meggyesy, who played linebacker for the old St. Louis football Cardinals from 1963 through 1969 before retiring and writing the book *Out of Their League*, a breakthrough critical look at the football industry. He later served many years as the NFLPA's western regional director.

Regarding the case of Brent Boyd — the proximate cause of Duerson's outburst during criticism of his role on the NFL retirement and disability review board, which rejected Boyd's application for mental disability benefits — Meggyesy said, "Duerson shows the impact of CTE, nothing more. Boyd's case should stand on its own, and no doubt be reevaluated."

I disagree with Meggyesy on that point. Duerson, and by extension the NFLPA, have been wrong, loud wrong, on the issue of football brain injuries and on taking the most aggressive and best steps to protect the community of retired players. The Brent Boyd case emphatically does not stand "on its own"; it must be viewed in the context of years of league-friendly, suppressed, and incomplete research on chronic traumatic encephalopathy.

16 AUGUST 2011 ------------------------

Alex Marvez of Foxsports.com has an important new piece up on Dave Duerson, which focuses on Duerson's battle with depression and uses as its main source former quarterback Eric Hipple.[12]

Credit Marvez with tackling a subject, mental health, which remains taboo. It's also good to see a prominent football journalist daring to talk at all about whether Duerson's service on the joint NFL/NFLPA disability claims review board was tainted by his own likely diminished capacity in his last years.

The FoxSports article quotes former defensive end Andrew Stewart, who has pending litigation against the Bert Bell/Pete Rozelle NFL Player Retirement Plan, using that exact phrase, "diminished capacity," to describe Duerson's state when he joined a unanimous board vote in rejecting Stewart's claim for an increase in disability benefits. At the May news conference announcing the autopsy finding of chronic traumatic encephalopathy after Duerson committed suicide, I used the same words in asking whether there should be a review of the case files on which Duerson helped the disability board rule.

What is unfortunate about the Marvez piece is that it quotes Duerson's friends as saying they perceived no "noticeable change in his demeanor or acumen," while failing to document his tirade against retired players who confronted him at a 2007 Congressional hearing in which Duerson downplayed concussion syndrome. (The article does note Duerson's 2005 domestic violence incident — but rather creepily puts distance between it and an observation by Belinda Lerner, executive director of NFL Player Care, that "he looked fine the last time I saw him.")

We can all have our opinions on how fine Dave Duerson was at any particular point before he took his own life and was found to have CTE. But the constellation of facts leads to the conclusion that ex-players with disputes over disability claims that were adjudicated, in part, by Duerson deserve rehearings. Period. That is elemental justice.

A second Marvez piece today, "NFL retirement plan faces challenge,"[13] is highly recommended. In it, Andrew Stewart's attorney, Michael Rosenthal, pounds hard on the theme that the entire process was corrupted by our retrospective knowledge that retirement board trustee Duerson, who committed suicide in February, himself had chronic traumatic encephalopathy.

I am less interested than some others in all the internal politics of the NFLPA. Maybe Duerson was a good guy, maybe he wasn't. But he was definitely brain-damaged, he was in denial about an already deep body of research on football and brain damage, and he was in a position of power, ruling on the disability claims of brethren. Stewart and others are right about this, and those calling them names for pointing this out are wrong. I hope the dissident retirees achieve justice, in this Maryland courtroom and elsewhere.

9 SEPTEMBER 2011 ----------------------
The pro football season opened last night with a game on NBC — coinciding, to the delight of Republicans, with President Obama's latest dithering televised address. Collectively, fans are wondering why kickoffs have to start at the 35-yard line this year rather than the 30. Most haven't given a second thought to the death last Sunday, at age

56, of Lee Roy Selmon, the Tampa Bay Buccaneers' Hall of Fame defensive end in the '70s and '80s.

They should. Selmon is Dave Duerson Lite.

Though no direct causal link can be established between Selmon's fatal cerebrovascular accident and the no-longer-quite-so-well-covered-up epidemic of traumatic brain injuries in football, the scenario in the round amounts to another grotesque twist on the fatal flaw of America's sport. And the sooner we have a real conversation about all this, the better. It is not a problem that can be willed away by hard counts, play-action fakes, or John Madden's belated brand of "concussion awareness."

A revered figure in the Tampa Bay community, Lee Roy Selmon had numerous business interests, including a popular chain of sports bars. He was athletic director at the University of South Florida from 2001 to 2004.

Early last week reports surfaced of a new lawsuit filed in Los Angeles Superior Court, on behalf of retired players, most of whom had played for the Bucs, against the NFL and two helmet manufacturers. Like other recent litigation — the mass action represented by Thomas Girardi of *Erin Brockovich* fame, and another in which the most prominent plaintiff is Super Bowl–winning quarterback Jim McMahon — this one alleges a cover-up of known evidence of the long-term effects of football-inflicted brain trauma.

Both Lee Roy Selmon and his brother Dewey (who also played for the Bucs) were listed as plaintiffs in this new action, but that turned out to be a mistake. Their attorney, David Rosen, who was representing the Selmons in other matters (notably, a contemplated lawsuit on behalf of retired players for non–head-injury disability claims), took public responsibility for a clerical error and amended the court papers to remove the Selmons.

Incredibly, Lee Roy Selmon then suffered a massive stroke on Friday and died two days later.

Was the stroke football related? I don't know, except to observe that it's for us to find out and for the NFL to hope we don't. Also that it's not a question the mostly timid and incurious mainstream sports media are eager to pursue.

Stroke, like spinal-cord injuries, is a different phenomenon than chronic traumatic encephalopathy. The delivery system, however, is identical. In pro wrestling, Bret Hart's 1999 stroke in his early forties, which partially paralyzed him, almost certainly was a byproduct of botched "sports entertainment" stunts. Last year another WWE legend, Ricky Steamboat, nearly died from a brain aneurysm — later euphemized to a "burst capillary" — caused by a fake beatdown by a posse of bad guys on live TV.

One exception to the list of journalists flinching from the implications of the Selmon story is Joey Johnston of the *Tampa Tribune*. In an email, Johnston told me that the potential parallel of the errant report of Selmon's involvement in a lawsuit, followed by his being stricken, was chronicled by his newspaper "the day of the stroke but not mentioned the day of the death. There's an element of conjecture there, sure, but it all makes you wonder."

Johnston led the reporting team for a lengthy and highly recommended July 25 article in the *Tribune* about the lifelong health price paid by Selmon's teammates on the 1979 Tampa Bay team that almost reached the Super Bowl.[14]

Unlike Duerson, Selmon did not loudly and publicly deny what was becoming widely known about concussion syndrome. Unlike Duerson, Selmon didn't live to see his judgment, businesses, personal finances, and family life go to pieces. Finally, unlike Duerson, Selmon didn't serve on a joint league-union board that reviewed disability claims and rejected many of them.

Of course, by that point Dave Duerson himself was not Dave Duerson. He had CTE.

10 SEPTEMBER 2011 -------------------

The Andrew Stewart case, as I suggested last month, might reveal more about the work on the disability claims review board of Dave Duerson. But it turns out that, while Stewart's attorneys have made a lot of progress in getting scrutiny in open court of the board's inner workings — a very good thing — Duerson himself did not participate in the deliberations of Stewart's case in August of last year.

The three NFL Players Association representatives on the board for Stewart's review were Andre Collins, Robert Smith, and Jeff Van Note. "I do not know why Duerson was not on the board that day," Stewart attorney Michael Rosenthal emailed me.

According to John Hogan, who represents many retired players from his disability law practice in Georgia, retirement board members occasionally designate others as proxies, and that is probably what happened here. The whole process is mysterious and secretive, which is why we need the drip-drip-drip of additional cases to break down the NFL and NFLPA's limestone wall.

12 SEPTEMBER 2011 -------------------

Why wasn't Dave Duerson, one of the three regular Players Association appointees on the review board for the Bert Bell/Pete Rozelle NFL Player Retirement Plan, not at the hearing in August 2010 at which a disability claim by former player Andrew Stewart was rejected?

If Duerson's absence were the result of a routine scheduling conflict — if he had to attend a wedding the same day, for example — that would be one thing. But we know that Duerson committed suicide six months later and that a study of his postmortem brain tissue showed he had chronic traumatic encephalopathy. So it is crucially important to determine if there is another explanation for his not having been at the Stewart review. What if Duerson suffered during this period from a flare-up of depression or general mental confusion?

Related question: how many *other* retirement board meetings did Duerson miss?

Writing about the Stewart case last month, FoxSports.com's Alex Marvez quoted an unnamed fellow board trustee as defending Duerson's performance in that role in the last five years of his life. The trustee said Duerson "never displayed impairments that reflected brain damage." Since both this trustee and Douglas Ell, the NFL attorney who talked to Marvez for his story, knew that its focus would be on Duerson's involvement in the Stewart matter, it seems odd that they wouldn't have mentioned that Duerson was not present at the August 2010 meeting.

Another source who is named — NFL Player Care Foundation executive director Belinda Lerner — told Marvez "that Duerson 'had his complete faculties working' and 'contributed to the conversation' at the last trustee meeting both attended six months before his death." What was the date of that meeting? I will ask Lerner.

Dave Duerson was in good spirits at the August 2010 NFL retirement board meeting. Or Duerson missed the meeting. Which is it?

Ever since Dave Duerson's February suicide and the finding of chronic traumatic encephalopathy, I have been calling for the reopening of all rejected National Football League disability claim files on his watch as one of the three NFL Players Association trustees of the Bert Bell/Pete Rozelle NFL Player Retirement Plan.

The first step is figuring out exactly when Duerson served in that capacity. We're making some progress — though today's information arrives with tantalizing ambiguity.

Back in the winter, NFL spokesman Brian McCarthy told me he didn't know the dates of Duerson's tenure and suggested I ask the NFLPA. But the NFLPA never responded to my inquiries.

Last month Alex Marvez of FoxSports.com reported on the

Maryland court case of retired player Andrew Stewart, who is suing to reverse the rejection of his disability claim by the retirement board. The Duerson angle, which I have been pushing, was a central element of Marvez's story. Belinda Lerner, executive director of the NFL Player Care Foundation, was directly quoted about seeing him at the trustee meeting six months before his death: "He seemed fine the last time I saw him. He was with his fiancée. To me, someone who is going to get married is someone who is feeling hopeful for the future."[15]

Six months prior to Duerson's death, of course, would have been August 2010.

Yet Michael Rosenthal, the attorney for Andrew Stewart, told me last week that disclosures by the NFL to his client now reveal that Duerson did not participate in the deliberation of that claim, which was at the August 2010 meeting.

On the chance that Lerner and Rosenthal were referring to two different meetings, I asked the former for the specific date and explained why I was asking.

I got this back, via NFL spokesman Greg Aiello: "The meeting referred to by Belinda was a Bert Bell/Pete Rozelle retirement board meeting — one of four quarterly meetings — February, May, August, and November. There was a retirement board meeting on August 18, 2010, in Boston. Belinda's comment referred to the last meeting Dave attended as a trustee for the Players Association."

I believe Aiello is confirming that Lerner was saying that the meeting where she saw Duerson was on August 18, 2010 — the one in which, according to the records provided to Stewart, Duerson was not a trustee but had been replaced by Andre Collins. If my interpretation is wrong, then Lerner or Aiello should tell me, and I will quickly reflect exactly what they were saying.

John Hogan, the Georgia disability attorney for many players, emailed me, saying, "I have the minutes of the August 2010 retirement board meeting from Jimmie Giles's case, which was considered at that meeting." (Giles, the ex–wide receiver, is a plaintiff in the latest of three lawsuits filed recently against the NFL alleging a cover-up of known evidence of the long-term effects of traumatic brain injuries from football.) "It confirms that Andre Collins was there in place of Duerson. It does not indicate why he was not present."

13 SEPTEMBER 2011 ----------------------
Belinda Lerner, executive director of the National Football League Player Care Foundation, has changed her story. Or if you prefer, she has clarified her statements about Dave Duerson last month to Alex Marvez of FoxSports.com. In one key respect, Lerner has admitted she was mistaken.

In my follow-ups with her, via NFL spokesman Greg Aiello, Lerner at first continued to insist that Duerson was one of the three NFL Players Association trustees at the August 2010 meeting. But after carefully reviewing the minutes, Lerner now acknowledges that alternate Andre Collins replaced Duerson. Duerson did attend the next meeting, in New Orleans in November, before committing suicide in February of this year.

Regarding Lerner's recollection that Duerson was fine "the last time" she saw him, NFL spokesman Greg Aiello said, "Dave also attended the November 17 board meeting in New Orleans, the last time Belinda saw him and last time he acted as a trustee. Belinda recalls that meeting as when he introduced his fiancée to the other board participants." That was three months, not six months, prior to Duerson's death.

The NFL's Aiello, whom I respect as a consummate professional, expressed pique at my line of questions. "We are trying to be helpful. This is not a deposition. Belinda was pretty clear that whatever comments were attributed to her were based on the last time she saw Dave

— precise date was unknown. Why are you more concerned about the dates than her observations of Dave?"

I responded to Greg: "To be clear, this all started because I'd read Alex Marvez's 8/16/11 coverage of the Andrew Stewart court case. One important focus of Marvez's story was whether Duerson's participation as a trustee matters in disputed disability claims — an issue I have been pushing, as you may know. I don't speak for Marvez, but as a reader of his work I know him to be a good and careful reporter, and I suspect he would have written his story quite differently had he known that Duerson didn't hear Stewart's particular case (which would come out at the pretrial hearing last week or in the discovery leading up to it)."

I added to Aiello: "Why the FoxSports.com article proceeded from a flawed premise is not something I'm going to speculate on in this email, except to note that Marvez had multiple NFL sources (not just Belinda Lerner). But I emphasize that my questions here were and are legitimate. No, I was not deposing Ms. Lerner; I was asking her questions for a piece of journalism, in the course of which I also openly answered your own questions as to why I was asking them. I am glad I got the right answers, even if it took a few rounds."

Further crucial questions remain. Why wasn't Duerson at the Boston meeting? And did he miss any other board meetings, and if so, why?

Meanwhile, Lerner's account of Duerson's introduction of his fiancée in November 2010 does fill in some gaps in the timeline of the last months of his life.

Retired player Dave Pear, leader of the dissident group Independent Football Veterans, cc'd me on an email today to DeMaurice Smith, executive director of the NFL Players Association. The message was spurred by this blog's coverage of the late Dave Duerson's role as one of the three NFLPA-appointed trustees of the Bert Bell/Pete Rozelle NFL Player Retirement Plan.

Here's the full text of the email by Dave Pear and his wife, Heidi.

Dear De Smith,

Dave Duerson was on the disability board as a voting member in 2008 when my claim for total and permanent degenerative disability was denied (again). I would like my case reopened and I would like a full report as to the merits of my denial and specifically why you think Dave was qualified (along with Robert Smith and Jeff Van Note) to make this decision.

How can an individual with severe brain damage and no disability training or legal expertise as were Robert Smith and Van Note allowed this abuse of power and breach of fiduciary duty? Or was Andre Collins filling that day (or moonlighting as a disability board voting member)?

Does ERISA law allow unqualified people the power to make these types of decisions?

Please explain.

Thank you.

Regards,

Dave & Heidi Pear

(The Pears don't even mention that Duerson, in 2007 Congressional testimony, was downplaying known evidence of the connection between football traumatic brain injuries and long-term mental-health problems.)

15 SEPTEMBER 2011 ---------------------

FoxSports.com's Alex Marvez now reports that a federal judge in Maryland has set a February 27, 2012, trial date in retired National

Football League player Andrew Stewart's lawsuit against the Bert Bell / Pete Rozelle NFL Player Retirement Plan.[16]

Marvez's story notes that, as I have reported — and in contrast to the strong suggestion of the collective NFL statements to him for FoxSports.com coverage of the Stewart case last month — "Dave Duerson didn't vote upon Stewart's claim as initially believed. Duerson — a star NFL safety who committed suicide in February — was one of the NFL Players Association's three trustee appointees on the board. The other three were appointed by the NFL."

This trial, the story says, "could reveal some of the NFL's retirement program's secretive inner workings."

Marvez writes that a proxy "is believed" to have taken Duerson's spot at the August 18, 2010, meeting of the board in Boston, where Stewart's disability claim was reviewed and unanimously rejected. From my reporting, I think it's pretty clear that that proxy was Andre Collins.

NFL lawyer Douglas Ell "declined comment to FoxSports.com."

Interestingly, Ell has filed a motion to remand the case to re-review by the NFL board. I support some kind of re-review of all Duerson-tainted cases. Stewart's attorney, Michael Rosenthal, however, opposes the motion — apparently because he feels, no doubt correctly, that at this point his client would get a fairer shake in a court of law than through a process now so despised and distrusted by many in the NFL retiree community.

19 OCTOBER 2011 ----------------------------

The Senate Commerce, Science, and Transportaton Committee held a two-hour hearing on sports concussions on Wednesday.[17]

Despite an annoyingly oily good-old-boy performance by the chairman, Senator Jay Rockefeller of West Virginia, the hearing had valuable moments. When we set aside the football element of the debate, the promotion of "concussion awareness" through such forums is immensely educational for participants in minor sports and especially for female athletes.

In my opinion, the most penetrating interlude was almost an aside: an exchange between Senator John Thune of South Dakota and one of the witness panelists, Dr. Jeffrey Kutcher, the director of Michigan NeuroSport, about the appropriate ages at which athletes can begin engaging in violent contact.

The star of the hearing, of course, was Senator Tom Udall of New Mexico, who has spearheaded the investigations by executive agencies of the Riddell football helmet company. But in two important ways, Udall seriously disappointed.

First, and as expected, Udall directed a lot of outrage against the spurious claims of Riddell and other "Concussion Inc." marketers — while saying nothing about how the National Football League and its operatives were in bed with many of those same companies.[18]

Udall also cited the suicide of Dave Duerson, the donation of Duerson's brain to chronic traumatic encephalopathy research, and the finding that Duerson had CTE. Udall said Duerson wanted to help others in the future, which is standard superficial commentary. But the senator went over the line when he went on to mention that Duerson had testified before the very same commerce committee in 2007.

Well, indeed he had, but Udall's suggestion that Duerson had the same intent in that appearance is shockingly misleading. As the senator well knows, the Duerson of the '07 testimony, in his role as a NFL Players Association–appointed trustee of the NFL's retirement and disability plan, had emphatically *downplayed* mounting evidence of long-term traumatic brain injury.

24 FEBRUARY 2012 -

The family of Dave Duerson has sued the NFL for its alleged liability for the brain damage he was found to have in the special autopsy he requested in his suicide note.

In recent months, more concussion-linked litigation has been filed by various groups of former players than even the 24/7 NFL Network could possibly cover. They add up to lots of confusing legal wrangling by professionals and their professional mouthpieces. The Duerson case is different, though — a bona fide potential game-changer in terms of both the NFL's exposure and the public's broader understanding of what I maintain is the bleak future of the sport of football.

All civil court actions involve two parties, a plaintiff and a defendant. But in this one, we have two institutional bystanders with more than a passing interest. The first is the community of disabled NFLers whose claims were rejected by the Bert Bell/Pete Rozelle NFL Player Retirement Plan — on whose board Duerson sat, denying the scientific evidence on chronic traumatic encephalopathy even as the disease ate away at his own brain, destroying mood, impulse control, and judgment.

The other spectator-stakeholders are all of the rest of us who are trying to sort out this concussion mess for the millions of kids who play football in peewee and high school leagues. Some believe the game, which is inherently violent, simply needs rule changes, better protective equipment, and smarter health and safety practices. I am in the camp holding that football concussion reform is oxymoronic, and that the medical, financial, legal, and educational bottom line is tobacco-like age restrictions, which would chop-block the knees out from under the NFL's $10-billion-a-year global marketing machine.

Duerson case discovery and testimony will subject key theories to empirical tests. As the process plays out, the Duerson family and their image will not emerge unscathed. Last year's suicide got spun as martyrdom because of the decedent's instructions to donate his brain tissue for research by Boston University's Center for the Study of CTE. The part about Duerson as a bad guy in his role as a NFL Players Association retirement board trustee got muted. That will no longer be the case, as the NFL's legal team submits for the court record and magnifies Duerson's every utterance in his years of denial.

Alan Schwarz of the *New York Times* is reporting Tregg Duerson's contention that his father had a private change of heart between 2007 — when he verbally and almost physically confronted other NFL retirees at a Congressional hearing — and his death. A change of some sort is manifest. Its effect on the entire Bell/Rozelle Plan mental-disability claim file, whose reopening and daylighting I have advocated? That is what remains to be seen.

The most devastating litigation against American football culture, our lay religion, is yet to come, from the parents of youth players who will continue to suffer catastrophic injuries and death, notwithstanding the medicine-wagon "solutions" being hyped by the cottage industries of "concussion awareness."

If you can't acknowledge which way the arrows are pointing, then you flunk your baseline neurocognitive test. You've been playing football for too long, with or without a helmet.

----

1   Since the original publication of this article, the site has been rebranded NFLevolution.com.

2   "A Suicide, a Last Request, a Family's Questions," www.nytimes. com/2011/02/23/sports/football/23duerson.html.

3   "'You Have to Accept My Pain,'" http://deadspin.com/#!5767609/ you-have-to-accept-my-pain-an-interview-with-dave-duerson-three-months-before-his-suicide.

4   youtube.com/watch?v=yeSsYOgGJW4.

5   This paragraph, reprinted here as originally published online, is incorrect. See the clarification in the next piece.

6   "Duerson's case highlights the limits of the N.F.L.'s disability plan," www.nytimes.com/2011/05/05/sports/football/05duerson.html:

7   Video of the press conference is available at www.bu.edu/buniverse/view/?v=1GIhOEcN.

8   sportslegacy.org/index.php/science-a-medicine/chronic-traumatic-encephalopathy.

9   "New technique targets ex-athletes' head injuries," December 1, 2010, www.cbc.ca/news/health/story/2010/12/01/brain-injury-virtual-biopsy-nfl.html.

10   The judge's opinion can be viewed at muchnick.net/boydruling52411.pdf.

11   www.usatoday.com/sports/columnist/lopresti/2011-05-23-dave-alicia-duerson-brain-injury-nfl_N.htm.

12   "Duerson didn't have to die to have impact," msn.foxsports.com/nfl/story/dave-duerson-didnt-have-to-die-to-have-impact-081511.

13   msn.foxsports.com/nfl/story/andrew-stewart-dave-duerson-nfl-retirement-plan-faces-legal-challenge-08151.

14   "Broken Bucs," at duke1.tbo.com/content/2010/jul/25/260710/bucs-first-success-came-costly-toll/sports-bucs-broken/.

15   msn.foxsports.com/nfl/story/dave-duerson-didnt-have-to-die-to-have-impact-081511.

16   See msn.foxsports.com/nfl/story/nfl-retired-players-injury-claim-court-date-set-091511.

17   You can view the video at www.c-spanvideo.org/program/Concuss.

18   More on this aspect of the hearing follows, in the chapter on Dr. Joe Maroon.

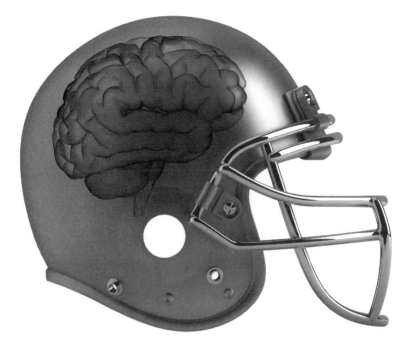

JOE MAROON
AND OTHER PITTSBURGH WITCH DOCTORS

14 DECEMBER 2009 ----------------------

In an article on ESPN.com about the brain damage of yet another dead pro wrestler, Andrew "Test" Martin,[1] World Wrestling Entertainment — the company of Connecticut U.S. Senate candidate Linda McMahon — stated in part: "WWE is unaware of the veracity of any of these tests, be it for Chris Benoit or Andrew Martin . . . WWE has been asking to see the research and test results in the case of Mr. Benoit for years and has not been supplied with them."

The second sentence is a grossly, and characteristically, misleading statement by the pro wrestling death mill. The following background reveals that "lie" may not be too strong a word.

Here's the full chronology.

In June 2007, WWE star Chris Benoit murdered his wife and their son, and killed himself. Chris Nowinski, a former pro wrestler who had been forced to retire because of the cumulative effects of in-ring concussions, had started a research and advocacy group, and Nowinski prevailed upon Chris Benoit's father, Mike Benoit, to donate his son's brain for studies by Dr. Bennet Omalu, a pioneering researcher of what is being called chronic traumatic encephalopathy. Later in the year Nowinski and Mike Benoit publicized Omalu's research.

In March 2008, WWE began baseline neurological testing for its performers, using an emerging system of sports-medicine protocols called ImPACT. WWE itself did not announce this change. However, in an April 11, 2008, news release, Sports Legacy Institute's Nowinski, citing "anonymous wrestlers," reported: "WWE management has instituted a concussion management program. At a mandatory meeting for all performers in early March WWE performers took a computerized neuropsychological testing protocol, which evaluates such things as memory, cognitive skills, and reaction time. They will be re-tested aggressively every six months to look for long-term health issues, as well as re-tested after suspected concussions to help determine when it is safe to return to in-ring action."

According to Dave Meltzer, publisher of the authoritative *Wrestling Observer Newsletter*, March 2008 corresponds with when Dr. Joseph Maroon was hired to coordinate WWE's ImPACT program and supervise the work of two doctors who henceforth traveled to all WWE shows.

On October 1, 2008, Dr. Maroon visited the Brain Injury Research Institute in Morgantown, West Virginia. The institute is co-directed by Dr. Julian Bailes, chair of the neurosurgery department at West Virginia University, and Dr. Omalu, a medical professor and coroner now based in California. Also present at the meeting were the brain institute's general counsel, Bob Fitzsimmons, and Peter Davies, a professor of pathology and neuroscience at Yeshiva University's Albert Einstein College of Medicine in New York.

On the phone with me this morning, Omalu was hopping mad about the WWE statement to ESPN. "Dr. Maroon was there with us and he was shown all our research information, slides, and specimens — on Chris Benoit and all the athletes' brains we studied," Omalu said.

The only possible confusion about any of this would be painfully hairsplitting. But that's WWE's M.O.

Maroon also has long been a team physician for the NFL's Pittsburgh Steelers and a familiar league consultant throughout the public debate in recent years — culminating in hearings earlier this year before the House Judiciary Committee — over football concussions. An impossibly tortured rationalization could be offered to the effect that when Maroon was in West Virginia, he was representing the NFL, not WWE.

The WWE corporate website prominently calls Maroon the company "medical director." Maroon's own website and bio at the University of Pittsburgh Medical Center say he became WWE medical director "in 2008," though not the month. Again, March 2008 was when the company hired Maroon with a brain-injury portfolio, whether or not the title at the time was "medical director."

Omalu pointed out that there is a lot more to how this story relates to the slow and grudging acceptance of his research by the NFL as well as by WWE. The October 2008 meeting was his third with Maroon dating back to 2006. Like WWE, the NFL started with a bureaucratic Alphonse and Gaston act of pretending to ignore Omalu or discredit his research.

For now, the story is that WWE's medical director was given full access to Chris Benoit brain studies, in person, 14 months before

WWE told ESPN that the company "has been asking to see the research and tests results in the case of Mr. Benoit for years and has not been supplied with them."

31 MARCH 2010 -

I've been exploring how a cluster of University of Pittsburgh Medical Center physicians came to join the medical staff of World Wrestling Entertainment.

In my view, these three doctors — WWE medical director and neurologist Joseph Maroon, cardiologist Bryan Donohue, and endocrinologist Vijah Bahl — have done little except give political cover to this billion-dollar publicly traded corporation and to the McMahon family, which runs and profits from it.

At the moment, I am especially interested in Dr. Bryan Donohue, who is supposed to be supervising cardiovascular screening of WWE talent under a 2007 revision of the company wellness policy. In December 2009, six months after being fired by WWE for refusing to go to drug rehab, wrestler Eddie "Umaga" Fatu died at age 36 of a massive coronary brought on by a toxic mix of prescription medications. Fatu's autopsy showed that he had an enlarged heart.

In addition, Dr. Donohue's overall portfolio of outside business interests may be a bit too entrepreneurial for my blood. Leveraging his medical credentials, he recently started a hype-happy company in the largely unregulated supplement industry.

In 2008, the University of Pittsburgh Medical Center (UPMC) published a new ethics policy, which has been widely praised for controlling the undue influence of pharmaceutical companies on the clinical decisions of doctors. However, when I viewed the text of the policy online, I noticed it included links to general University of Pittsburgh guidelines for faculty conflicts of interest — and those links did not work.

Yesterday I spoke to Frank Raczkiewicz, a UPMC media relations director, about getting access to the blocked documents. Raczkiewicz referred me to Dr. Barbara Barnes, the UPMC vice president who authored the ethics policy. Dr. Barnes told me that the links within the UPMC ethics policy to the University of Pittsburgh policies were designed not to be publicly accessible because the latter are "internal" documents.

In our phone conversation yesterday, Dr. Barnes did not have time to get into the substance of my reporting on the relationship between UPMC and WWE. I emailed her with my contact information but did not hear back. Later yesterday I sent around to all the principals an email with the following text:

TO:

Ed Patru / Linda McMahon for Senate campaign, media relations

Robert Zimmerman / World Wrestling Entertainment, media relations

Bryan C. Donohue, M.D.

Joseph C. Maroon, M.D.

Barbara E. Barnes, M.D. / University of Pittsburgh Medical Center, Vice President of Continuing Medical Education, Contracts and Grants and Intellectual Property

Frank Raczkiewicz / University of Pittsburgh Medical Center, media relations

I am about to post to my blog a report headlined, "Umaga Autopsy Turns Focus to Linda McMahon's WWE Cardio Program and Docs." The post — to which I invite all of your comments (see my contact information below) — includes the following points:

* The autopsy report on wrestler Eddie "Umaga" Fatu — a WWE performer until six months before his December 2009 death from a heart attack caused by prescription drug toxicity — showed that he had an enlarged heart. This raises questions about the cardiovascular screening under the WWE wellness policy. Dr. Maroon is WWE's medical director. Dr. Donohue is the consulting cardiologist.

* Dr. Maroon, Dr. Donohue, and a third member of the WWE medical team, Dr. Vijay Bahl, have UPMC practices. This raises questions about the UPMC ethics policy that took effect in February 2008.

* The UPMC ethics policy seems primarily aimed at the issue of pharmaceutical companies' inducements to doctors, which can compromise patient care. However, there are also general conflict-of-interest issues, as well as specific ones involving physicians' relationships with the non-regulated supplement industry. Dr. Donohue is a co-founder of a supplement company, which he aggressively promotes in media appearances. Dr. Maroon has written a book touting the same supplement and is cited prominently on its website.

* Dr. Maroon's professional associations in pro football — as a doctor for the Pittsburgh Steelers and as a member of the National Football League's concussion policy committee — are also noted. I point out the case of Richard Rydze, yet another UPMC physician who was dropped by the Steelers after he was found to have purchased huge quantities of growth hormone from the internet

gray-market dealer Signature Pharmacy. I also review my previously published reports that Dr. Maroon's NFL concussion work has been criticized as too passive, and that he and WWE last year gave ESPN misleading information about his access to the postmortem brain studies of WWE performer Chris Benoit, who committed double murder/suicide in 2007.

9 SEPTEMBER 2010 -
We have more information on Dr. Joseph Maroon and WWE's failure to disclose the October 1, 2008, meeting of experts at the West Virginia University Brain Injury Institute — where Maroon was shown studies of dead wrestler Chris Benoit's brain.

Among the participants in that meeting was Peter Davies, professor of pathology and neuroscience at Yeshiva University's Albert Einstein College of Medicine. Davies holds an endowed chair in Alzheimer's disease research and directs a center on Alzheimer's and memory disorders. Here is Davies' full statement to me:

> I was at a meeting in West Virginia in October 2008, originally at the request of Dr. Ira Casson, who at the time was a member of the NFL Head Injury Committee (I'm not sure exactly what it was called then). Ira asked me to try to look at the material collected by Dr. Omalu and Dr. Bailes, because I am considered to be an expert in the kind of pathology that Dr. Omalu had reported seeing in the brains of ex-NFL and WWE cases. Dr. Omalu was not an expert in this kind of pathology, and Dr. Casson wanted an outside expert to see if there was anything significant going on. I was

not then nor am I now affiliated with the NFL. I flew to West Virginia at my own expense: Dr Maroon (who was also a member of the NFL committee) "brokered" the meeting, arranging for me to meet with Dr. Omalu and Dr. Bailes, and I did have the chance to examine several brain sections.

It was clear that there was pathology in these cases, although Dr. Omalu had not done the kind of extensive staining of tissues that my lab has developed. I suggested to Dr. Omalu that my lab could do much more extensive staining on these cases to better define the pathology. Dr. Omalu readily agreed and sent me samples from several brains. We stained them and reported on our findings to the NFL committee in June 2009; a brief summary report was prepared ahead of the meeting and sent to Dr. Maroon, Dr. Omalu, Dr. Bailes, and the NFL committee. The issue I had been asked to address was the nature and extent of the pathology in these cases. I reported that there was a unique and very serious pathology. I did not and do not discuss individual cases in a manner that can lead to their identification, although others involved with examination of this material have done so.

At the same time, the Boston University group also obtained samples of these cases from Dr. Omalu and has published extensively on their findings. There is no doubt that what is called CTE exists and is a serious concern for professional athletes in sports where the risk of concussions is high. Quite how common CTE is remains a question, as are the nature of the risk factors for development of CTE. I am now part of an NFL Players Association group trying to further investigate this.

Having read your blogs, I should add that I have never had any involvement with the WWE, and that I have never been contacted by anyone with a declared interest in the WWE.

4 JANUARY 2011 ----------------------------

The entrepreneurial careers of Dr. Bryan Donohue and Dr. Joseph Maroon expose a giant loophole of the University of Pittsburgh Medical Center's ethics policy: the role of physicians in outside ventures, including with unregulated supplement companies. Donohue directs talent cardiovascular screening for WWE. Maroon, a team physician for the Pittsburgh Steelers and a member of the NFL concussion policy committee, is WWE's medical director.

Both are proponents of the red-grape extract resveratrol for its asserted benefits for a healthy heart, energy, and fighting cancer and aging. They have taken to hyping, for their own profit, a particular brand called Vindure.

Though many among us might wonder if we could achieve just about the same effect by drinking a glass of grape juice every morning, as Larry King used to recommend in his radio commercials for Welch's, the larger issue of supplement regulation is far from the only eyebrow-raiser for the UPMC clinicians affiliated with WWE. Equally troubling is Donohue's exploitation of his UPMC credentials on behalf of Vindure even as the med center congratulates itself for more rigorous conflict-of-interest rules with respect to pharmaceutical companies. In at least some of his promotional efforts, Donohue doesn't even disclose to potential medical patients and supplement consumers his equity interest in Vindure's company, Vinomis Labs.

Vinomis Labs, headquartered in the Pittsburgh suburb of Sewickley, launched Vindure in 2009. Donohue and Vindure were featured in a January 2010 article in a Pittsburgh lifestyle magazine called *The Whirl*, which was accompanied by a news interview — essentially an infomercial — on television station KDKA.[2]

Donohue, who is listed on the Vinomis website as the company's "chief medical advisor," is one of its five founding investors, according to a 2009 article in the *Pittsburgh Tribune-Review*. In the original report on this blog on Donohue's Vinomis connection last March, I noted that his Pittsburgh TV interview was a testimonial for Vindure, amounting to what people on Madison Avenue call a "Victor Kiam" (after the one-time owner of the New England Patriots who famously said on commercials that he liked Remington electric shavers so much, "I bought the company").

When I reviewed the YouTube clip for this current post, however, I did not see a reference there to Donohue's part-ownership of Vinomis; either the original video got edited or my March report was mistaken about a detail that at least would give Donohue credit for having disclosed his stake.

There is no disclosure by Donohue that he owns the product he is pushing in other elements of the campaign for Vinomis coordinated by EMSI Public Relations, which describes itself as a "pay-for-performance" firm. In a news release headlined "Could Compound in Red Wine Help Cancer Patients? Resveratrol Being Tested for Effectiveness in Treatment and Prevention of Cancer," he is quoted at length about "an abundance of very well done basic preclinical science" on resveratrol.

"I have had occasion to introduce hundreds of patients to daily resveratrol supplementation, ranging from healthy adults interested in health maintenance and prevention to more elderly individuals with specific health concerns," Donohue says. "The experience to date has been very gratifying. People have experienced greater energy, increased exercise tolerance, crispness and clarity of thought, and a general bounce in their overall level of well-being."

Donohue adds, "I prefer the product line from Vinomis, because their products contain a concentration of 98 percent resveratrol plus pure red wine grape concentrate, and their website is an outstanding resource for independent studies and scientific information about natural compounds."

The doctor is among the "food and health industry clients" who are available for media interviews through EMSI — in his case on the suggested topic "Overworked & Stressed Out? Top Cardiologist Gives Tips on How to Stay Healthy Under These Conditions." Bullet-point answers are "eat better," "sleep better," "exercise," and "take supplements," especially those at Vinomis.com.

Dr. Maroon's résumé raises related ethical flags. The company website promotes his book *The Longevity Factor* and says he "assisted Vinomis in the formulation of Vindure." The *Pittsburgh Tribune-Review* story identifies Maroon as a partner in Xenomis LLC, which licensed the Harvard Medical School research on which Vindure is based, receives royalties from Vinomis, and shares "five to ten percent" of those royalties with Harvard.

(The product itself, one of many resveratrol supplements on the market, is manufactured in South Carolina by a subsidiary of General Nutrition Centers. The Harvard medical research, spearheaded by David Sinclair, has just moved from experiments on mice to human trials.)

According to his UPMC bio, Maroon also is on the board of directors of Mylan, a Pennsylvania company that markets generic pharmaceuticals. Since Maroon wouldn't talk to me, I can only speculate on how he or UPMC might rationalize his outside business activities. In the case of generic drugs, they certainly save patients money over name-brand equivalents. Maroon may well be a true believer in the benefits of Vindure, too. But even in that event, he owes the public transparent disclosure of his financial interest.

Maroon's most visible hat is with the Steelers and the NFL. He was among the league spokesmen who testified last year at hearings of the House Judiciary Committee, which focused public criticism of the early deaths and mental illness of former football players who had suffered serial untreated concussions during their careers.

The proportions in which Maroon is part of the solution and part of the problem remain open to debate. At UPMC, he has helped develop a patented system of concussion prevention and treatment programs, known as ImPACT, which includes baseline neurological testing and more precise protocols for determining when an athlete is ready to return to action following a head injury. In 2010, the NFL donated $1 million to Boston University to study dead athletes' brains and further CTE research, and more recently NFL Charities added nearly as much for independent research on such related topics as youth sports concussions and post-career dementia.

At the same time, many concussion reform advocates do not place Maroon on the aggressive end of the continuum of experts acknowledging CTE. After last year's scathing criticism by the Judiciary Committee, the NFL shook up the leadership of its concussion committee; Maroon, who was not one of the co-chairmen, still serves on it, according to league spokesman Greg Aiello.

I asked Aiello whether team physicians were governed by a formal ethics policy similar to UPMC's. Aiello said, "The doctors are obligated to follow the code of ethics of their profession and of their specific medical societies (i.e., AMA, American Orthopaedic Society of Sports Medicine, American Medical Society for Sports Medicine, etc.)."

One passage of the American Medical Association policy which applies to Donohue and Maroon is Opinion 5.02, "Advertising and Publicity": "A physician may publicize him or herself . . . provided that the communication shall not be misleading because of the omission of necessary material information . . ."

WWE spokesman Robert Zimmerman has not responded to an

email query on whether the company considers its wellness team practitioners bound by the same standards as those of the NFL.

WWE created Maroon's title of medical director in 2008. In the past
generation, pro wrestling has had an astronomical rate of occupation-
related deaths under age 50 — multiples higher than even football's.
In 2006, shortly after one of its biggest stars, Eddie Guerrero, had a
fatal heart attack at 38, WWE instituted what it calls a "wellness policy." The WWE program includes testing for steroids and other drugs.

In 2007, another WWE headline performer, Chris Benoit, murdered his wife and their seven-year-old son before killing himself at
their home in suburban Atlanta. In his postmortem toxicology, Benoit
had a testosterone-to-epitestosterone ratio of 59 to 1 (the Olympic
pre-doping maximum is 4 to 1), but he had been deemed clean under
wellness policy tests because of a "therapeutic use exemption." Two
months earlier, Benoit's wife, a victim of domestic violence at various
times, had texted him, "We both know the wellness program is a joke."

During the Linda McMahon Senate campaign last year, Maroon
told the *Hartford Courant*, "We have no talent now on steroids." Dave
Meltzer, publisher of the *Wrestling Observer Newsletter*, called the
inaccuracy of that statement "mind-boggling."

In terms of Maroon's medical specialty of neurology, the matter
of closest interest was his response to a study of Benoit's brain tissue,
which showed a large accumulation of tau proteins, the sign of CTE.
The examination was conducted by a forensic pathologist, Dr. Bennet
Omalu, one of the pioneers of this research, at the behest of the Sports
Legacy Institute. SLI had been started by a former WWE performer
and Harvard graduate, Chris Nowinski, who retired from the ring as a
result of his own concussions.

Much like Maroon and the NFL originally, WWE tried to
discredit or downplay CTE research. But the hiring of Maroon to
coordinate WWE's wellness policy coincided with the addition of

Maroon's ImPACT testing and of Donohue's area of expertise, cardiovascular screening. In total, five out of the wellness program's eight medical professionals listed at the WWE website are from UPMC.

Whatever progress has been achieved by the wellness policy is sullied by questions about the overall integrity of WWE's investment in the occupational health and safety of its talent in light of its long history of inaction coupled with misleading or false public statements. From 1996 to 2006, WWE had *no* comprehensive steroid testing, which had originated in the wake of the 1991 federal conviction and imprisonment on steroid-trafficking charges of George Zahorian, one of WWE's Pennsylvania ringside doctors.

The year before hiring Maroon, WWE founder and chairman Vince McMahon told both CNN and investigators for Congressman Henry Waxman's House Committee on Oversight and Government Reform that the promotion was banning "chair shots" to the head from its arsenal of physical theater. In fact, WWE wrestlers continued to bash steel chairs on each others' craniums until January 2010 — by which time Vince's wife, Linda, was already deep into her unsuccessful self-funded $50 million Senate campaign.

Besides sometimes joining WWE in criticizing CTE research as hyped, Maroon has given UPMC-credentialed cover to other corporate statements of dubious faith. In October 2008, Maroon met with Dr. Omalu and Dr. Julian Bailes at the West Virginia Brain Injury Research Institute, where Maroon was shown slides from the Benoit brain study. Five months later, another WWE wrestler who had been fired earlier, 33-year-old Andrew Martin, died from a prescription drug overdose, and Martin's father donated his brain for a similar study by the West Virginia doctors. They found CTE — making it two for two among dead wrestlers tested.

Yet in a statement to ESPN, which reported the findings, WWE said it was "unaware of the veracity of any of these tests, be it for Chris Benoit or Andrew Martin . . . WWE has been asking to see the research and test results in the case of Mr. Benoit for years and has not been supplied with them."

Maroon, who knew otherwise, said nothing. In the course of legal threats directed at me for my reporting, WWE lawyer Jerry McDevitt has maintained that what the statement to ESPN really conveyed was that WWE challenges the "chain of custody" of the Benoit brain tissue purportedly under study — in other words, the company demands further proof that the histologic slides produced by Drs. Omalu and Bailes were not from the brain of someone other than Benoit.

The nexus of Donohue's and Maroon's controversial consultancies for WWE is two wrestlers' dramatic deaths during the Linda McMahon Senate campaign. In December 2009 Samoan-American wrestler Eddie Fatu — age 36, stage name "Umaga" — died of a heart attack, which was blamed on the familiar pattern of steroid and painkiller abuse. The autopsy found that Fatu, 406 pounds, had an enlarged heart. Had the WWE cardio screening program not detected the condition? If not, why not? Six months earlier, Fatu had been fired by WWE for refusing to go to drug rehabilitation. Two years before that, he had been suspended for being one of the dozen-plus company performers found by prosecutors on the customer list of the internet steroid dealer Signature Pharmacy.

And in August 2010, Lance McNaught, who had wrestled for WWE as "Lance Cade," died of "heart failure" at 29. There is reason to wonder whether Fatu or McNaught, or both, had CTE. Regardless, the latter's prescription pill addiction could be traced at least in part to an October 2008 segment on the cable show *Raw* in which he was smashed 19 times with a chair, including once flush on the head. This, of course, occurred during the period between Vince McMahon's 2007 public statements about banning chair shots to the head and the actual imposition of the policy in 2010.

Meanwhile, a closer examination of Chris Benoit's July 2007

autopsy report, produced by the Georgia Bureau of Investigation, reveals that he, too, had an enlarged heart — as did the wrestlers Davey Boy Smith, Eddie Guerrero, and many others who died young prior to the start of both the WWE wellness policy and its cardiovascular screening component.

One thing Senator Richard Blumenthal, who defeated Linda McMahon for his seat, and others probing pro wrestling need to examine closely at this point is whether WWE cardiovascular screening under Drs. Maroon and Donohue is meaningful, transparent, and effective. In general, more information must be generated on this industry's "cocktail of death" — different permutations and interactions, in individual cases, of heart disease, steroid abuse, prescription pharmaceutical toxicity, and CTE/concussion syndrome. The history of the problem, along with its scale and public health implications, suggests that the leading pro wrestling promotion has forfeited the argument that it can be trusted to regulate itself.

The University of Pittsburgh Medical Center, meanwhile, should answer for some of its best-known doctors' outside interests with both Vinomis Labs and WWE.

11 JANUARY 2011 ------------------------
Joe Maroon is a member of the NFL's concussion policy committee, which came under withering criticism by the House Judiciary Committee for lax research and questionable ethics during the emergence of awareness of serial-concussion syndrome. The league responded last year by booting its policy committee chairs and installing new ones. (Maroon, not a chairman, remains a committee member.)

But even before CTE became part of the general public discussion of safety in football, hockey, and other sports, Maroon had been parroting passive and misleading company lines on concussions.

In his groundbreaking 2006 book *Head Games*, Chris Nowinski, founder of Boston's Sports Legacy Institute, told of how Maroon led the chorus of the NFL's attempts to pooh-pooh the early findings of CTE in the brains of prematurely dead ex-Steelers Mike Webster and Terry Long.

In an example of what seems to pass for the corporate physician's Hippocratic oath, Maroon attacked the "fallacious reasoning" of CTE research pioneer Dr. Bennet Omalu (a forensic pathologist who is now chief medical examiner of San Joaquin County, California). Specifically, Maroon said, "I was the team neurosurgeon during Long's entire tenure with the Steelers, and I still am. I re-checked my records; there was not one cerebral concussion documented in him during those entire seven years."

Nowinski (a former WWE wrestler who had to retire from the ring due to his own cumulative brain trauma) proved Maroon dead wrong: Omalu found in Long's records a letter, written by Maroon, recommending that Long be given two weeks off following a concussion incident. (Thanks to Dustin Fink of the invaluable TheConcussionBlog. com for this catch.)

20 JANUARY 2011 -------------------------
Eric Adelson of the ThePostGame.com is reporting that the National Football League ordered new Oakland Raiders head coach Hue Jackson to sever his ties with a supplement company called Sports with Alternatives to Steroids (SWATS), whose product IGF-1 contains a banned substance.[3]

"We have a long-standing policy that prohibits coaches from any relationship with a supplement company," said Brian McCarthy, the NFL's director of corporate communications.

Curiously, no such policy applies to team or league physicians, such as Dr. Joseph Maroon, a long-time neurologist for the Pittsburgh Steelers and member of the NFL concussion policy committee. I have been reporting that Maroon endorses a supplement called Vindure, which is based on the red-grape abstract resveratrol, and is an owner of the company that licensed Harvard Medical School research to Vindure's producer, Vinomis Labs.

So far as I know, Vindure contains no substances banned by the league. But Vinomis Labs is a supplement company.

In addition — and as I am reporting here for the first time — Dr. Maroon endorses another supplement called Sports Brain Guard, described as a "daily tri-delivery bioactive protection program" for concussed athletes, from Irvine, California–based Newport Nutritionals.[4]

Maroon also is medical director of WWE. Dr. Bryan Donohue, WWE's consulting cardiologist, is an owner of Vinomis Labs. Both Maroon and Donohue are at the University of Pittsburgh Medical Center, whose officials refuse to comment on whether Vinomis Labs and other outside business interests are covered by a recently revised and much-publicized ethics policy.

When I asked NFL spokesman Greg Aiello if the league had a parallel ethics policy for team physicians, he said they were bound only by the codes of their professional medical societies. I will forward this post to Aiello and invite comment on why the NFL bans its coaches but not its doctors from relationships with supplement companies.

WWE has not commented on whether it has an NFL-modeled or any other conflict-of-interest policy for its consulting doctors.

This is all of particular relevance because the Federal Trade Commission, on the request of Senator Tom Udall, just opened an investigation of the promotional claims of the NFL's official helmet supplier, Riddell. Those claims are based on NFL Charities–funded research conducted by Maroon.

Greg Aiello, the NFL's conscientious media liaison, got back to me quickly in response to my post earlier today. Aiello said, "The league's supplement endorsement policy applies only to league and club employees. If any club or person affiliated with a club engages in or promotes conduct that violates our policy on performance-enhancing substances, all involved would be held accountable."

The language here recalls that of Commissioner Roger Goodell at the October 2009 hearings of the House Judiciary Committee. Pressed about questionable denials of chronic traumatic encephalopathy research issued by the NFL concussion policy committee, Goodell insisted that the committee doctor-members — Maroon among them — are not league employees. But they are certainly league *consultants* who draw fees and ancillary commercial benefits.

I'm not saying that the supplements endorsed by Dr. Maroon contain substances listed as performance-enhancing. But the principle that came through at the Judiciary Committee hearings applies: he is a walking infomercial, not someone whose word on player safety and on the NFL's vigilance on its behalf earns the benefit of the doubt.

23 JANUARY 2011 ----------------------

The *New York Times* story today on the federal football helmet investigation[5] fails to make the important connection to its own recent big story: the Federal Trade Commission investigation of safety claims by Riddell, the official helmet supplier of the National Football League, for its Revolution model.

Reporter Alan Schwarz leads today's account of action by the National Operating Committee on Standards for Athletic Equipment by stating that it was spurred by the Consumer Product Safety Commission. Yet the piece doesn't mention at all the FTC probe of Riddell initiated earlier this month by Senator Tom Udall.

The concussion story is more than the sum of the blocking and tackling by dueling experts. It is also the story of a process: the ecosystem of clinical research, an interdependent web of leading doctors, research journals, and commercial interests.

Today ground zero is an article in the February 2006 issue of *Neurosurgery*, "Examining Concussion Rates and Return to Play in High School Football Players Wearing Newer Helmet Technology: A Three-Year Prospective Cohort Study." One of the co-authors was Dr. Joseph Maroon. Two of Maroon's three co-authors were University of Pittsburgh Medical Center colleagues Micky Collins and Mark Lovell; they are also partners in the concussion management software company ImPACT Applications, Inc. The article's other co-author, Thad Ide, is chief engineer at Riddell. The Pittsburgh research was underwritten by NFL Charities.

As news of the FTC investigation broke, Maroon threw Riddell under the bus, claiming that the company's promotion of the Revolution helmet emphasized the blue-sky findings of the *Neurosurgery* article while ignoring its disclaimers. But is that explanation good enough?

Here is the full text of the abstract of the article:

OBJECTIVE: The purpose of this study was to compare concussion rates and recovery times for athletes wearing newer helmet technology compared to traditional helmet design.

METHODS: This was a three-year, prospective, naturalistic, cohort study. Participants were 2,141 high school athletes from Western Pennsylvania. Approximately half of the sample wore the Revolution helmet manufactured by Riddell, Inc. (n = 1,173) and the remainder of the sample used standard helmets (n = 968). Athletes underwent computerized neurocognitive testing through the use of ImPACT at the beginning of the study. Following a concussion, players were reevaluated at various time intervals until recovery was complete.

RESULTS: In the total sample, the concussion rate in athletes wearing the Revolution was 5.3% and in athletes wearing standard helmets was 7.6% [[chi]2 $(1, 2, 141) = 4.96$, $P < 0.027$]. The relative risk estimate was 0.69 (95% confidence interval = 0.499–0.958). Wearing the Revolution helmet was associated with approximately a 31% decreased relative risk and 2.3% decreased absolute risk for sustaining a concussion in this cohort study. The athletes wearing the Revolution did not differ from athletes wearing standard helmets on the mechanism of injury (e.g., head-to-head strike), on-field concussion markers (e.g., amnesia or loss of consciousness), or on-field presentation of symptoms (e.g., headaches, dizziness, or balance problems).

CONCLUSION: Recent sophisticated laboratory research has better elucidated injury biomechanics associated with concussion in professional football players. This data has led to changes in helmet design and new helmet technology, which appears to have beneficial effects in reducing the incidence of cerebral concussion in high school football players.

2 FEBRUARY 2011 ------------------------

I don't think Dr. Joe Maroon gets off the hook in the Federal Trade Commission investigation of Riddell helmets just by asserting that the company inflated the claims of the assessment of the helmets' safety in *Neurosurgery*. After all, Maroon co-authored the piece for the journal of the Congress of Neurological Surgeons.

Nor do I think *Neurosurgery* itself gets off the hook for publishing a decade's worth of research, much of it funded by the NFL, that arguably retarded rather than accelerated professional and public awareness of the magnitude of CTE and related issues.

Here are unanswered questions I've submitted to Dr. Nelson Oyesiku of Emory University, the current editor-in-chief of *Neurosurgery*:

1. There is currently a Federal Trade Commission investigation of promotional claims by the Riddell football helmet manufacturer that were based on data in a 2006 article in *Neurosurgery*.

   Does the journal have a comment on this controversy?

   Are there historical examples of allegations of exaggerated claims from *Neurosurgery*-published research by another marketer of a consumer product? I exclude here the categories of professional debates over the efficacy of particular pharmaceuticals, surgical techniques, therapies, and the like; I am referring only to products sold in general consumer markets. If the answer is yes, could you provide some parallel examples?

2. Questions have arisen concerning the relationships of authors of articles published in *Neurosurgery* with the National Football League.

   Particular controversy surrounded work by Dr. Elliot Pellman, then chair of the NFL's concussion policy committee, with a series of articles, beginning in 2003, in *Neurosurgery*, which at the time was edited by Dr. Mike Apuzzo, a consultant for the New York Giants. Dr. Robert Cantu, then a senior editor of the journal, suggested that the sample size of the data would not have warranted publication of a similar article about a subject other than football head injuries. And according to reports, Dr.

Pellman revised one of the articles post–peer review and prior to publication, and without consulting co-authors. Did the Congress of Neurological Surgeons publish any subsequent correction or clarification? Was any other action taken?

Was this scenario covered by the Congress's existing code of ethics? If so, in what particular passages? If not, were changes contemplated in the wake of the Pellman episode?

3. Dr. Kevin Guskiewicz, director of the Sports Research Laboratory at the University of North Carolina, was quoted by ESPN as saying, "The data that hasn't shown up makes [the NFL doctors' work] questionable industry-funded research." What is your response to that allegation?

25 MARCH 2011 --------------------------

As long ago as a 2007 article in *ESPN The Magazine*, Peter Keating has written extensively about the start-up company ImPACT Applications, whose concussion management software was by then being used by 30 of the 32 National Football League teams.

Two of ImPACT's co-founders, Drs. Joseph Maroon and Mark Lovell of the University of Pittsburgh Medical Center, were members of the NFL's Committee on Mild Traumatic Brain Injury.

Christopher Randolph, professor of neurology at Loyola University Medical Center in Chicago, and former team neuropsychologist for the Chicago Bears, told Keating, "It is a major conflict of interest, scientifically irresponsible."

Other key points:

- Lovell and a third Pittsburgh Medical Center colleague
  and ImPACT stakeholder, Michael Collins, were co-
  authors of all 19 of the publications listed in the "Reliability and Validity" section of the ImPACT website.
- In 2005, Loyola's Randolph published a study in *Journal
  of Athletic Training*, which found that only one peer-
  reviewed article involving a prospective controlled study
  with ImPACT had been published.
- Another then unpublished study by Stephen Broglio,
  professor of kinesiology at the University of Illinois at
  Urbana-Champaign, concluded that ImPACT and two
  other tested computerized systems were "less than optimal."
- Without disclosing their financial interests, Maroon and
  Collins published laudatory comments on a 2006 *Neurosurgery* article about ImPACT that was co-authored by
  Lovell and three other members of the NFL concussion
  committee.
- Lovell declined to be interviewed for ESPN's investigative
  series *Outside the Lines*.

23 APRIL 2011 --------------------------
Author-journalist Matt Chaney's piece today, "Critics, Evidence
Debunk 'Concussion Testing' in Football," suggests that I have been
far too kind in my criticisms of the ImPACT system.[6] Some highlights:

- A peer-reviewed article in *Current Sports Medicine Reports*
  by Loyola University's Dr. Christopher Randolph details
  ImPACT's "glaring faults," with unacceptable rates of false
  positives and false negatives.
- Chaney writes, "An overwhelming majority of journalists,
  politicians, educators, and football experts ignore the accu-

mulating evidence rebuking concussion testing as invalid and unreliable, choosing instead to endorse the quick-fix notion and push it for mandate by law."

- Generally speaking, the neuropsych tests on the market "are unsuitable for clinical work with concussions," according to Dr. Lester Mayers of Pace University.

- Dr. Bennet Omalu, who discovered chronic traumatic encephalopathy in athletes in contact sports, says, "ImPACT testing is not a diagnosis tool . . . Using [computerized] testing in the acute phase of injury can actually make the symptoms *worse*."

11 JUNE 2011 ----------------------------

The NFL's new PR website, NFLHealthandSafety.com, has a video demonstrating how Dr. Joseph Maroon, team neurosurgeon for the Pittsburgh Steelers, might examine a player who has been concussed. The clip, which Maroon describes as a kind of "two-minute drill" showing how a trained professional can check out a player "efficiently and expeditiously," is unintentionally comical.[7]

The obvious flaw here is that the person Maroon is examining passes all his markers perfectly. Is the NFL representing this as a typical outcome?

A companion piece might be a skit with the cast of *Saturday Night Live* reenacting the anecdote about the player who, the coach is told, doesn't know his name. "Well, tell him his name and get him back out there!" the coach says.

24 JUNE 2011 ----------------------------

Dr. Richard Ellenbogen, co-chair of the NFL's reconstructed concussion policy committee, now has done his own star turn at

NFLHealthandSafety.com.[8] It contradicts the buffoonish demonstration of Dr. Joe Maroon.

The Ellenbogen video has useful information, but its message is muddled.

Ellenbogen emphasizes taking your time in an on-field evaluation of an injured player; Maroon, with no disclaimers, emphasizes how fast you can do such an evaluation ("efficiently and expeditiously" is his assonance). These two positions are not reconcilable. Will Ellenbogen use his authority to remove and disavow Maroon's video?

Ellenbogen's "first principle" is unassailably correct: "tailor approach to level of athletic play." But this principle is undercut by the overall topic, which is a guide on returning athletes to play after they suffer concussions.

We all get it that NFL return-to-play protocols are being tightened (except, of course, when they aren't). The question Mom and Pop Football urgently want to hear the experts discuss, however, is not how to manage Johnny Gridiron's second concussion. It is whether they should be exposing their precious bundle of shoulder pads to a possible *first* concussion and to scores, hundreds, or thousands of lethal subconcussive blows. In short, is the sport of football a viable activity at all for youngsters? That would be the most fundamental "tailoring of the approach to level of athletic play."

No one expects Richard Ellenbogen, speaking on an NFL website, to trash his client. But rather than handing down education about baseline neurological testing for little squirts — a concept both flawed overall and, specifically, impossible to reproduce at the amateur level — he should be making the broadest and most professionally responsible disclaimer of all: that everything he says on behalf of the league about return-to-play applies only to those so dedicated to football that they are willing to play Russian roulette with their mental health. Failure even to acknowledge the existence of a controversy on this crucial point exposes his lack of independence.

As the old National Public Radio comedy segment "Dr. Science" used to demonstrate, you don't need "a master's degree in science" on your résumé in order to have a beakerful of common sense. A new study of neuropsychological (NP) testing as a tool of concussion management — soon to be published in the *American Journal of Sports Medicine* — provides further evidence that Dr. Joseph Maroon's ImPACT software has little going for it except its University of Pittsburgh Medical Center team's tainted National Football League connections, plus a doctorate in B.S.

In "The Influence of Musculoskeletal Injury on Cognition: Implications for Concussion Research," four University of Toronto researchers conclude that athletes recovering from orthopedic injuries, which have nothing to do with traumatic brain injury, "also display a degree of cognitive impairment as measured by computerized tests." The clinical relevance of this finding: "[A]thletic injury, in general, also may produce a degree of cognitive disruption. Therefore, a narrow interpretation of scores of neuropsychological tests in a sports concussion context should be avoided."

On top of everything else we now know about how savvy athletes game the ImPACT system — by taking Ritalin to improve superficial cognition post-concussion, or simply by tanking their initial "baseline" tests to come off as naturally stupider than they are — we can see what the Maroonization of concussion management is all about. Like standardized testing of academic achievement, it is creating its own closed system of gimmicks, which measure mental acuity far less accurately than they measure how resourceful and well prepared the taker was in having been "taught to the test."

With iPads, that principle is fine for developing a new-tech economy of "killer apps." With public health, it's just a killer.

No matter how you slice and dice it, when it comes to youth concussions there is no substitute for reasonably knowledgeable and concerned people — coaches, trainers, doctors, parents — making sure their kids are OK . . . really, really OK . . . through use of their own powers of observation. Standardized NP testing misses the point badly, lets the NFL's multibillion-dollar marketing off the hook, and, not incidentally, further lines the pockets of doctors like Joe Maroon who brought us to this pass.

Which reminds me that Dr. Richard Ellenbogen, co-chair of the NFL's concussion policy committee, still hasn't gotten back to me on the dangerously mixed messages at the website NFLHealthandSafety. com. In Maroon's video there, he shows off getting a concussed player back to action "efficiently and expeditiously" with a "two-minute drill" evaluation. In Ellenbogen's video, he emphasizes that you need to evaluate the head-injured athlete across time.

So . . . which one is it, Dr. Chairman?

FoxSports.com's Alex Marvez reports that last night the league held mandatory conference calls with team officials to review new tightened-up protocols promulgated by Ellenbogen and his co-chair, Dr. Hunt Batjer. The slogan is "When in doubt, keep them out," according to Gene Smith, general manager of the Jacksonville Jaguars.

"When in doubt, keep them out" is also the mantra of Ellenbogen's NFL safety video for the general public. But as long as phony solutions like ImPACT continue to cast a falsely reassuring shadow on the national concussion conversation, Ellenbogen's words are empty.

28 JULY 2011 -----------------------------

Dr. Joe Maroon's interview with the *Intelligencer/Wheeling* (West Virginia) *News-Register* has all the standard Maroon tropes and a couple of new whoppers.[9]

On NFL return-to-play protocols, Maroon says that the league has mandated, as the first of three standards, that "you must be completely asymptomatic, in other words no headaches, nausea, vomiting, fatigue, sleepiness, drowsiness, at rest." Funny, but in Maroon's video at the PR website NFLHealthandSafety.com, he says nothing about the athlete being "completely asymptomatic."

Perhaps it could be argued that this point is so obvious that it doesn't even need to be said — but if so, then why does Maroon feel it is important enough to articulate today in his West Virginia interview but not in his official NFL website video of a few months ago?

Maroon makes this stunning remark: "I saw some statistics a few years back, if you look at the time that kids . . . spend in automobiles at the same time they could be on the practice fields . . . the incidence of injury from being in car accidents would be significantly higher than participating in sports."

Even if Maroon is attempting to commingle brain injuries with all injuries, this assertion intuitively makes no sense. Of course, over time while in a car, as either driver or passenger, you run the risk of serious injury or death in a crash. But I would like to see the citation of "some statistics a few years back" suggesting that such incidence is "significantly higher" than the day-to-day injuries, minor and major, in football practices and games.

18 AUGUST 2011 -------------------------

"The ImPACT test, widely regarded as the go-to neurological exam to measure concussive blows, doesn't always accurately gauge a player's readiness to return to action. And you can cheat on it."[10] That is one of the bullet points from an excellent article in the current *LA Weekly* that highlights why "concussion awareness" is not the answer.

> In 2008, Ryne Dougherty, a 16-year-old high school linebacker in Essex County, NJ, sat out three weeks following a concussion. But after taking an ImPACT test, he was cleared to play. During his first game back,

he suffered a brain hemorrhage; he died within a week.

Dougherty's ImPACT results were ominously low, the family has claimed in a lawsuit against the school district. Additionally, according to the test results, Dougherty reported feeling "foggy" but still was cleared to play.

Further, reporters Jansen and Garcia-Roberts note, ImPACT's "real-world snags" include "price: At packages costing roughly $600 per school for the first year, ImPACT is too expensive for some districts. And many of those that do buy the program cannot afford to pay a specialist to administer it. Instead, that duty tends to fall on coaches or trainers."

13 OCTOBER 2011 ----------------------

Don't believe that ImPACT is worse than useless for high school football programs? The case in New Jersey of Ryne Dougherty, a kid who was killed in a game in 2008 — after suffering a concussion and being cleared to return to play three weeks later, with the assistance of ImPACT — illustrates how the tool will provide a veritable road map to the string of lawsuits that will bring down prep football.

And check out this unintentionally comical report from the Jackson County (Michigan) *Citizen Patriot*, under the headline "Orthopaedic Rehab Specialists 'ahead of the curve' in helping treat athletes with concussions."[11]

No one knows that better than Sullivan Evans, a Lumen Christi High School sophomore who suffered two concussions last year playing freshman football. The first one occurred after a helmet-to-helmet hit in the season opener.

"The ImPACT test proved it [was a concussion]," said his mother, Kristin Evans. "He said, 'Now that I know what that feels like, I bet I've had six of those playing hockey.'"

It took four weeks before Sullivan's ImPACT test scores showed he was ready to return to action. Then in his first game back, he suffered another concussion. This time, it was six months before he was cleared to play contact sports again.

Wow, give these docs a Nobel Prize! They sent the kid back out there for a second concussion four weeks after his first one . . . but they sure guarded against that vaunted *third-concussion syndrome*!

The article proceeds, deadpan: "So far this fall, 89 athletes have suffered concussions, and Chamberlain said every school in the county had at least one football player out with a concussion for three to four weeks."

19 OCTOBER 2011 ----------------------------

At today's Senate commerce committee hearing, Senator Tom Udall, as expected, directed a lot of outrage toward the spurious claims of the Riddell helmet manufacturer and other "Concussion Inc." marketers — while saying nothing about how the NFL and its operatives were in bed with many of those same companies. With respect to Riddell, Udall noted that a doctor involved in the now-infamous 2006 *Neurosurgery* journal study of Riddell's Revolution helmet had distanced himself from the way Riddell went on to quote the article in its commercials and promotions. But Udall couldn't spit out the name of this doctor: Joe Maroon.

Dr. Jeffrey Kutcher's testimony included a point glossed over by Udall: *the problem isn't just how Riddell exploited the Maroon/UPMC/*

NFL–funded study of the Riddell Revolution. The problem is that the study itself was shoddily designed and scientifically unsound. In January, Maroon told the *New York Times* that the company's promos should have been more careful about his study's "limitations."

Limitations, my foot — as Kutcher told the commerce committee, the *Neurosurgery* article had lousy controls in the first place and proceeded to play fast and loose with claims of percentages of reductions in the incidence of concussions among those who used the helmet.

Udall should haul Maroon before the commerce committee for a defense of his work, not just a secondhand and unnamed renunciation of the supposed bad faith exhibited by a patron and exploiter of his work. Maroon also needs to explain why, if Riddell's promos were so heinous, he never complained about them over a period of years, until the *Times* and Udall came along to ask questions about them.

Also at the hearing, Udall ripped the marketer of the supplement Sports Brain Guard — but conveniently without mentioning that Maroon is a prominent endorser of that product, too.

The approach of our government to the concussion crisis reminds me of the "fix" of the radio payola scandals in the 1950s. Back then we made sure to criminalize the acts of disc jockeys in accepting bribes for giving particular songs more airplay. Decades later, television producers would barter entire blocks of commercial time to station licensees and exploit numerous other loopholes in newly loosened Federal Communications Commission rules. But payola at that level, owner to owner, was perfectly legal. It was just business.

Now Udall and the commerce committee are devoted to bashing "sports equipment manufacturers [which] are exploiting our growing concerns about sports concussions to market so-called 'anti-concussion' products to athletes and their parents," as the senator's press release put it.

Though my bête noire has been Dr. Joseph Maroon, the most amazing one-man medical conglomerate since Dr. Welbeck of Paddy

Chayefsky's *The Hospital*, the issue is larger than Maroon. There is growing evidence that ImPACT is expensive and unreliable and — to get straight to the prompt of Udall's hearing — preys on the fears of parents, as well as the liability jitters of educators, while providing a false sense of security.

Unfortunately, Udall seems intent on getting to the nitty-gritty later rather than sooner.

21 OCTOBER 2011 -----------------------

A popular new reform is the call for "independent neurologists." However, there is no such thing as a medical authority empowered to make return-to-play decisions, especially within games.

The Philadelphia Eagles maintain that an "independent neurologist" cleared Michael Vick before the October 6 game against the New York Giants, but refuse to name him or her. Last Sunday, Vick got "dirt in the eye" and "the wind knocked out of him" against the Washington Redskins.

Well known but not well reported is the fact that a number of team physicians, or the institutions employing them, have tangled financial relationships with their clubs. These call into question their ability to provide down-the-middle player diagnoses and return-to-play prognoses.

For example, the University of Pittsburgh Medical Center is a corporate sponsor of the Pittsburgh Steelers, in addition to being its preferred health care and sports medicine provider. (UPMC has the same relationships with University of Pittsburgh sports teams, but those are intra-institutional and more intuitive.)

NFL spokesman Greg Aiello told me that sponsorships do not compromise medical care: "League policy is that team hospital, medical facility, or physician group sponsorship cannot involve a commitment to provide medical services by team physicians." Aiello also pointed out that Article 39 of the new collective bargaining agreement (CBA) with the NFL Players Association details "Players' Right to Medical Care and Treatment," stating: "The cost of medical services rendered by Club physicians will be the responsibility of the respective Clubs, but each Club physicians' primary duty in providing player medical care shall be not to the Club but instead to the player-patient."

The CBA does seem to attempt to tighten the principle that a team physician's primary duty is the care of the player, regardless of contractual relationships with teams outside the four corners of the medical-services contract itself. As a pro football beat writer put it to me, "All players are allowed to choose their own surgeons for surgeries, but clearly teams like when players use the teams' docs."

The NFL's position is that there is no linkage between sponsorship contracts and medical services. But breaches of the league's professed new culture of "concussion awareness" and extra caution reach ever-more-farcical levels. Heavily lawyered verbiage on doctor independence and true Hippocratic independence are not one and the same.

24 OCTOBER 2011 -----------------------

Mark Lovell — consultant for the NFL and WWE, director of the University of Pittsburgh Medical Center Concussion Program, and co-owner of ImPACT Applications, Inc., the Pittsburgh-based company that markets concussion management software — may not have disclosed financial conflicts of interest in grant applications to the National Institutes of Health over the past decade.

The substance of the applications themselves is accessible online, but the module relating to conflicts is blocked under old NIH rules. Those rules were recently revised to make conflict disclosures publicly viewable on grants moving forward.

Lovell has not responded to an email requesting clarification of his conflict disclosures. Susan Manko, the UPMC media relations specialist on sports concussions, has not responded to the same message, or to a fax or phone messages.

Examination of NIH's online database shows that between 2002 and 2005 Lovell was listed as the project leader on at least four grants from the federal agency for research on sports concussions and fMRI (functional magnetic resonance imaging). These grants totaled more than $2 million: $538,499 in 2002; $554,652 in 2003; $571,292 in 2004; and $588,429 in 2005.

We already know that Lovell (a Ph.D. neuropsychologist, not a medical doctor) was the NFL's director of neuropsychological testing at the same time his company was selling testing software to teams. This new development raises the additional issue of whether undisclosed financial conflicts supported Lovell in securing public funding to underwrite research and development for a for-profit company, ImPACT Applications. (ImPACT stands for immediate post-concussion assessment and cognitive testing.)

Lovell joined UPMC to coordinate the efforts of, among others, Maroon (then vice chair of neurosurgery, as well as Pittsburgh Steelers neurosurgeon) and Charles Burke (an orthopedist who was team physician for the Pittsburgh Penguins hockey team). Another charter program staffer was non-M.D. neuropsychologist Michael Collins, who had published a multi-part, multi-site study of concussion effects and return-to-play evaluation methods in the *Journal of the American Medical Association.*

Asked about NIH conflict-of-interest disclosure policies, the NIH Office of Extramural Research said, "Investigators are expected to disclose their significant financial interests to their institution." However, at the time of these grants, those disclosures were not part of the records released to the general public on request.

28 OCTOBER 2011 ------------------------

A program entitled "Town Huddle: Concussions in Sports" was scheduled for next Tuesday at the Western Pennsylvania Sports Museum in Pittsburgh. The event (co-sponsored by the University of Pittsburgh Medical Center, ImPACT Applications, Inc., the Western Pennsylvania Interscholastic League, and television station KDKA) has been postponed until further notice — "due to some scheduling conflicts," a museum spokesman told me.

I was especially amused by the note, "High school athletes are encouraged to wear their jerseys or team colors."

Panelists were to have been Andy Russell, a linebacker on the Pittsburgh Steelers 1970s Super Bowl teams, plus the Big Three of ImPACT: Dr. Joe Maroon and his UPMC/NFL/WWE business partners Mark Lovell and Micky Collins.

31 OCTOBER 2011 ------------------------

The chairman of the Senate commerce committee — which twice failed to mention Dr. Joseph Maroon by name at obvious junctures of its October 19 hearing on sports concussions — was the recipient of a $2,000 campaign contribution from Maroon in 2007, Federal Election Commission records show.

During discussion of the Riddell claim that its Revolution helmet reduced the risk of a football concussion by 31 percent, Senator Tom Udall of New Mexico noted that this figure came from an article published in the February 2006 issue of the journal *Neurosurgery*. Udall went on to explain that the co-author of the article had told the *New York Times* that he disagreed with Riddell's use of the 31 percent figure without also acknowledging the "limitations" of the study.

That co-author of Riddell's study, unnamed by Udall, was Maroon.

Later in the hearing Udall *did* name Tim Bream, head trainer for the Chicago Bears, as someone who had spoken favorably of the

Riddell Revolution helmet in one of its promotional videos.

Udall also gave Maroon a pass on his endorsement of the supplement Sports Brain Guard, whose marketer claims that it "protects against concussions." Earlier this year, as reported here, the company's website, SportsBrainGuard.com, included a photo of Maroon and a testimonial quote from him. He is no longer there.

Maroon donated $2,000 to Rockefeller on May 29, 2007 — the largest of Maroon's four most recent campaign contributions totaling $4,500. The others were, in 2010, $1,000 to Joe Manchin, West Virginia's other U.S. senator, and $500 to Senator Arlen Specter of Pennsylvania (who is no longer in office), and in 2011, $1,000 to Senator Orrin Hatch of Utah.

According to the database maintained by the Center for Responsive Politics, Maroon over the past 20 years has contributed to various politicians, the Democratic National Committee, and the American Neurological Surgery PAC. One of Maroon's employers, the University of Pittsburgh Medical Center and its corporate parent UPMC Health Systems, has spent millions of dollars on Washington lobbying.

According to the Sports Brain Guard website, the product was created by Dr. Russell Blaylock and developed by Newport Nutritionals, a company based in Irvine, California. There is no contact information listed for Blaylock either at his personal website (RussellBlaylockMD.com) or at the Sports Brain Guard site.

1 NOVEMBER 2011 ------------------------
In a finding that exposes just how aggressively, misleadingly, and perniciously ImPACT concussion management software is being marketed, *Concussion Inc.* has uncovered ImPACT and University of Pittsburgh Medical Center documents advising potential purchasers that not even baseline neurocognitive tests are needed in order to safely use their expensive, for-profit product.

Baseline testing is the holy grail of "concussion awareness." The evidence of its fraudulence, as usual, is hiding in plain sight. Examples:

- In talks at medical conferences, neuropsychologist Jamie Pardini of the UPMC Concussion Program discusses "How I Manage Concussions." At Muchnick.net/pardini .pdf, you can download a PDF file, which appears to include slides shown to the audience, perhaps a PowerPoint presentation. Look at slide number 8, "Clinical Protocol: Neurocognitive Testing." The first point on the timeline, pre-concussion, states, "Baseline Testing (Not necessary for decision making)."

- The lead story of the December 2005 issue of the *CIF News*, the newsletter of the California Interscholastic Federation, was a promo for ImPACT under the headline, "ImPACT Technology Ensures Safe Return to Play After Concussion." The article was written by the company's director of sales and marketing. It states, "[I]n the event that baseline testing is not possible, ImPACT has a normative database of thousands of non-injured athletes, and such data can be used effectively for adequate comparison and deciding safe return to play. Thus, ImPACT may now be used effectively in a clinical setting when baseline data is not available for comparison."

- ImPACT Applications, Inc.'s own website tackles the question head-on (so to speak). Here's the explanation from the FAQ page (ImPACTtest.com/faq): "Yes, the program can, and should, be used even without a baseline. In the report summary scores (composite scores), the norms are printed out and automatically tabulated. The raw score is accompanied by a percentile which indicates where they fall relative to healthy age and gender-matched controls.

For example, if the composite score falls at the 5th percentile . . . that would indicate 95 out of 100 non-concussed individuals would perform better than the athlete that is being tested. By understanding their pre-injury status, this data can be extremely informative and helpful. For example, a typical A/B student should be around the 60th percentile or higher on all composite scores, those that are C students should typically fall around the 40th percentile or higher and those with learning disability or very poor students could fall as low as the 20th percentile or so and be considered within normal limits. We use the program all the time without baselines and the data is very helpful for clinical management."

I don't think UPMC and ImPACT would be able to find many, if any, experts who were not already on their payroll who would be willing to assert that a "normative database" could responsibly substitute for individual baseline tests. Young people's brains are still growing and changing, and their responses to standardized tests fluctuate year to year, even month to month, with variances that make the UPMC and ImPACT claims here almost criminally unsupportable.

All this does not even to get to the general flaws of subjective neurocognitive tests, which have already been widely discussed: the reality that test-takers sandbag the baseline tests with deliberately dumb answers and boost their scores on repeat tests with the help of Ritalin.

30 NOVEMBER 2011 ----------------------

The National Institutes of Health yesterday fulfilled my Freedom of Information Act request and supplied five documents from the University of Pittsburgh Medical Center's multimillion-dollar grant application and progress reports on concussion research for the period 2001–06.[12]

This is no mere underwriting of purchases of lab equipment or travel to scientific conferences. It is a major subsidy, including compensation breakdowns, for a monumental public health study. The grant shows tens of thousands of dollars of annual remuneration for Mark Lovell, Dr. Joseph Maroon, Micky Collins, and others.

As noted previously, the NIH conflict-of-interest disclosure by UPMC is not included with this document release. The federal rules put the control of the public release of that disclosure in the hands of the grant recipient itself.

One of the more intriguing loops left unclosed by this release is: What happened at the back end? Did UPMC ultimately report out conclusions from its fMRI study?

28 FEBRUARY 2012 --------------------------

Neurosurgery has published a new paper claiming that healing time from a concussion now can be predicted with more precision. Remember that *Neurosurgery* is a virtual house organ of the NFL and historical repository of canned, cooked, and unethically produced articles on traumatic brain injury. UPMC today put out a press release:

> The study, one of the first to examine concussion prognoses, showed that specific neurocognitive "cut-off" scores derived from ImPACT™ (Immediate Post-concussion Assessment and Cognitive Testing) improved clinicians' ability to predict which sports-related concussions could take longer — as much as five times longer — to rehabilitate than others. They found, in as many as 85 percent of the cases, the scores could warn

athletes, parents, coaches, schools, teams, and health professionals when a concussion is likely to take on average a month to heal.

Micky Collins, the UPMC program director who co-owns the for-profit ImPACT Applications, calls the study "a game-changer" because it augurs "a way of determining within two days of injury who's going to take a month or longer to recover."

Meanwhile, in the neglected common-sense wing of youth concussion research, another journal, *Brain Injury*, has published a paper by Université de Montréal neuropsychologist Dave Ellemberg buttressing the intuitively obvious case that teenagers are far more vulnerable than adults in this area. Furthermore, Ellemberg says, a first sports-related concussion "will result in six months to a year of neurophysiological side effects for adolescents, adults, and children alike."

29 FEBRUARY 2012 -
Pittsburgh is the national capital of Concussion Inc. — and proud of it!

"Health care is booming business in Western Pennsylvania," says the *Pittsburgh Tribune-Review*:

> The industry's impact in the region last year was $15.8 billion, and health care employed more than 112,000 workers, according to a report published by the Hospital and Healthsystem Association of Pennsylvania. The number represented 10.5 percent of the total workforce in Allegheny, Westmoreland, Washington, Beaver, Butler, Fayette, Armstrong, and Green counties.
>
> Health care continues to dominate the local landscape as UPMC and West Penn Allegheny Health

System, the two largest providers, fight for patients and insurance customers in the region.

Highmark Inc., the region's largest insurer, has proposed acquiring West Penn Allegheny for $475 million. Because of that merger, UPMC intends to terminate agreements between its doctors and Highmark.[13]

UPMC owns 19 hospitals and had 2011 operating revenue of $9 billion — up from $8 billion in 2010. "The system employed 54,000 people in Western Pennsylvania, including more than 5,000 physicians. Its hospitals admitted and observed more than 234,000 patients. CEO Jeffrey A. Romoff earned $4 million in 2009, according to public tax disclosures."

The part about the UPMC turf war with West Penn Allegheny Health caught my eye. In 1999, Dr. Maroon made regional business news when he and his celebrity-studded practice at Allegheny General Hospital — West Penn Allegheny Health's flagship — jumped to UPMC.

As it happens, last October I was contacted by Dr. Jack Wilberger, the neurosurgery chair at Allegheny General and a vice president of West Penn Allegheny Health. "Our Concussion Center is becoming more robust as more and more realize the issues you describe," Wilberger told me. I have since noticed that Wilberger occasionally lands a dissenting quote in the Pittsburgh press coverage of UPMC's management of hockey star Sidney Crosby's long recovery from a series of concussions.

None of this should be taken as an endorsement of Jack Wilberger; I don't know Jack Wilberger from Jack. But "health care is booming business in Western Pennsylvania." That much I know.

6 MARCH 2012 -------------------------

The UPMC media relations department never responds to my inquiries, and that hurts my feelings. Peer-reviewed studies show that I get between 30.07 and 43.24 percent madder than baseline every time UPMC flacks ignore me.

However, the indefatigable Dustin Fink of the *Concussion Blog* yesterday did receive an unsolicited email from Chuck Finder, who joined the UPMC staff recently after years as a sportswriter for the *Pittsburgh Post-Gazette.*

Last week Fink wrote an unflattering analysis of UPMC's hype of its new "concussion recovery predictor" model.[14] Whereupon Finder contacted Fink. Below, as a public service, I reproduce Finder's entire message, including the memo from UPMC's Brian Lau responding to Fink's questions.

In Nos. 1 and 5, Lau asserts that symptoms such as fatigue and headache can exist without concussions and are sometimes confused with them. Of course, the same point makes the "sensitivity" percentage claims for the ImPACT system — to the hundredths of a percent! — meaningless. We have no way of knowing if concussion symptoms are abating or if mere "concussion-like symptoms" are abating. Two can play this circular logic game.

In No. 4, UPMC explains that its recovery-predictor study has no "traditional control group." English translation: There is no control group.

> Dustin,
>
> First, please allow me to introduce myself. My name is Chuck Finder, and in my previous life as a sports writer I penned more than a few concussion stories/series in my 25 years at the *Pittsburgh Post-Gazette.* I joined UPMC in mid-January to help represent their Sports Medicine and Concussion Program work.

Folks here noticed your Feb. 29 blog questions prompted by their Cut-Off Study news release, and Brian Lau — one of the co-investigators — typed up answers for you.

Use them however you choose: They can be for your edification solely or, if you wish, you have UP-MC's approval to post them as they are . . .

Chuck Finder

UPMC Media Relations

*****

[BRIAN LAU MEMO]

1. *Why would you neurocognitive test anyone with symptoms, while still recovering?*

The symptoms after a concussion — fatigue, headache, etc. — are non-specific findings that may or may not represent a concussion. Moreover, some athletes have some of these same symptoms at baseline. Neurocognitive testing has traditionally been used to determine the presence or absence of a concussion. This study adds to other preliminary evidence that neurocognitive testing while an athlete has symptoms during recovery may also assist in predicting length of recovery. A previous study showed that symptoms used alone had a 40.81% sensitivity in predicting protracted recovery. When neurocognitive testing was used with symptoms, the sensitivity in predicting protracted recovery increased to 65.22%.

2. *Are the numbers based upon the ImPACT "norms" or a baseline calculation?*

There are no numbers in this study requiring the use of norms or baseline calculations. We used the numbers from the first ImPACT tests and determined cutoffs off that.

3. *Is this experiment repeatable with other measures?*

This is the first study to attempt to set cutoffs for prognosticating return to play early after injury. As recommended in the discussion section, we hope that this study encourages other groups to conduct similar studies to evaluate the value of cutoff scores.

4. *Where are the control groups?*

It should be noted that this was an observational study that followed athletes, whom underwent a structured recovery program. It was not designed to compare two different diagnostic modalities or treatment intervention. Therefore, the traditional control group vs. study group that compares traditional practice with a novel diagnostic tool or treatment is not represented in this study. However, recovery from a sports concussion usually takes less than 14 days. In this study, the athletes were divided into protracted and short-recovery based on this time frame. As such, the short-recovery group may be considered the control group because it represents the natural recovery time following a sports concussion.

5. *Is the accuracy of ImPACT that sensitive (is there even one accurate enough to make this assessment)?*

ImPACT testing has been shown previously to have a high degree of sensitivity (81.9%) and specificity (89.4%) in diagnosing concussions (Shatz et al., *Arch Clin Neuropsychol*, 2006). The sensitivity and specificity in prognosticating the recovery time following a concussion has only recently been studied. A recent study showed that when ImPACT testing and symptoms were evaluated together, there was a sensitivity and specificity of 65.22 and 80.36%, respectively. The effectiveness of ImPACT testing as a prognosticating tool should be further validated and we hope that this study will encourage others to do so.

6. *What did each individual do for management of the concussion in the two days?*

All athletes were followed by certified athletic trainers who made the initial on-field diagnosis of a concussion. These certified athletic trainers were also trained in the graded exertional activity protocol used in this study which requires athletes to be symptom free at rest and to be cleared by clinical concussion specialists. Therefore, in the time frame prior to initial neurocognitive testing (mean: two days), athletes were kept out of practice and game situations.

25 SEPTEMBER 2012 ----------------------
The *Pittsburgh Post-Gazette* is in the middle of examining how "UPMC has come to dominate Pittsburgh's landscape, much like the steel industry did."

Part 1 of the series includes the following account of a questionable land deal between UPMC and my favorite physician-piñata, Dr. Joseph Maroon, in 1999, the year Maroon was recruited away from Allegheny General Hospital:

> Dr. Maroon also was a prolific real estate investor and had bought about three dozen parcels on the North Side.
>
> At the same time UPMC announced that Dr. Maroon was coming to work for the hospital, the surgeon sold UPMC a group of his properties for $5.2 million — real estate which cost him a fraction of that to acquire.
>
> UPMC still owns all but two of the parcels it bought from Dr. Maroon in the deal. But 13 years after UPMC completed the transaction, the property is valued about $1 million less than the purchase price.
>
> In 1999, both UPMC and Dr. Maroon denied there was any tie between his move to UPMC and the purchase of the property.
>
> Dr. Maroon did not return calls seeking comment for this story.[15]

Give that *Post-Gazette* reporter, Sean D. Hamill, an ImPACT baseline test at once!

19 OCTOBER 2012 ----------------------
The feds have indicted Dr. Joe Maroon's former UPMC and Pittsburgh Steelers colleague, Dr. Richard Rydze, for human growth hormone trafficking.

Rydze made six-figure purchases of HGH by credit card from internet gray-market drug dealer Signature Pharmacy. He was busted by ESPN's Mike Fish.[16]

----

1   sports.espn.go.com/espn/otl/news/story?id=4724912.

2   The interview is viewable at youtube.com/watch?v=g8jqCZ4yUrs.

3   See www.thepostgame.com/features/201101/tpg-exclusive-nfl-orders-raiders-head-coach-hue-jackson-end-ties-company-linked-bann.

4   See Maroon's piece of the hype at www.sportsbrainguard.com/sbg.aspx.

5   www.nytimes.com/2011/01/23/sports/football/23helmet.html?ref=sports.

6   blog.4wallspublishing.com/2011/04/23/critics-evidence-debunk-concussion-testing-in-football.aspx.

7   Video was originaly available at nflhealthandsafety.com/2011/01/20/performing-a-neurological-exam/.

8   Video was originaly available at nflhealthandsafety.com/2011/07/13/dr-ellenbogen-on-concussions/.

9   www.theintelligencer.net/page/content.detail/id/557704/-Sunday-Sit-Down—TODAY-S-GUEST–Dr–Joseph-Maroon.html?nav=510#. Tj_rrgQagV0.twitter.

10   "Concussions Take a Terrible Toll on America's Young Athletes," by Steve Jansen and Gus Garcia-Roberts, www.laweekly.com/2011-08-18/news/concussions-take-a-terrible-toll-on-america-s-young-athletes/.

11   www.mlive.com/sports/jackson/index.ssf/2011/10/orthopaedic_rehab_specialists.html.

12   The documents are available at muchnick.net/upmcgrantyr1.pdf, muchnick.net/upmcgrantyr2.pdf, muchnick.net/upmcgrantyr3.pdf, muchnick.net/upmcgrantyr4.pdf, muchnick.net/upmcgrantyr5.pdf.

13   www.pittsburghlive.com/x/pittsburghtrib/business/s_779870.html.

14   See theconcussionblog.com/2012/02/29/upmc-and-recovery-predictor/.

15   www.post-gazette.com/promohomepage/2012/10/02/PG-Special-Report-UPMC-Forging-a-Giant-Footprint-1/stories/201210020227.

16   sports.espn.go.com/espn/otl/news/story?id=3831956.

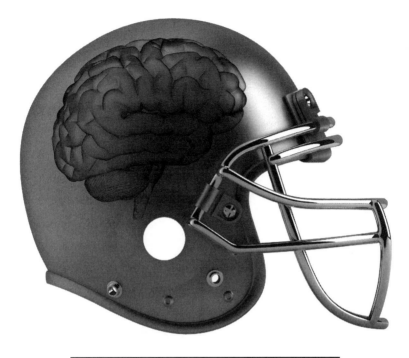

CHRIS NOWINSKI AND ALAN SCHWARZ

Having lambasted Dr. Joe Maroon for his sundry commercial associations, I cannot fail to explore a controversy last week sparked by
articles in the Boston business press reporting that Dr. Robert Cantu
had some kind of advisory status with the innovative Xenith helmet
company. Cantu, of Boston University, the physician who diagnosed
Chris Nowinski's concussions prior to the launch of his Sports Legacy
Institute, is one of the leading lights in chronic traumatic encephalopathy research. Fasten your chinstraps for a complicated tale of hype in
the world of venture capital.

I am not alleging here the kind of blatant corruption suggested by the deep-seated symbiosis of Maroon with the Pittsburgh Steelers, the NFL, WWE, UPMC, ImPACT, the unregulated supplements Vindure and Sports Brain Guard, and the Riddell Revolution helmet. That particular custodian of the Hippocratic oath has turned himself into a walking infomercial.

But do Cantu and Xenith themselves pass the "Caesar's wife" test of discouraging even the appearance of impropriety? You decide.

Xenith, LLC is a Lowell, Massachusetts, based company started by Vincent Ferrara, who played quarterback at Harvard in the 1990s and, indeed, lost most or all of one season to a concussion. (He happened to be four years ahead of Nowinski at Harvard.) Ferrara then got his M.D. and, upon finding himself most interested in the business side of health care, his MBA at Columbia.

I am not an expert and I have no opinion on the benefits of Xenith's helmet model. If it has the potential to prevent injuries and save lives, then great. In a phone conversation with me last Thursday, Vin Ferrara said all the right things about the primacy of education — how no piece of head hardware can substitute for safer playing technique and a smarter athletic mindset.

In a 2007 *New York Times* story on Ferrara's company — written by concussion beat writer Alan Schwarz — Dr. Cantu said a good bit more.

Schwarz's article asserted that the Ferrara helmet's 18 thermoplastic shock absorbers filled with air "can accept a wide range of forces and still moderate the sudden jarring of the head that causes concussion." In addition, unlike traditional foam helmet lining, the disks do not degrade after hundreds of impacts, according to laboratory tests.

Cantu told the *Times* this was "the greatest advance in helmet design in at least 30 years." He was identified as an informal advisor during the helmet's development with "no financial relationship with the product."

In September 2010, Xenith issued a press release announcing it had raised $10.5 million in equity financing. The release cited the marketing inroads of the company's X1 football helmet. Dr. Cantu was nowhere mentioned.[1]

However, until very recently — that is, some time past the September round of PR — Cantu was still on the Xenith website (Xenith.com). Ferrara told me that Cantu had asked that references to him be removed several months ago.

By law, Xenith was required to submit paperwork to the Securities and Exchange Commission about its $10 million financing threshold; the filing became public on February 25. Three days later — a week ago Monday — a spate of articles about Xenith appeared in online versions of Boston business magazines. Citybizlist.com, for example, wrote:

> Xenith helmets have been recorded to reduce the risk of concussion by as much as 60%, and players have reported a 70% reduction in the incidence of headaches. Xenith advisor Dr. Robert Cantu, co-director of the Center for the Study of Traumatic Encephalopathy at Boston University School of Medicine and one of the nation's leading experts in concussion management, called it "the greatest advance in helmet design in at least 30 years."[2]

The *Boston Business Journal* and its offshoots also erroneously reported (and subsequently retracted) NFL Hall of Fame quarterback Warren Moon's participation in the Xenith investment group.

Ferrara shared with me his email to the leadership of the National Operating Committee on Standards of Athletic Equipment, in which he said he had "absolutely no idea why anything came out today, and Xenith had no involvement in this whatsoever. . . . [Xenith's September press release] in no way mentions concussions, concussion reduction, the NFL, Warren Moon, Bob Cantu, or anything else that is being printed in these recent posts. I have received numerous calls, emails, etc., about these releases, and I am truly baffled as to how this transpired. I have already emailed Jeff Pash [NFL attorney] to inform him of this as well."

I also spoke last Thursday with Cantu, who reinforced that he has never been a paid advisor for Xenith. "Have I talked with people from that company about their products? Yes. I do that with a lot of companies," Cantu said. "But I have not received money from any of them."

I'm not sure what to make of all this. In my experience, business journalists don't ordinarily have the enterprise to research and publish deep backgrounders with short turnarounds — let alone inaccurate ones — every time a company makes a routine SEC filing.

I also think that, while the root 2007 *Times* article carefully disclaimed Cantu's equity interest in Xenith, the story as a whole smells of social networking in the old-fashioned sense — the kind involving Ivy League elites well practiced in planting high-toned hype in the Newspaper of Record. Would a start-up elsewhere located and with a worse-connected CEO have been able to get this kind of ink?

It was wrong for Riddell Helmets, aided by NFL-funded research conducted by Joseph Maroon, to be making the kinds of statistical safety claims now under investigation by the Federal Trade Commission.

It was also wrong for Robert Cantu and Xenith to have gotten mixed up in their own brand of fledgling and unverifiable braggadocio.

As the public witnesses a statistically significant population of athletes dying young, often by their own hands, leading doctors cautiously emphasize how much is yet to be understood about the scope and magnitude of traumatic brain injury in contact sports. I just wish the same doctors would be correspondingly modest about the commercial products designed to mitigate it.

18 MAY 2011 ----------------------------

The *New York Times* and the *New Yorker* are responsible for elevating the concussion issue from the sports pages to the national agenda. However, in my view, they frame the story inadequately.

The *Times* would prefer to spur much too gentlemanly an outcome: a reprise of President Teddy Roosevelt's football reforms of a century ago. The problem is that this sport and associated ones are no longer character-building rituals by Ivy League elites buffing their résumés in anticipation of careers on Wall Street and in other ruling-class institutions. Football today is a global multi-layered mega-industry. The urgency of reducing the human toll of this culture, across all classes and races, exceeds the scope of legislating helmets or any other piece of hardware, or mumbling bromides about changing the way that players block and tackle.

In its January coverage of the controversy surrounding Riddell helmets, the *Times* quoted Dr. Maroon — co-author of the *Neurosurgery* article that was the basis for the company's promotion — as claiming Riddell quoted him out of context. But Maroon was not asked if he ever so complained, in public or in private, prior to the initiation of a Federal Trade Commission investigation of Riddell.

In his January article in the *New Yorker*, "Does Football Have a Future?", writer Ben McGrath quoted Maroon as calling the *Times'* Schwarz "the Socratic gadfly in this whole mix." Maroon added, "What we're seeing now is [a] major cultural shift, and I think Alan took a lot of barbs, and a lot of hits, initially, for his observations."

26 MAY 2011 ----------------------------

Chris Nowinski has done valuable work on the concussion crisis in sports. That work is also limited and flawed.

He is the subject of a profile in today's edition of the *Harvard Crimson*, the student newspaper of his alma mater.[3] Clearly and deservedly, *Crimson* reporters Emily Rutter and Scott A. Sherman take note of Nowinski's value. They may not realize that the Old Ivy orientation of their account also reveals his limitations and flaws.

The story has it all: Nowinski's Harvard and football pedigree; his fascination with and employment by World Wrestling Entertainment — which led to his debilitating, career-ending concussions; and his decision to write a book about brain trauma in sports and start the Sports Legacy Institute.

The revealing passage, from my perspective, was this:

> With the help of Alan Schwarz, at the time a freelance sportswriter for the *New York Times*, he got in touch with publishers.
>
> "I thought his manuscript was great," says Schwarz, who had written one book on baseball statistics and was working on another.

As I reflect on what I find both inspiring and dissatisfying about Nowinski's career advocacy, the (obviously indispensable) Schwarz/ *Times* connection is instructive. It reminds me very much of the phenomenon surrounding *Freakonomics: A Rogue Economist Explores the Hidden Side of Everything*, a 2005 bestseller by Steven Levitt and Stephen J. Dubner.

For my money, *Freakonomics* is a pedestrian book, but my opinion doesn't matter. In any case, I'm more interested in the process of its creation. *Freakonomics* grew out of a profile of Levitt by Dubner in the Sunday magazine of the *New York Times*. The two Steves then decided to collaborate on a book. And get this: *the epigraph of every chapter of the book wound up being a quote from Dubner's* Times *magazine profile of Levitt.*

Talk about a hall of mirrors!

I wish Nowinski the very best, both with his brave personal battle to survive post-concussion syndrome, and his likely as-yet-undiagnosed own case of chronic traumatic encephalopathy, and with his campaign to spread the word about and temper the brutality of football and other sports.

However, with respect to the latter, I also observe that his voice is skewed, at times even muted, by his ready access to the resources of both our Newspaper of Record and the National Football League (the latter thanks to a $1 million NFL grant to the Sports Legacy Institute's sister Center for the Study of CTE at Boston University Medical School). You can see it in the increased corporatization of SLI's message and in the current carefully adumbrated coverage by the *Times* of football helmet safety and promotion. So much more remains unsaid: the accounting for the tobacco-level scandal of NFL-branded research over the last generation, and the structural solutions we must be devising as a society, outside of willy-nilly litigation on behalf of the many lives ruined and prematurely ended by this system.

Above all, I'm convinced there is a need for more than just Chris Nowinski's voice on this critical issue.

27 MAY 2011 ---------------------------

Today I received the following email, with the subject line "What you don't know":

> is that all I did — based solely on the public-interest aspect of his message, and long before I was even an employee of the *Times* — was introduce him to a few people. And they quickly blew him off. He didn't find a publisher for his book for another 12 months, and completely independent of me.
>
> More importantly, your comparison to Leavitt and Dubner is incorrect, misleading and borderline offensive.

(Despite the fact that both of them are friends of mine.) Regardless of how they might have met, those two are collaborators and business partners, and make no bones about it. Your strong implication that Chris and I are either of those two things is something I recommend you correct.

Third, and most serious, your characterization of the *Times* coverage as "carefully adumbrated" — which, I'm assuming for now that you know, means presented somewhat incompletely in an effort to be vague or misleading. As far as I know your concern with the coverage stems only from your Maroon-connection-to-Riddell-study issue. Even if that were an issue, which I know it is not for reasons of which you are totally unaware, you have some nerve casting the entire work that way.

I kill myself for six months to expose a serious safety problem — and even conspiracy — in youth football, cause sweeping changes (some about to be announced) and investigations by the CPSC and the FTC, and you sit back and decide that one small issue you think you've found with it makes it "carefully adumbrated"? Wow.

I am not above criticism. But misinformed and careless criticism pisses me off. When you accomplish one-tenth of the good for the world and kids that I — or for that matter, Chris — have on this subject, then you'll really have something.

— Alan Schwarz.

Schwarz was responding to the item here yesterday in which I expressed discomfort with the amount of space he and Chris Nowinski were taking up in the national concussion conversation (while also pointing out, as I do repeatedly, their deserved credit for raising that conversation to its present level).

At the bottom of Schwarz's disagreement with me is a difference of opinion on the forward thrust of federal investigations of the National Football League. I will begin by explaining that disagreement from my perspective. If I may say so, the Schwarz account *carefully adumbrates* it. More on this fatal phrase as we move along.

"As far as I know," Schwarz says, "your concern with the [*Times*] coverage stems only from your Maroon-connection-to-Riddell-study issue."

Well, that's one way to read it. Another way is to note that Maroon is a connection that could help push the current probes by executive agencies and members of Congress from their focus on football helmet safety to a wider scope of NFL accountability for a public health tab we are just beginning to tote up. Schwarz is entitled to the opinion — if his opinion it is — that scapegoating helmet manufacturers gets to the heart of the problem. And I am entitled to mine: that the investigations, plural, need to go much higher up the food chain.

I am not sure which dictionary Schwarz consulted for the definition of the word "adumbrate"; nor is it clear whether he ever got his nose out of the air long enough to look at one at all. According to *Merriam-Webster*, the verb means "to foreshadow vaguely: *intimate*"; "to suggest, disclose, or outline partially"; to "*overshadow, obscure.*"

Schwarz says my use of the word means that I think he has presented the story "somewhat incompletely in an effort to be vague or misleading." I have never speculated as to his intentions. A less malignant interpretation of the phrase *carefully adumbrated* could also mean that a *Times* reporter, in contrast to an independent author, journalist, and blogger, lines up his work with certain calculations about the size of his news hole, the number and timing of his investigative angles, and — finally and critically — the internal political demands of the *Times* editing machine.

Again, it should be obvious that Schwarz's resources and methods have distinct advantages over my own, as well as less obvious drawbacks. Having clarified as much, let me go on to say that if Schwarz's interpretive shoe of having been accused of being willfully vague or misleading fits, then he should wear it. Schwarz asserts by fiat that the Maroon link to the Riddell issue is of little or no importance, "for reasons of which you are totally unaware." I beg to differ, and I also beg Schwarz to enlighten us all on these alleged reasons instead of *carefully adumbrating* them.

My comparison of the Nowinski/Schwarz relationship to that of the co-authors of the book *Freakonomics* "is incorrect, misleading and borderline offensive," Schwarz says. "[T]hose two are collaborators and business partners, and make no bones about it. Your strong implication that Chris and I are either of those two things is something I recommend you correct."

This is another great example of inflating a barb into a crime. The point of the *Freakonomics* analogy was not and is not that Levitt and Dubner are ethically challenged. It is that they reside in an echo chamber. This puts their egos in the foreground and their insights in the background. With or without Schwarz's permission, I will continue to worry publicly that he and Nowinski might be doing something similar.

Speaking of ego, all praise is due Schwarz for spurring the involvement of the Consumer Product Safety Commission and the Federal Trade Commission. I rather doubt, however, that he's "killing" himself in the effort. Evidently *Times* reporters, like the rest of us, employ the occasional figure of speech.

By the same token, your humble blogger is proud to be the named respondent of the landmark United States Supreme Court case *Reed*

Elsevier v. Muchnick, the latest step in a 17-year-long public-interest fight. So there, and onward.

30 MAY 2011 --------------------------

In the course of his whiny, egotistical, and largely fact-free email complaint, Alan Schwarz said that, as far as he knew, "your concern with the coverage stems only from your Maroon-connection-to-Riddell-study issue. Even if that were an issue, which I know it is not for reasons of which you are totally unaware, you have some nerve casting the entire work that way."

One striking aspect of this passage is that it raised the issue of Dr. Joseph Maroon in response to an item by me that itself did not mention him. Moreover — as anyone plugging the term "Alan Schwarz" into this blog's search engine can confirm — I never frontally criticized the *Times* for its Maroon coverage (as opposed to exhorting the *Times* and all media to pick up on my exposure of the fuller context of his work for the National Football League and World Wrestling Entertainment, and to connect it to the Riddell helmet investigation in a way that would make it, in my view, more meaningful).

Once again: I have not once ripped Schwarz for what he has written about Maroon.

On January 13, I wrote:

> The *New York Times'* Alan Schwarz, whose investigative article last October on the unreliable work of the National Operating Committee on Standards for Athletic Equipment (NOCSAE) helped spur Senator Udall's call to the FTC, reported that Maroon "disagreed with Riddell's marketing the 31 percent figure without acknowledging its limitations, and supported Udall's request for a formal scrutiny."

Maroon told the *Times*, "That was the data that came out, but the authors of that study on multiple occasions have recommended further investigations, better controls and with larger numbers. If one is going to make statements relative to the paper we wrote, it should be with the limitations that we emphasized, and not extrapolated to studies that we suggest should be done and haven't been done yet."

I went on to document that Riddell had been aggressively exploiting the Maroon-co-authored and NFL-funded study of its Revolution model since no later than July 2008, and wondered why neither the doctor nor the league had raised a peep about it before it became a federal case.

The piece also included this paragraph:

I asked the *Times'* Schwarz if he had sought elaboration from Dr. Maroon as to where, when, and to whom he had ever objected to Riddell's advertising claims exploiting his research. Schwarz declined comment.

After the article was posted, Schwarz emailed me: "Nicely done."

On January 24, I emailed Schwarz, in part, "On or off the record, your choice: do you intend to explore the Maroon/Riddell fault line? If not, why not? Any insights from your valuable perspective would be appreciated."

Schwarz again declined comment — but not before first going out of his way to say that Dr. Maroon had been "obviously (and surprisingly) quite generous to me" in comments in a recently published *New Yorker* article, and to make sure that he, Schwarz, was satisfied that my "motives" in asking the question were pure.

Now that Schwarz's thin skin has been pierced and he is giving his crypto-assurance that Joe Maroon is a non-story, it's time to reemphasize that Maroon is not a good guy in the NFL concussion narrative and has not been for years. Why *didn't* Schwarz press Maroon on the history of his enabling of Riddell helmet hype, rather than allow the doctor to get away with a quote triangulating the FTC investigation and distancing himself from the company? Intuitively, this made no more sense than Maroon's parallel survival as a member of the NFL's Mild Traumatic Brain Injury Committee for years (up to the present) beyond the exposure of his and other league doctors' commercial conflicts of interest in Congressional hearings and in the media (some of them well-drawn stories by Schwarz himself).

This is not an attempt to brand a triviality into the main timeline. As the Pittsburgh Steelers' neurosurgeon, Maroon was on the front rank of the apologists and deniers when Dr. Bennet Omalu identified the breakthrough cases of chronic traumatic encephalopathy in Mike Webster and Terry Long. Is there a better word in the English language than "lie" for the statement by Maroon that Long's team medical file showed no concussions — a falsity chronicled by Chris Nowinski in his book *Head Games*? (After Maroon's categorical denial, Omalu produced a 1987 letter by Maroon about treating Long for a concussion.)

Any way you slice it, Schwarz's Mount Olympian dismissal of the very idea that Maroon might be more than a bit player in the national sports concussion scandal ignores a clear and chilling through-line. Maroon's and colleagues' articles for the journal *Neurosurgery* (whose editor-in-chief through much of the period was a New York Giants consultant) downplayed concussion syndrome, beat the drum for pseudo-objective neurocognitive testing in return-to-play standards, and were the direct antecedent of the current state-by-state campaign to put the costs of newfangled concussion management software on the backs of high school sports programs. (The runaway market leader in this field is the for-profit ImPACT system owned by Maroon and some of his University of Pittsburgh Medical Center colleagues.)

The DNA of this whole process is evident again in Maroon's work for Riddell. That is why I argue that the federal government will solve nothing, and indeed will be aiding a whitewash, if it stops at a probe of the helmet industry.

Finally, if Alan Schwarz's "reasons" for treating Dr. Joseph Maroon with kid gloves in the pages of the *New York Times* cannot be articulated even though the reporter initiated a reference to them in an unsolicited communication, then I am not the only reader with "reasons" to question whether the reporter's impenetrable code here is a public service.

3 JUNE 2011 ----------------------------

In a January *New Yorker* article on the concussion crisis in football, writer Ben McGrath quoted Pittsburgh neurosurgeon Joseph Maroon speaking admiringly of Alan Schwarz, the *New York Times* reporter who created this beat and more recently was nominated for a Pulitzer Prize. Schwarz, said Dr. Maroon, is "the Socratic gadfly in this whole mix."

Unlike Socrates, however, Schwarz asks questions that are carefully and corporately adumbrated. The resultant national spirit of cautious inquiry into a stunningly broad public health story is being driven by our Newspaper of Record. This process has the effect of protecting powerful and moneyed interests.

I don't think anyone from the Riddell helmet company is going to jail after Congress, the Consumer Product Safety Commission, and the Federal Trade Commission are finished probing how the company ran hard and fast with ambiguous data from a safety study underwritten by the NFL. Nor do I think anyone should, based on what we so far know, despite the Purple Heart that Schwarz awarded himself last week in a bush league email complaint about my blog's coverage: "I kill myself for six months to expose a serious safety problem — and even conspiracy — in youth football, cause sweeping changes (some about to be announced) and investigations by the CPSC and the FTC . . ."

Schwarz, who used to write books analyzing baseball stats, is in his element when he verbally slaps around the leadership of the National Operating Committee on Standards for Athletic Equipment. He is obviously less comfortable confronting figures like Dr. Maroon, a team physician for the Pittsburgh Steelers who remains, inexplicably, a quotable authority even though he is facemask-deep in the concussion scandal.

It would behoove the most celebrated concussion reporter in American journalism to press Maroon for better answers. Instead, Schwarz has allowed Maroon to distance himself from the NFL's Riddell helmet study, which the doctor co-authored with, among others, the company's chief engineer, and which Riddell then exploited in its promotion.

Ah, but Maroon is not an issue, Schwarz asserted to me — "for reasons of which you are totally unaware." If that's true, then this titan of communications needs to do some more communicating.

One upshot of Schwarz's incomplete coverage is that ImPACT has been purchased by an estimated 10 to 15 percent of high school football programs across the country, often under the mandates of new state "safety" legislation. I believe that, rather than shifting the NFL's public health tab to already financially beleaguered school districts, we should be talking seriously, not as a throwaway line, about whether high school football is medically, legally, and educationally sustainable.

Somehow the *Times* has not seen fit to print the devastating critique of ImPACT by Christopher Randolph, a neurology professor at Loyola University Chicago's Stritch School of Medicine, in the journal *Current Sports Medicine Reports*. (Credit for first publicizing Randolph's work goes to Matt Chaney.)

Randolph wrote, "There is no evidence to suggest that the use of baseline testing alters any risk from sport-related concussion, nor is there even a good rationale as to how such tests might influence outcome." He added that independent studies of ImPACT show a level of reliability "far too low to be useful for individual decision making." In sum, youth sports programs using it are investing in a false sense of security.

And what, I ask Alan Schwarz and the *New York Times*, would Socrates have to say about *that*?

8 JUNE 2011 --------------------------------

No doubt some readers think I'm doing an excessive metaphorical tap dance on Dr. Joe Maroon. The same readers may also wish I'd call a halt to my proverbial soft shoe on Alan Schwarz of the *New York Times*, the baseball statistical nerd who, by his own modest account, "[killed] myself for six months to expose a serious safety problem — and even conspiracy — in youth football." Maroon praises Schwarz in the *New Yorker*, Schwarz quotes Maroon uncritically in the *Times*, and Schwarz tells me flatly that Maroon is a not an issue in the larger national sports concussion scandal "for reasons of which you are totally unaware."

I point these readers and others to author-journalist-blogger Matt Chaney's January 28 post, "Brain Expert Omalu Wants Longer Rest for Concussed Football Players."[4] The subhead of Chaney's article is "Sideline concussed juveniles for three months, says the breakthrough neuropath; Neuropsychological testing lacks validation and might be harmful, critics caution; NFL players rebuke theory of 'safer' football through their 'behavior modification.'"

Here's most of the section headed "Critics Doubt Efficacy of NP testing for concussion diagnosis, 'return to play'":

> Today's general view that concussion management
> works or can work in tackle football is rendered highly

suspect, if not effectively discredited, by independent review and mounting adverse opinion of experts and witnesses like players.

Linebacker [Scott] Fujita notes he hasn't been measured on neural baseline for two NFL seasons. Might not matter, anyway, for NP testing has taken a systematic beating by reviewers of late. Observations and findings of medical literature from 2005 to 2010, listed without full author groups or first names, include:

* Randolph et al., 2005, for *Journal of Athletic Training*: "Despite the theoretic rationale for the use of NP testing in the management of sport-related concussion, no NP tests have met the necessary criteria to support a clinical application at this time. Additional research is necessary to establish the utility of these tests before they can be considered part of a routine standard of care . . . until NP testing or other methods are proven effective for this purpose."

* Patel et al., 2005, for *Sports Medicine*: "Numerous guidelines have been published for grading and return-to-play criteria following concussion; however, none of these have been prospectively validated by research and none are specifically applicable to children and adolescents."

* Mayers, 2008, for *Archives of Neurology*: "Current guidelines result from thoughtful consensus recommendations by expert committees but are chiefly based on the resolution of symptoms and the results of neuropsychological testing, if available. Adherence to this paradigm results in most

injured athletes resuming competition in one to two weeks."

* Duff, 2009, for *ASHA Leader*: "Indeed, the identification and management of concussion has become a growing public health issue. Considered to be the fastest-growing sub-discipline in neuropsychology, concussion management poses unique challenges and opportunities for those working with school-aged children. . . . There is no consensus on the best course of action for concussion management. In fact, there are as many as 22 different published guidelines for grading concussion severity and determining return to play. . . . Developers are working to collect data regarding reliability, validity, and clinical utility of these (NP) tools; independent replication is still forthcoming."

* Echemendia et al., 2009, for *British Journal of Sports Medicine*: "Post-injury assessment requires advanced neuropsychological expertise that is best provided by a clinical neuropsychologist. Significant international differences exist with respect to the training and availability of clinical neuro-psychologists, which require modification of these views on a country by country basis."

* Covassin et al., 2009, for *Journal of Athletic Training*: "little is known about the use of baseline neurocognitive testing in concussion assessment and management. . . . We found that the majority of ATs (athletic trainers) are interpreting ImPACT results without attending a neuropsychological testing workshop. . . . The use of baseline testing, baseline testing re-administration, and post-concussion

protocols among ATs is increasing. However, the ATs in this study reported that they relied more on symptoms than on neurocognitive test scores when making return-to-play decisions."

* Maerlender et al., 2010, for *The Clinical Neuropsychologist*: "Although computerized neuropsychological screening is becoming a standard for sports concussion identification and management, convergent validity studies are limited."

* Piland et al., 2010, for *Journal of Athletic Training*: "Obtaining (self-reported symptom) statements before a concussion occurs assists in determining when the injury is resolved. However, athletes may present with concussion-related symptoms at baseline. . . . In other words, some post-concussive symptoms occur in persons who have not sustained concussions, rendering the specificity of alleged post-concussive symptoms suspect."

* Schatz, 2010, for *American Journal of Sports Medicine*: "Computer-based assessment programs are commonly used to document baseline cognitive performance for comparison with post-concussion testing. There are currently no guidelines for how often baseline assessments should be updated, and no data documenting the test-retest stability of baseline measures over relevant time periods."

* Comper et al., 2010, for *Brain Injury*: "Despite the proliferation of neuropsychological research on sports-related concussion over the past decade, the methodological quality of studies appears to be highly variable, with many lacking proper scientific rigor. Future research in the area needs to

be carefully controlled, repeatable, and generalizable, which will contribute to developing practical, evidence-based guidelines for concussion management."

* Eckner et al., 2010, for *Current Sports Medicine Reports*: "The sports medicine practitioner must not rely on any one tool in managing concussion and must be aware of the strengths and limitations of whichever method is chosen . . ."

Unfortunately, software packages like ImPACT, long criticized for its direct connections to the NFL, are widely employed as *cornerstone* for concussion evaluation and typically by untrained clients, as literature and news reports confirm.

17 JUNE 2011 ----------------------------

New York Times reporter Alan Schwarz, May 27 email to me: "As far as I know your concern with the coverage stems only from your Maroon-connection-to-Riddell-study issue. [I know that is not an issue] for reasons of which you are totally unaware . . ."

New York Times columnist George Vecsey, June 14 email to me: "The *NYT* has led that story for three years. What are you talking about?"

We all realize that the *New York Times* is the worldwide leader in worldwide leadering. But on the story of the pandemic of traumatic brain injuries in sports and entertainment, exactly where is the *Times* trying to lead us?

An examination of the Newspaper of Record's coverage over the past six months suggests that the answer is it is leading us to a world made safe for the NFL and its $9-plus billion in annual revenues.

Pay plenty of lip service to the alleged mental-health toll for the thousands upon thousands of professional and amateur athletes employed by the NFL or in its orbit — but also make sure all the opinion-making honor and commercial benefits are reaped by the very league-connected doctors whose corrupt research and false public statements brought us to this pass.

Last December 8 the *Times* led a story headlined "NFL Invites Helmet Safety Ideas" with these words: "With the federal government, state legislatures, and football helmets' regulatory body already focusing on concussions and head protection, perhaps the most influential group of all — the NFL — convened its own summit of experts Wednesday to discuss possible reforms."

Try to imagine a *Times* story in the 1960s, subsequent to the surgeon general's report on the dangers of cigarettes, with a lead characterizing the Tobacco Institute as "perhaps the most influential group of all."

One of the NFL's "summit of experts" — quoted in paragraph three of the *Times* account with the searing insight "there's still more questions than answers" — was Dr. Joe Maroon. (The line in Maroon's résumé about being the medical director of WWE is scrubbed in *Times* coverage.)

There are already plenty of answers about Maroon himself, one of the root liars of the concussion saga. Yet the *Times* continues to inflict unfiltered Maroon on the concussion education of its readers. Most recently, Maroon, who says he welcomes the federal investigation of his NFL-funded safety study of Riddell football helmets, has been given *Times* news real estate for the lame explanation that he studied good but Riddell promoted bad.

Meanwhile, Dr. Bennet Omalu, who overcame Maroon's obstacles to identify chronic traumatic encephalopathy in dead football players, has not appeared even one time this year in print editions of the *Times*. On February 26, the *Times* did run a blog item by Toni Monkovic, which allowed that Omalu once upon a time "figured prominently" in a breakthrough finding of brain damage in NFL players. Monkovic also quoted author-blogger Matt Chaney's report on Omalu's call to sideline all concussed athletes for three months.

In lieu of conducting this threshold debate in print, however, the *Times* has chosen to go yawn and on about football helmets and neurocognitive testing. The latter is a field that Maroon and his UPMC colleagues, with their NFL affiliation, dominate via their for-profit concussion management software, ImPACT. This despite a substantial body of research — also unreported in the *Times* — arguing that neurocognitive testing in general, and ImPACT in particular, are at best ineffective.

And it's not as if Omalu hasn't been heard from lately in the CTE field: after several years of effective exile from the pages of the NFL-doctor-controlled journal *Neurosurgery*, he returned there under new management with a recent major article.

There's no new management at the NFL itself. For the *New York Times* and reporter Alan Schwarz (whom the *New Yorker* quotes the corrupt Dr. Maroon praising), that seems to be what counts most.

19 JUNE 2011 -----------------------------

Let's move beyond my criticism of Alan Schwarz and the *New York Times*. I want to impress upon everyone not just that the Gray Lady recently has fumbled the ball in the red zone, but also how to regain the lost momentum of its generally excellent coverage of the concussion crisis prior to this year.

The *Times* website's March 13, 2010, interactive timeline, "The NFL's Embattled Concussions Panel," with references dating back to 1994, remains a great historical resource.[5] Several things have gone wrong since then, in my view, beginning with the subtle co-optation of Schwarz, an inexperienced investigative reporter, which has paralleled that of his friend Chris Nowinski. It is hard to hear people nominating you for a Pulitzer Prize in Schwarz's case, or to find yourself brokering a $1 million National Football League grant in Nowinski's case, and retain your outsider's edge. Someone whom the *New Yorker* quotes corrupt NFL doctor Joe Maroon calling "the Socratic gadfly" of concussion discussion is receiving accolades with strings: he also is being unofficially appointed the amanuensis of the ruling class.

Add to all this last fall's loss of Democratic control of the House of Representatives, whose Judiciary Committee had conducted the most penetrating public hearings drawing the parallel between the NFL and the tobacco industry, and you have a recipe for tepid and hyped measures like helmet reform, along with acquiescence in spurious and cost-shifting post-concussion "management."

I am not the only observer who, in his own mind, damns the *Times* with such faint praise. I am just one of the few doing so out loud.

Coincident with the *Times*' squishy coverage of the past year has been the NFL's appointment of new co-chairs of its concussion policy committee. I'm still searching for the new leaf that the league has claimed to turn via its association with Drs. H. Hunt Batjer and Dr. Richard Ellenbogen.

29 JUNE 2011 ---------------------------------------

Word is leaking to the general public that "concussion management" software systems are magic shows, not public health solutions.

The *Chicago Tribune*'s solid health reporter, Julie Deardorff, was the first major newspaper journalist I noticed writing about the clinical journal research which casts doubts on programs like ImPACT (developed by Dr. Joe Maroon's UPMC team).

Today Fox News picked up the story of the new *American Journal of Sports Medicine* article finding that an athlete undergoing a computerized neuropsychological evaluation, which is designed to measure the effects of a traumatic brain injury, could get low marks because he was depressed about a sprained ankle.[6]

Meanwhile, the *New York Times* remains silent on the controversy over the reliance on neurocognitive testing. Indeed, of late the *Times* has been strangely light on concussion issue coverage in general, even as the NFL lockout has ended and pro football training camps have opened.

Dr. Bennet Omalu discovered chronic traumatic encephalopathy in football players. The last time a print edition of the *Times* mentioned Omalu was more than a year ago, June 29, 2010.

2 AUGUST 2011 ---------------------------

Alan Schwarz seems to have been taken off the concussion beat. Was it a promotion or an exile?

I just received the following email:

> Irv—
>
> My move out of Sports has been in the works since December. After four years of covering concussions — and after my entire 20-year career being spent in Sports, mostly baseball — I requested a new challenge, and the *Times* masthead was wonderfully supportive, to the point that they encouraged me to tackle one of the more important beats on the paper, National Education. I did not make the switch until July 5 because there were many loose ends to be tied up — the Duerson situation, some helmet things, some other non-concussion stories, and various personnel shuffling. I also took some time off to recharge my batteries. But the wheels began turning on this in late 2010 and were essentially rolling by February.

The break is clean — I am no longer, officially or unofficially, part of the Sports department. Of course I will contribute things here and there, as I do to other sections — for example, the essay about my son, and the obit on John Mackey. But I have moved — mentally and physically, given my new desk on the third floor — to National Education.

It is not for me to say what the Sports department will do regarding concussions and other head-injury/football matters in the future. Mine was never any sort of concussion "beat" — I just did the work and pursued it with my superiors' support and guidance, like dozens of other reporters at the paper. You'll notice I did a lot of other work (baseball, Paralympics, etc.) interspersed during my four years; concussions was my prime focus when it made sense, which was obviously rather often. I am extremely confident that the subject will be covered just as skillfully in my absence.

My leaving Sports was a promotion, not an exile — it was my decision alone, facilitated by a masthead that wanted to reward my work with the prestigious challenge of National Education. They couldn't have been nicer about it.

Hope this helps. Take care.

— Alan.

I responded:

Alan,

Thanks. I'll post your statement. Happy trails. Whether it's known as a beat or anything else, I hope the *Times* carries forward well the important work you pioneered.

Irv

Yesterday I asked Chris Nowinski, head of the Sports Legacy Institute, and Dr. Robert Cantu, Nowinski's co-director at Boston University's Center for the Study of Chronic Traumatic Encephalopathy, to comment on the wildly propagandistic statement by Dr. Joseph Maroon that the incidence of kids' injuries in car accidents is "significantly higher than playing in sports."

Nowinski and Cantu have not responded. That is both disappointing and revealing.

Talking about the new collective bargaining agreement between the NFL and its players, Nowinski has said that it is good if the professional athletes got what they wanted, and now there are additional questions of whether amateur athletes and their families will get what they need in terms of a sports system that protects them from undisclosed risks of permanent and disabling brain trauma. (I am paraphrasing.) There is no problem with Nowinski's stance, so far as it goes. But it doesn't go far enough, and he, more than anyone, should know that.

The NFL has given Nowinski's center a $1 million grant, but with each muted and equivocal public statement by the guiding light of contemporary concussion reform, the tacit strings attached to the league's discount generosity are showing.

Nowinski realizes — and he used to articulate this powerfully — that the NFL doesn't merely set the tone for the incentives and style of play in high school and youth football. It also buys and sells them. No example is starker than the thoroughly tainted Maroon and his ImPACT "concussion management" system. So when Maroon spews more public nonsense, as he did this week, it is Nowinski's responsibility — not just his job description — to rebut it.

Nowinski bristles at the charge that NFL money has compromised his mission. He says the steps initiated in recent years by Commissioner Roger Goodell and the owners have been "game-changers" in the national concussion narrative. Maybe so — but if one of those changes was to squelch the voice of Nowinski and his Boston group, then it was a bad bargain for the rest of us.

17 SEPTEMBER 2011 ----------------------
On September 8, National Public Radio's *Talk of the Nation* with Neal Conan featured a discussion of the concussion issue by guests Alan Schwarz of the *New York Times* and Buzz Bissinger, author of *Friday Night Lights*.[7]

It's an excellent dialogue, though also an incomplete one from my perspective. In addition, it provides some important interpretation by Schwarz of his groundbreaking and, unfortunately, now past-tense coverage.

Schwarz and Bissinger trade topping each other with the points that define the debate over the future of football. Schwarz gets to the heart of the unacceptable risks of traumatic brain injuries for pre–legal consent amateurs, and even the impossible real-world task of helmets in protecting against them. Often he does so with quite a bit more clarity than he achieved in his published news reports and analyses.

Bissinger, I think, effectively presses Schwarz on the bottom-line futility of changing football rules to address the problem. (Bissinger comes to a different conclusion than I do on whether the upshot is that tackle football should continue to be part of the public high school agenda — let alone its 900-pound gorilla.)

Now, back to Schwarz and what I have found so inadequate about the *New York Times* on concussions. Or was, before the *Times* moved

Schwarz to the position of national education reporter and became just another pack outlet on a story he and they had made.

It's a shame so much of Schwarz's intelligence is used for caginess instead of communication. For example, on the subject of the spate of lawsuits against the NFL, he says on NPR, "I think the question is, you know, what did you know, and when did you know it? And that's very debatable. I think those of us who have spent a long time studying not only the evidence but the history of the unfolding of the evidence, there's a point at which it becomes reasonable to think that the employer should have told the employees. However, a lot of people want that to start a lot earlier than I think is reasonable. So we'll see. It's for a jury and a judge to decide."

That is certainly one hermetically impenetrable way to put it. But is an underlined disclaimer about how the lawyers are going to slug it out, while we all sit back and watch, the most illuminating way? In my own interview on a Toronto radio station the very day the first of these lawsuits became news, I acknowledged that the specifics of that case needed more scrutiny. But I also emphasized that litigation, this one and others, collectively and inevitably, would drive the public's better understanding of the NFL's responsibility for a tobacco-like public health tab.[8]

This is the difference between someone employed by the *New York Times* and someone employed by himself.

Generally speaking, Schwarz devotes a lot of verbiage to his skepticism about the strongest claims of the links between football and traumatic brain injury. I think it's mostly a matter of style — but again, at a point the style becomes less about projecting credibility than about being disengaged and unhelpful. He says on NPR, "I think all we were certainly trying to do at the *New York Times* was give people the information, whether they were professionals or the parents of kids, on which to base their decisions of whether to take a risk — that particular risk or not. They can take whatever risks they want. We don't care."

Well, I for one care which risks are undertaken — by the parents of other kids as well as my own — in heavily funded and promoted activities run by the gatekeepers of our educational system. Because those risks will affect all of us in maintaining national mental hygiene and a civil society.

12 OCTOBER 2011 -----------------------

Minus Alan Schwarz, *New York Times* football concussion coverage has evolved from "flawed" to "missing in action."

Since Schwarz was promoted to national education reporter, the *Times* has not run a single story about the National Football League's relation to the national concussion issue that was not prompted by a press release.

I think it's fair to interpret this as showing that Schwarz was exiled, not promoted.

8 NOVEMBER 2011 -----------------------

I appreciate the fact that Chris Nowinski doesn't perceive his mission to include making the case against public high school football. But someone should tell Nowinski that the public conversation doesn't begin and end with making the case for chronic traumatic encephalopathy, either.

Right now the hockey community is pushing back at the Boston research group's finding that retired player Rick Martin had early onset CTE when he died earlier this year of a heart attack at 59. Even though the face of the sport, Sidney Crosby, continues to sit out the aftereffects of his nearly year-old concussion, and other recent hockey deaths do clearly link in some fashion to contact-induced brain degeneration, doctors and journalists from points north are right to be noting holes in claims by the Center for the Study of CTE. To oversimplify only a little, tau protein buildup in brains is like plaque buildup around hearts — further study will surely show that it affects individuals with different intensities and at different rates.

That a debate so narrow should be bogging down general understanding of the sports concussion crisis is a crying shame — and also so unnecessary. Sadly, Nowinski, not long ago one of the great public health advocates of his generation, seems to be devolving into a Concussion Inc. bureaucrat as he stubs his toe in defense of the research turf of Dr. Robert Cantu and colleagues. What we all could really use from Nowinski is a little less "peer review" pomposity and a little more common sense.

The hype that Martin's so-called stage 2 CTE would have led to Martin's eventual dementia ("no question," Nowinski said in one credibility-crippling sound bite) is "incomplete . . . fragmented," neurosurgeon Dr. Charles Tator told Randy Starkman of the *Toronto Star*, adding, "We need more science and less grandstanding." The intellectual rift between hockey doctors and the Boston group was further explored in a very good three-part series by *Yahoo Sports'* Nicholas J. Cotsonika.

Let me be clear about my own position. I think the pattern of CTE — that new and more all-encompassing nomenclature for what once was known only in ex-boxers as "punch-drunk syndrome" — is unmistakable in football players especially. But in the course of chasing research dollars (including the National Football League's not-so-unrestricted $1 million gift to the Boston center), Nowinski has pushed the envelope in the Martin case and undermined the larger cause.

My view is that we don't need this non-scientific spokesman, with his own scary brain-sloshing experience and testimonials from college football and WWE, fronting for narrow institutional interests. We need him leading from the bully pulpit on the heart of the matter: ending the annual carnage of disability and death — including but not limited to traumatic brain injury — in the football programs of our public high schools.

To reduce the whole shootin' match to "CTE or no CTE?" is to give away the game just when the good guys' team was building momentum. There is a known heavy toll in other injuries sustained by young people in pursuit of American gladiatorial blood sport: strokes, seizures, aneurysms, brain bleeds, subdural hematomas, and, lest we forget, spinal injuries, as well as garden-variety concussions. (Never mind steroid abuse: that horse is so far into the next county that the barn door has petrified.) These add up to a significant public bill, whose significance would be even better grasped if Nowinski's mentor, Cantu, would compile catastrophic injury reports as comprehensively as my colleague in independent journalism, Matt Chaney.

It would also help if the Boston crowd stopped giving aid and comfort to the fiction that football safety measures and baseline neurocognitive testing were real solutions at the Pop Warner and prep levels. The former undoubtedly can reduce the volume of serious injury and death at the margins. The latter is part of a sham, preying on football mania, to turn the whole crisis into a marketing opportunity for frauds like the pushers at UPMC.

6 DECEMBER 2011 -----------------------

If the *New York Times'* superb three-part series by John Branch on the death of 28-year-old hockey player Derek Boogaard had only added vestigially to what's being called "concussion awareness," then it would rate no more than a gentleman's C. I'm happy to be praising Branch for accomplishing so much more — putting chronic traumatic encephalopathy in the context of what I have called the "cocktail of death" in contact sports and entertainment. Give the Gray Lady and its reporter an A+.

Give credit, also, to the Boston University Center for the Study of CTE and to concussion go-to guy Chris Nowinski for coming back from the credibility hit they took for overhyping the CTE findings of another recently deceased ex–National Hockey Leaguer, Rick Martin.

The hockey establishment had scored a TKO in its debate with Nowinski over the claim that Martin, a non-brawler in his late fifties, had "stage 2" CTE, from which the public was asked to extrapolate that he "definitely" would have faced hockey-related dementia had he not died first of a heart attack. As I argued at the time, that was a stretch — more about the Boston group's territorial claims to concussion research than about deepening public understanding.

But I try to call 'em as I see 'em, and I see the Boogaard story, as sketched by the *Times*, very differently. Here I think the hockey mavens' attempts to disclaim its implications come off not as healthy skepticism but, rather, as classic and unfortunate defensiveness in the face of facts.

The key difference rests with the word "story." Branch doesn't present bloodless, atomized lab reports and expect general readers to accept them as the teachings of the priesthood. Instead, he weaves a compelling narrative of Boogaard's violent life and work, leading to episodes documenting his mental deterioration.

As a result, the story has no need to choose or champion any single cause of the player's specific and final demise. Was it the concussions? The booze? The painkillers? The clinical depression, somehow divorced from all of the above?

Correct answer: it was all of them, as it almost always is, in different measures in different people.

I hope the hockey industry now moves more aggressively and effectively than the football industry has to date on stemming the lifelong damage inflicted by the system on everyone from highly paid, eyes-wide-open pros all the way down to clueless kids and their parents.

I also hope Nowinski and company recognize a good model for public education when they see one, and in the future don't push robotically past complexities outside the four walls of their funded research grants.

7 FEBRUARY 2012 ------------------------

Two days before the Super Bowl, Dr. Robert Cantu and Chris Nowinski's Boston University research group and their sister advocacy organization, the Sports Legacy Institute, announced a "bold initiative." Their findings were transparently a lot less than bold. And their choice of setting, the NFL's official media control center in Indianapolis, ensured that their proposals would be neatly folded into the NFL's public relations counteroffensive 2.0 on traumatic brain injury — an enterprise all about buffing image and limiting legal exposure.

Of course, just because Cantu and Nowinski are establishment dudes who play the corporate game doesn't mean that the SLI "Hit Count" white paper is without any value. I'm sure they sincerely believe that their private interests and improved public health policy overlap. Let's take a look at what they said.[9] Here's the thesis:

> We believe that the fastest and most effective path to safer youth sports is to regulate the amount of brain trauma that a child is allowed to incur in a season and a year. Like youth baseball has widely adopted a "Pitch Count" to protect the ulnar collateral ligament of the elbow from wear and tear, we urgently call for the development and adoption of a *Hit Count* to limit the frequency of repetitive brain trauma. Theoretically, a lower *Hit Count* would reduce the risk of concussion, risk of brain damage from sub-concussive blows, and would theoretically reduce the risk of Chronic Traumatic Encephalopathy (CTE), a degenerative brain disease linked to repetitive brain trauma.

Guidelines include defining a "hit"; limiting the number of hits permitted by day, week, season and year (with all counts stratified by age); developing a "total force" threshold "when the technology is available"; and mandating days of rest for a young athlete following "a minimum brain trauma exposure."

Like mom and apple pie, all this is close to critic-proof. If, tomorrow, 100 percent of the country's thousands upon thousands of youth and high school football programs were to magically summon both the political will and the material means to adopt and enforce each and every one of these proposals, they would reduce the gross national football mental-health toll, without a doubt. They wouldn't do much, if anything, about the annual incidence of discrete catastrophic injuries (whose most widely accepted accounting, co-directed by Dr. Cantu, seriously lowballs the carnage, according to journalist Matt Chaney). But they would take a bite out of cumulative subconcussive injury and CTE. So in five years, or 10 or 20 or 50, we could do another study and assess the "legacy" in "Sports Legacy Institute."

Others and I have a better idea: end tackle football in public high schools. (Private schools and club programs, which don't operate with taxpayer funds, could continue to do what they do.)

Also, issue a surgeon general's style warning that no one under age "xx" should be strapping on helmets under the delusion that they will be protected while playing a sport that inevitably and systematically involves knocking heads, with levels of bad outcomes that are both morally and economically unacceptable. Every now and then, Cantu and colleagues tiptoe to the edge of such a warning, but they seem too beholden to the NFL to issue it in plain English.

Cantu and Nowinski want to make football safer, and good for them. But there's a difference between safer and safe. The ultimate safety here is that of their own entrenched positions.

My last observation on the white paper, for now, is the revealing way it cites as a model the already evolving practices of Ivy League college football programs. Revealing in several ways:

- The Ivy League is the cradle of popular American football, and this echo of President Teddy Roosevelt's early 20th century reforms there is conscious. I argue that the parallel is flawed and without relevance in today's era of globally marketed sports and superstars.

- Nowinski and company hold up the Ivy League's brain-trauma practices without also promoting our most esteemed academic institutions' total "student-athlete" model. How about turning every NCAA Division 1 football program into a Division 3 program? Oh, right, that's outside the scope of their advocacy.

- And finally, the analysis of football and concussions is assumed to rest, with definitive authority, in the hands of experts. I don't buy that. I think there is a larger problem with sports in this country, and that is its rampant professionalization — money-wise, health-wise and otherwise. (I deliberately didn't say *professionalism*.) Thus, if the NCAA is trampling educational values, then the only solution isn't to trim its sails but to make sure it pays its players. Did I hear someone complain that baseball's Little League World Series exploits little kids? Well, then don't think about eliminating the exploitation of little kids on international television — just make sure you cut them (and their moms and dads) in on the profits.

- When it comes to football safety, we — parents, citizens, all of us — are being manipulated into unleashing "solutions" that will cost vast sums of money, which we are supposed to apply to amateur athletics without a debate over cost, proportion, or priority.

Last summer Dan Wetzel of *Yahoo Sports*, a really good overall columnist, made an odd proposal that I find sadly characteristic of the
state of our culture, in which there is no demarcation between adults
and children — and in which, as a consequence, adults are expected to
behave like children and children like adults. "Pay the Little League
World Series players," Wetzel wrote.[10] Don't protect 'em. Just pay 'em.
It's the American way.

With somewhat less caricature, the same dynamic infuses the debate
over paying athletes in the so-called college revenue sports. I wrote a
supportive article about this issue for the *Los Angeles Times Magazine*
in 2003, years before Taylor Branch came along to brand it and Joe
Nocera to backstop it. (And by no means do I claim to be the first.)
I'm bothered, though, by the breezy confidence with which our leading
voices — Branch, Nocera, Wetzel, all of them — seem to believe that
giving a fair share to young people who are professional athletes in all
but name will solve the American sports problem. For the American
sports problem, as I see it, is that it is a perpetual growth industry: fun
and character building by faith, and without accountability.

It's not too big a reach to relate this theme to the Cantu-Nowinski
white paper on youth football solutions. I'm all for having coaches who
have some idea of what they're teaching, and I'm all for having safety
guidelines and background checks. (One of these days I'll tell you about
my daughter's USA Swimming club coach, who turned out to be one of
the many across the country later ID'd as child rapists.) But we're doing
this sports thing backward. Professionals and Olympians might set the
dream bar for our kids, but they shouldn't be setting the standards for
the youth sports industry. That's the job of the rest of us: the parents.
Yet, time and again, we are seeing the consensus of the football concussion debate reduced to a game of gotcha with the National Football
League — as if the stupidity of Michael Vick's and Troy Polamalu's
and Colt McCoy's health care matters because it "sets a bad example."

It matters, all right. But it matters because the NFL, which pays out a few dozen short-term multimillion-dollar contracts to its hired help, is so blatantly pulling the strings anywhere and everywhere, from the Congress of Neurological Surgeons to the Senate Commerce Committee to the Centers for Disease Control.

The NFL-coopted Cantu and Nowinski are playing right along with hit counts, politically calculated silence about the expensive awfulness that is Dr. Joe Maroon's ImPACT "concussion management system," and state-by-state "Zack Lystedt Laws." This mutual massaging of the leading players in Concussion Inc. is not, in the end, about the kids; it's about the cottage industries and self-congratulation created around gestures for the kids.

(Notice in the white paper where they foresee calibrating the "total force" on young-uns' noggins as soon as "the technology is available." The very first post on this blog to use the term Concussion Inc., months before the blog itself was so named, talked about the confused relationship between Cantu and the *Rollerball*-esque Xenith Helmet Company.)

Even the best-intentioned children's advocates have it backward. We don't need to be dedicating disproportionate capital to the best and the brightest so that they can reinvent football's answer to the better mousetrap. We need to be exercising common sense — summoning the political will to take this blood sport back where it belongs, several notches below a national obsession.

It's now a cliché of the concussion discussion that the sport has gone through this kind of thing before, and TR stepped in and saved it from itself, and it's happening again today. To that analogy I say, not so fast.

A hundred years ago the Ivy League was both the spiritual and the financial center of the football universe. There was no NFL, no television, no $10-billion-a-year marketing juggernaut. Lads from Harvard brawled on the gridiron with lads from Yale. These representatives of the ruling class used the manly man's arts, with all their good qualities and all their pretense, to polish their résumés for destinies on Wall Street and elsewhere. In that environment, containing death and disability was achievable.

But that is no longer the case, in my view, and not just because athletes are bigger, stronger, faster, and therefore more menacing to each other's lives and limbs. Football long ago graduated from the Ivy hothouse to the too-much-is-never-enough demands of turbo-charged capitalism. *Friday Night Lights* dramatizes how football has lost its cultural homogeneity, as well, and become a brass ring, a lottery ticket, a vehicle to greater things for all the classes.

Except when it's not.

26 APRIL 2012 ---------------------------------

After nearly two years, the name "Dr. Bennet Omalu" is once again fit to print.

New York Times op-ed columnist Nicholas Kristof today wrote a piece about Dr. Bennet Omalu's work on military service persons' traumatic brain injuries.[11]

Omalu is also the researcher who discovered chronic traumatic encephalopathy in football players. Yet in the 22 months since Omalu's name was last invoked, I counted 22 quotes or mentions of Dr. Robert Cantu in the *Times* archive. Cantu, of course, directs the Center for the Study of CTE at Boston University, which two years ago this month received a $1 million grant from the NFL.

"$1 million, and zero strings," *Times* reporter Alan Schwarz wrote in celebration that day.

In the wake of Schwarz's promotion (or exile), *Times* concussion coverage remains sparse, opaque, mysterious. We could use the kind of sharp investigation and cogent analysis that can be provided only by our leading newspaper and unofficial house organ of the ruling class. Unfortunately, we're not getting it. Instead, we're gorging on reactive coverage of the New Orleans Saints' NFL-concocted "Bountygate" scandal, pro retiree litigation, peer-reviewed studies of CTE autopsies 501 through 999.

7 MAY 2012 -----------------------------

Next Tuesday, May 15, is the night of the premiere, in Chicago, of a new documentary, *Head Games*, which was inspired by the 2006 Chris Nowinski book of the same title.[12]

Billed as an account of the "public health issue of our time" — a characterization I wholeheartedly agree with — the film seems to have a substantial budget. Steve James, of *Hoop Dreams* fame, directed. Billy Corgan composed the score, which I am guessing employs a lot of violins.

Needless to say, I was not invited to the red-carpet opening, but I am looking forward to seeing the movie. Based on my screening of the trailer, I have some concerns over whether *Head Games* will get past the long-running self-congratulation phase of the work of Nowinski, Boston sports doctor Robert Cantu, and on-again off-again *New York Times* concussion writer Alan Schwarz. I also doubt that the film will push for more formidable reforms than have been advanced by this group ever since the Center for the Study of Chronic Traumatic Encephalopathy at Boston University started accepting National Football League money two years ago.

All the usual suspects/role players make appearances in the trailer. These include Schwarz, who, in keeping with his romantic curation, is billed as "The Reporter," and is listed on the website as the film's associate producer. Bob Costas supplies an appropriately measured sound byte. In February, Costas teed up Schwarz in the audience at a pre–Super Bowl town hall meeting in Indianapolis for the NBC cable sports network. As he has been doing in a very unfocused fashion ever since formally leaving the *Times* concussion beat last summer, Schwarz used that opportunity to further promote the idea that he and his buddies invented the concussion issue. It is a stance I find journalistically unseemly, and I fear *Head Games* will offer additional such preening.

My larger concern is that this slick, and no doubt competent and compelling, film will monopolize the oxygen for the off-season national conversation on the future of football and frustrate the funding and progress of other documentaries on the subject.

Email exchange with Alan Schwarz:

> [Muchnick to Schwarz]
> . . . Please answer a few questions. (I wanted to cc Bruce Sheridan in case he is better positioned to answer the first question in particular. But the Columbia College Chicago website directory is balky right now. I'll forward this to him later.)
>
> There is no information on the website about the funding of *Head Games*. Can you provide it?
>
> Also, I'm sure the *Times* has policies on outside projects by staffers, so I would assume that there was a process by which you disclosed your involvement and secured permission from the editors. Please share with my blog's readers how and when this played out.
>
> Finally, does the film project relate in any way to your departure from the concussion beat? And what is your current role at the *Times*? The last time I looked at your Twitter profile, it no longer said you were National Education Correspondent, as the bio at the film's website says.

[Schwarz to Muchnick]

1. Questions regarding the funding of *Head Games* should be directed to the producers.

2. Yes, the *Times* has policies regarding projects like this, and yes, I went through that process and received permission. As for the substance of that process, please direct your questions to the *Times*.

3. This film has nothing to do with any "departure from the concussion beat," as that very voluntary process had begun in early 2011 (and perhaps before, I don't remember) and had been long completed when a producer approached me last summer. I agreed to participate in September, months after I had joined the Education department.

4. I am now a National Correspondent, period. I do not have any formal attachment to any particular subject, although I remain very interested (and encouraged by the *Times*) in covering news regarding education issues. I have been heading a massive project regarding children's health for the past several months, hence my few bylines during that time.

5. I have never "promote[d] the idea that he and his buddies invented the concussion issue" [...] I have repeatedly stated that this was news long before I ever showed up, and fantastic work had been done at least 10 years before, specifically by Michael Farber of *Sports Illustrated*. I agree with you that OTHERS have cast me as having invented it, but I have repeatedly, when possible, corrected them in that misperception. You might not find proof of this on the Web — I know you will look, so I did —

but it's not my fault that the many people who have interviewed me have not included that comment in their stories. At the very least I can send you the following note I sent to Mr. Farber back in 2009:

——Original Message——
From: Alan Schwarz
Sent: Wed 12/2/2009 3:07 PM
To: Farber, Michael – Sports Illustrated
Subject: from Alan Schwarz / New York Times

Michael–

I hope this note finds you well. I just wanted to let you know that through my three years of covering head-injury stuff for the *Times*, and watching all sorts of change take place, I have been very aware of the fantastic story that you did way back in 1994. I still think it's one of the best treatments of the subject that I've ever seen; people treat me as if I've invented concern for this subject, but you obviously were around far earlier than I, and long before what much has been learned since was known. It's a damned shame that your story didn't effect the change it should have, making my work unnecessary.

I've been meaning to write you for a long time just to say that your story was great.

–Alan.

[Muchnick to Schwarz]

Thanks. [...]

One follow-up: since becoming associate producer of the film, you have had, I believe, one co-byline on a concussion story, and a solo byline earlier this year on the report of the Duerson family lawsuit against the NFL. I can understand the thinking of the editors that, since you are so knowledgeable on the subject, it was helpful to return you to it on an ad hoc basis. What is potentially troubling, though — and let's not make too much of this, nor, frankly, too little — is the failure to disclose your role in the *Head Games* film. Any thoughts?

Alan Schwarz, who almost exactly a year ago took great umbrage at my comparing his relationship with Chris Nowinski to that between the co-authors of the bestselling book *Freakonomics*, has become exactly what he insisted he wasn't in May 2011 (and what, by the way, I had never accused him of being): a business partner of Nowinski.

Schwarz is the associate producer of the new documentary, *Head Games*.

Here's the *New York Times*' explanation. Eileen Murphy, vice president for corporate communications, told me:

> The *New York Times* has a detailed and comprehensive ethics policy. There is a specific section that deals with consulting agreements on films or television programs.
>
> It states: "Staff members offered consulting agreements by agents, producers, studios or others must consult the standards editor or the deputy editorial page editor before accepting. No staff member may serve as a consultant to a film or program that he or she knows in advance is tendentious or clearly distorts the underlying facts. In no case should a consulting role be described in a way that invokes the *Times* or implies its endorsement or participation."
>
> Alan's role on *Head Games* was approved in advance and meets with all other aspects of this policy.

Murphy did not answer my second question: why the *Times* didn't disclose to readers Schwarz's involvement in the Nowinski film project after Schwarz, who had putatively left the concussion beat, continued to byline stories on such subjects as the Dave Duerson family's recent lawsuit against the National Football League.

When I suggested that *Times* standards editor Phil Corbett might be asked for a fuller explanation, Murphy got testy: "Thank you for your instructions on how to do my job. . . . We're not commenting further on this."

I don't advise anyone to hold his breath waiting for commentary by Arthur S. Brisbane, the *Times* ombudsman (or, as the Gray Lady calls that position, with perfectly pitched pomposity, the Public Editor). The Public Editor's column, you see, is better suited for things like busting freelancers who accepted perks while working on travel articles. *Times* ethics are like NCAA compliance — meant for the players more than the coaches.

8 MAY 2012 -------------------------------

In an email, Steve James, director-producer of the film *Head Games*, told me its funders are anonymous:

> As is increasingly the case in documentaries these days, funding has come from private investors, many of whom commonly prefer anonymity. What I can say is that funding did not come from any sports league, SLI, *NYT* or the Center for the Study of Chronic Traumatic Encephalopathy. We really are scrambling right now to prepare a version of the film for this showing. So beyond this, you'll really need to wait until we get our publicist on board.

Let's see what *Head Games* brings to the screen. James, the director of *Hoop Dreams* and *The Interrupters*, has done sterling work on subjects in which I am not as intimately connected. If his new documentary moves the ball down the field in the concussion debate, his oeuvre will boast a fine new entry. If he limits his story to counterposing those who want to make football safe with those who don't, he'll have stalled an important national conversation.

My reset, in extended bullet points:

- While Alan Schwarz (an associate producer of *Head Games*) will never die of chronic traumatic modesty, whether he is a self-promoting egotist or a self-effacing genius is just a squabble between a couple of bar mitzvah boys.
- We are not even having this discussion today if Schwarz and the *Times* hadn't devoted assets and front-page real estate to it as early as 2007. That ain't chopped liver.
- Schwarz states repeatedly that his grasp of statistics was a game-changer. His newspaper in an unkind review of the excellent new off-Broadway play *Headstrong* perpetuates this myth. I think that's an elitist load. The public health narrative of the boys of America turning their brains into mush in service of their parents' *panem et circenses* is not the Bill James Annual TBI Abstract. It is a story best told by classic investigative journalism: cumulative and progressive anecdotes, plus relentless probing of powerful institutions and players.
- Since, oh, let's say the spring of 2010 — right around the time Schwarz's Boston pals, Chris Nowinski and Dr. Robert Cantu, started receiving National Football League money — *Times* coverage has been poor. There has been an assumption that "concussion awareness" legislation is efficacious; there has been bent-knee attention to the efforts

of the CEO of the same multibillion-dollar corporation that has lied to its employees and the public, across decades, in "peer-reviewed scientific literature"; there has been no heat on the Senate Commerce Committee for its fealty to the NFL and University of Pittsburgh Medical Center lobbying lines. Excuse all this, if you must, on the grounds that the NFL is "too big to fail" and this is about what we should expect from the *New York Times*. But do me a favor and don't idealize it.

14 MAY 2012 ----------------------------
The principal funder of the new documentary film *Head Games* is Steve Devick, a billionaire music and technology entrepreneur, who co-invented and is marketing a sports sideline concussion tool called the King-Devick Test.

On the virtual eve of the first preview screening of the movie in Chicago — originally billed as a "red-carpet premiere," now called a "private sneak peek" — Devick is listed as an executive producer on the film's website (HeadGamesTheFilm.com).

According to a knowledgeable source, Devick controls all rights to *Head Games*. The documentary is directed by Steve James, whose previous credits include the acclaimed *Hoop Dreams*.

Among the other listed executive producers of *Head Games* is Anthony Athanas, a Boston restaurateur who is a friend of Robert Kraft, owner of the New England Patriots. Athanas and Kraft serve together on the executive council of the Catholic Schools Foundation.

A former optometrist, Devick made his fortune developing Platinum Entertainment, a record label, which became a pioneer of digital music transmission systems. He is a trustee of Columbia College Chicago, whose faculty member Bruce Sheridan produced *Head Games*.

. . .

I'm ramping up my knowledge of the origins of and scientific to-and-fro regarding the King-Devick Test, which billionaire Steve Devick is promoting via the Steve James film he underwrote. A good place to start is an article in the October 2011 issue of *Philadelphia* magazine, "Penn Researchers Study Football Concussions."[13]

The Penn researchers are neuro-ophthalmologists Steven Galetta and Laura Balcer. The *Philadelphia* story describes their work and their relationship with Devick.

The piece also includes this grumpy assessment of the King-Devick Test from Boston's Dr. Robert Cantu, one of the protagonists of *Head Games*:

> They don't have any background in concussion research. They don't have a good feel for what concussions are all about. They talk about finding nearly 100 percent of concussions . . . We'll see what the data shows . . . I doubt it will be able to predict more than 75 or 80 percent of the time. That's good enough to rule somebody out, but not good enough to rule somebody in [for return to play]. And we don't want simplistic tests to let people go back in.

Another researcher, whose views I respect, thinks Cantu "is not wrong" on this point. "There is a lot of interest in both balance and neuro-ophthalmology. We have been looking at these things for years and it just has not proven scientifically reliable," this source says.

---

1   The document can be viewed at muchnick.net/xenithpr.pdf.

2   boston.citybizlist.com/article/vin-ferrara-xenith-raises-105m-safer-helmet-cbl-0.

3   www.thecrimson.com/article/2011/5/26/commencement2011-feature-nowinski/.

4   blog.4wallspublishing.com/2011/01/28/brain-expert-omalu-wants-longer-rest-for-concussed-football-players.aspx.

5   www.nytimes.com/interactive/2010/03/17/sports/football/20100317_CONCUSSION_TIMELINE.html?ref=football.

6   "Study: Non-Head Injuries May Impact Thinking Skills," http://www.foxnews.com/health/2011/07/29/study-non-head-injuries-may-impact-thinking-skills/.

7   The audio and transcript are at www.npr.org/2011/09/08/140297255/nfl-season-kicks-off-with-new-safety-rules?sc=emaf.

8   Hear it at www.youtube.com/wrestlingbabylon#p/a/u/1/hrXZLpK-vAAQ.

9   The executive summary is at www.sportslegacy.org/policy-2/hitcount-whitepaper/. The full document is at http://www.sportslegacy.org/wp-content/uploads/2012/02/Hit-Count-White-Paper.pdf.

10 sports.yahoo.com/top/news?slug=dw-wetzel_little_league_world_series_pay_kids_082411.

11 See www.nytimes.com/2012/04/26/opinion/kristof-veterans-and-brain-disease.html.

12 See www.headgamesthefilm.com/.

13 www.phillymag.com/articles/penn-researchers-study-football-concussions/.

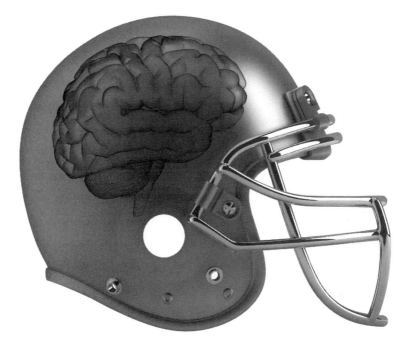

CONCUSSION INK
(IN OTHER WORDS, MISCELLANEOUS)

Our real national concussion problem is that the NFL is too big to fail. You can see that in the willfully ignored corollaries of the groundbreaking work of Dr. Bennet Omalu.

Omalu is saying that anyone who suffers a concussion should sit for three months, period. The reason is that a concussion, often involving violent head rotation rather than (or in addition to) a blow to the skull, can cause tearing of brain tissue all the way down to the brain stem, and it can take 90 days for brain fluid to return to normal.

Along with others, Omalu also comes very close to calling for an out-and-out ban on youth football. Growing brains should not be subjected to a diet of concussive and subconcussive blows, any more than growing arms should throw baseball curveballs — and the stakes of the former activity are a lot higher. As awareness and reporting improve, I am convinced we are going to see ramifications of traumatic brain injury in American youth going to the root of indexes of academic performance, workplace productivity, and criminal behavior.

This leads to a problem no easier to solve than the ingrained and corrupt ways of Wall Street. There was a time when a heavyweight boxing championship fight could galvanize the land, not just with a million pay-per-view buys but as a truly unifying cultural experience. That day passed, and we became more aware of "punch-drunk syndrome" — the forerunner to CTE — and boxing dipped in spectatorship and influence.

In the America of 2011, only football's Super Bowl is a comparable national hearth, blending hard-core, soft-core, and kitsch. Except that now we are learning that football, especially in the steroid era and with the sophistication of industrial training and the might of global marketing, literally involves armies of athletes daily and systematically inflicting CTE on each other.

If we were to eliminate football under, say, age 18 (and is that really what Chris Nowinski means when he talks about "changing how football is played"?), what will happen to the high school and youth leagues that develop skills and grease recruitment to college and the pros? Who will hire the coaches? Dress the cheerleaders? Market the lines of pint-sized blocking sleds and shoulder pads? In *Miracle on 34th Street*, the political advisor to the judge, who was trying to decide whether to declare Kris Kringle insane, ticked off all the categories of Christmas-related constituents who would be up in arms. But Santa Claus is a kindly myth — football is head-delivered death.

And without that intergenerational thread, how will the NFL carnival, with its sexually predatory quarterbacks, its diva wide receivers, its human-missile defensive secondary personnel, remain a national obsession? Especially when the legal bills start piling up. Wrongful death goes for seven figures. As the late Senator Everett Dirksen once observed, a million here and a million there, and pretty soon you're talking about real money.

Such is the crisis of our football economy, whether anyone out there wants to talk about it seriously or not.

22 JUNE 2011 --------------------------------

In March 2010 the NFL's concussion policy panel, called the Mild Traumatic Brain Injury Committee, got a new name and new co-chairs. Now known as the Head, Neck and Spine Medical Committee, it is jointly chaired by Dr. H. Hunt Batjer of Northwestern Memorial Hospital outside Chicago and Dr. Richard Ellenbogen of Harborview Medical Center in Seattle. Batjer and Ellenbogen replaced the disgraced Dr. Ira Casson and Dr. David Viano, who in turn had replaced the disgraced Dr. Elliot Pellman.

Batjer and Ellenbogen promised a new direction: to sweep out the Augean stable of league head-injury custodians. They have done nothing of the sort. For example, Dr. Joe Maroon remains on the committee.

And last July the two new co-chairs reversed a commitment not to release an ambiguously worded NFL helmet safety study with limited or no value for the broader universe of amateur helmet consumers. In the good coverage of this narrow issue by the *New York Times'* Alan Schwarz, Ellenbogen explained that he decided the study was OK "as long as statements were phrased very carefully."

Batjer and Ellenbogen — who are supposed to be independent but whose public statements get screened by the NFL office — forged ahead with uncontroversial projects, such as the toughening up of language in posters warning players of the risk of brain injury.

Last month Ellenbogen told the *Wall Street Journal.* "I defer to the guys who are the experts at football: the competition committee, people like John Madden who actually know the game." (The money-grubbing Madden knows the game so well that the new edition of his bestselling video game bows to the new "concussion awareness.")[1]

28 JUNE 2011 ----------------------------

The absolute power of the NFL has corrupted our sports culture absolutely. Since at the very latest 1994, but in reality long before that, the league has been served ample forensic notice that the sport it markets was growing out of human and medical control. These are not ACLs and torn shoulder capsules we're talking about, people; they are the brains of frighteningly large numbers of American males who have participated, in organized fashion and from very early ages, in an activity that is a staple of adult approval and social status.

"Conspiracy" is a tepid term, indeed, for the pervasive self-delusion that has gripped all of us for years, for decades. The title of one of historian Barbara Tuchman's books says it better: *The March of Folly.* The title of Randy Shilts' chronicle of the AIDS epidemic says it better still: *And the Band Played On.*

We continue to have no evidence — none — that the league leadership grasps this problem at a level more profound than public relations. The new co-chairs of the NFL's concussion policy committee, Drs. H. Hunt Batjer and Richard Ellenbogen, were supposed to be making a complete break with the conflicted and unsavory work of their predecessors when they were appointed last year. Don't make me laugh — it might snap a synapse in my own still barely functioning noodle.

Once the owners' lockout of players is out of the way, commissioner Roger Goodell can get on with the task of loading up the NFL season with more games and more gambling opportunities while he touts the league's total $20 million investment — taxicab money for a $9-billion-a-year industry — in scandalously dependent and controlling research on brain trauma. Before you know it, he'll be as comfortable in retirement as his predecessor, Paul Tagliabue, and it'll be the next regime's turn for "catch me if you can."

In December 2009, a Cincinnati Bengals wide receiver named Chris Henry was killed when he fell out of the back of a truck while stalking his fiancée. Henry was in the circle of bad boys out of West Virginia University and his five-year NFL career was marred by legal scrapes. In June 2010, an autopsy by the West Virginia Brain Injury Research Institute found that Henry had the accumulations of tau protein associated with CTE.

Here is what Ellenbogen told Schwarz for a *Times* "news analysis": "I'm really worried that we're going to get to where if you have a challenging personality, it must be CTE — that's really a dangerous way of going. We really need to be careful to parse out the underlying personality issues from the underlying injuries. This is probably just one factor among many that can put someone over the edge."[2]

Really on a roll here, analyst Schwarz clucked, "[I]f concussions turned every player felonious, Troy Aikman and Steve Young would be broadcasting games from C-block. Many players later found with CTE managed not to commit crimes." The *Times* man concluded, "To be truly valuable moving forward, the legacy of the Chris Henry finding will not be to look back and assign blame for players' past acts, but to look ahead at how future behavior among players at all levels will derive from a cocktail of factors — psychological, neurological, societal, genetic, or sometimes, just being a jerk."

And thus the disclaimer, which could have been tossed off with a phrase, becomes the centerpiece of the analysis.

At least football participants have the excuse of brain tissue deadened by tau proteins. What is the excuse for all us spectators?

You don't have to be an ambulance chaser to know which way the sports-head-injury litigation winds are blowing. The *San Francisco Chronicle*'s Kevin Lynch has provided some instructive background on the woes of San Francisco 49ers center Eric Heitmann.

Heitmann, who missed all of last season after injuring his neck and breaking his leg in training camp, will sit out all of 2011, as well, lockout or not, with a ruptured neck disk. Lynch's blog post on the *Chronicle*'s website, "Eric Heitmann — victim of the nutcracker,"[3] tells "the rest of the story":

> Heitmann's injury is another lasting legacy from Mike Singletary's infamous nutcracker drill. The exercise in which two players clashed into each other and tried to push the other one back, like a pair of mountain rams, resulted in a series of injuries. None more serious than Heitmann's; he felt a tweak in his neck after a nutcracker encounter in last summer's training camp.
>
> According to tackle Joe Staley, Heitmann ignored the injury but was slowed by it. The next day in a team drill, Heitmann broke his leg when he wasn't quick enough to escape a falling teammate. The shattered fibula might have prevented possible paralysis with his vulnerable neck. While recovering from the leg injury, numbness and shooting pain persisted from his neck. When the symptoms refused to abate, Heitmann underwent surgery last month.

In his two-plus years as the 49ers head coach, Singletary convincingly established that he was one of the 25 or so NFL field generals who have no idea what they're doing, rather than one of the seven or so who have a clue. The Heitmann anecdote adds another dimension to the persona that Singletary (a teammate of Dave Duerson on the defense of the Chicago Bears' 1986 Super Bowl champions) parlayed into a career on the Christian motivational-speaker circuit and then in the NFL coaching ranks.

Nor is it reassuring to hear the ballyhooed concussion-awareness culture shift of 2010 did nothing to prevent this men-among-men barbarism.

21 JULY 2011 --------------------------
The National Operating Committee on Standards for Athletic Equipment (NOCSAE) has partnered with the federal Centers for Disease Control (CDC) on a "Heads Up to Parents" campaign — described as "a new educational initiative designed specifically to provide parents with the facts about how to protect, prevent, and respond to youth and high school athlete concussions."

Nice. The problem is that with the concussion crisis in football, parents need more than niceness from officials charged with protecting public health. How can you keep your heads up when they're in the sand?

Someone at CDC seems to have done focus-group work leading to the conclusion that its mission is accomplished if it alerts the public to protecting kids from second concussions. But even assuming the new "awareness" significantly reduces second concussions, this all says nothing about first concussions — or about growing evidence that the problem may not be concussions per se, but rather the repetitive subconcussive blows that are the very air football breathes.

The literature quotes CDC's Dr. Richard C. Hunt saying, "Parents, when in doubt, keep the athlete out of play. It's better to miss one game than the whole season." Left unsaid is, "It's better to miss one season" or even, "It's better to pass on this particular activity altogether."

When CDC starts adding value to the debate over eliminating

contact football below a certain age, that's when it will be time to start listening to the feds. The rest is blather.

26 JULY 2011 ----------------------------

When the NFL lockout ended, the head of a fledgling organization called the Sports Fans Coalition couldn't wait to get its message out. "NFL Lockouts End, Blackouts Won't," blogged its executive director, Brian Frederick.

Frederick made the same narrow point last September in a piece for *Huffington Post* under the headline "Ahead of Possible Lockout, NFL Owners Giving Big Bucks to Politicians." Frederick cited research by the Center for Responsive Politics showing the unsurprisingly large NFL lobbying presence in Washington and campaign contributions by NFL owners.

But in case you were wondering, the "blackouts" to which the Sports Fans Coalition refers are not the ones causing early and violent deaths of football players and diminishing the mental health and future productivity of American youth. No, siree. Frederick is talking about the league's policy of blacking out local-market telecasts of home games of teams that didn't sell out their stadiums in advance.

20 AUGUST 2011 -------------------------

Yahoo Sports' Jason Cole had a feel-good story about how Green Bay Packers quarterback Aaron Rodgers, the most valuable player of the Super Bowl, used the time when he was sidelined last fall with a concussion to "refocus." The piece also highlighted the wise management of Rodgers' second concussion by coach Mike McCarthy. The whole package combined "concussion awareness" and a happy ending so seamlessly that it earned a link at the NFLHealthandSafety.com website.

Left unsaid is that many knowledgeable observers believe Rodgers suffered a *third* concussion during the National Football Conference championship game against the Chicago Bears, just two weeks before the Super Bowl. It came on a vicious helmet-to-helmet hit by the Bears' Julius Peppers early in the fourth quarter.

According to some, the subsequent Fox television footage showed the Packers medical personnel sitting on the opposite end of the bench when Rodgers came to the sidelines at the end of that drive. Throughout Super Bowl hype week there were rumors, which Rodgers denied, that he'd sustained a concussion.

In an article headlined "Conspiracy of silence over possible Rodgers concussion?" Shawn Dougherty of the *Capitol Times* in Madison, Wisconsin, wrote that after the Peppers hit "Rodgers was woozy and wobbling about with dazed eyes. If you didn't notice he was wobbling, surely you noticed his football was wobbling. His magic was gone for the rest of the game. He couldn't even hit the mark with a couple of short passes. And yet for all the conscious-ness-raising lately about the dangers of concussions in football, hardly anybody seems to be talking about the possibility that our star quarterback suffered another one."[4]

Dustin Fink of the *Concussion Blog*, a high school athletic trainer, told Dougherty, "If this had happened to one of my players on Friday night, I would have pulled him off the field, just based on his gaze. We call it 'the gaze' when we see somebody concussed. It's like they're look-ing right through you. Their eyes don't look like they're as focused."

I'm less bothered by whatever executive decisions the Packers might have made about the handling of their multimillion-dollar property than I am about how the story of whatever had transpired got steamrolled into a story with a false moral. Rodgers even added an explicit marketing element, telling Peter King of *Sports Illustrated* that he had escaped a concussion in the NFC championship game thanks to a recent switch from a Riddell to a Schutt helmet. Conveniently,

this broke just as the NFL and Joe Maroon were distancing themselves from the FTC investigation of Riddell.

24 AUGUST 2011 ------------------------
Below is an edited exchange I had the other day with a sports columnist for a major newspaper. I am not identifying the columnist except
to say that he had written something in opposition to a new rule in the
National Football League this year — moving kickoffs from the 30- to
the 35-yard line to facilitate more touchbacks instead of runbacks; the
latter type of play has been shown to lead to a high incidence of concussions. I'll continue to hope he gives the subject additional thought
and eventually comments more profoundly in his column.

> [Muchnick to columnist]
> The new kickoff rule is, indeed, intellectually dis-
> honest. You articulate very well the case against it.
> I want to ask you a different question, about the
> very viability of football. To my knowledge, you have
> not addressed it.
> Yes, head-on collisions and the thrill of lethal vio-
> lence — either the survival or the skillful avoidance of
> it — are fundamental to the game. Again, good of you
> to so define it.
> But has this become unsustainable? Once upon a
> time boxing was the most popular sport in the country.
> But middle-class kids, by and large, no longer aspire
> to become boxers. I think something like that is evolv-
> ing here. What say you? As fans, do we just sit around
> and wait until, say, Tom Brady murders his family and
> himself on the 50-yard line on national television? (Of
> course, it doesn't count if it's 10 years after he retires.)

The argument that multimillion-dollar professionals do what they do for our entertainment is OK, so far as it goes, but the reach of pro football in our society goes much further, as we are seeing. Do you have any suggestions? Or is it just not your problem?

[columnist to Muchnick]

I wouldn't align with the boxing comparison because the sports are so different. Kids play football because it's glamorous, sexy, because they "get the girl," as they say. It's a chance to excel in the coolest sport in town, and in some cases, it has only to do with pure love of the game. There's seldom much general outcry from the public about football violence at any level. There are individual cases that deservedly draw a ton of attention, but football is the most popular sport in the country because people LOVE to watch such intense conflict. I don't see the sport changing, in essence. In fact, I'd expect to see another change in the kickoff rule within a couple of years, making returns more possible.

[Muchnick to columnist]

The boxing analogy is, obviously, imprecise. The facts about brain damage and death, however, are not. The question is whether such information with respect to football's systematic (not random) delivery of traumatic brain injury trumps the popular romance about getting the girl.

Whether there is or will be a public outcry against football's violence — with "public outcry" defined as defensively as possible by the sport's followers — doesn't really answer the question. We have moved to an era of plausible multibillion-dollar tobacco-style litigation, for both wrongful death and restitution of public-health costs. Without resorting to things like cheap lawyer jokes, can you explain how you think football will remain medically, legally, and educationally viable? Will it be simply by force of bread-and-circuses will?

[columnist to Muchnick]

If I were to make a public comment on the issue, I'd give it considerably more thought.

24 AUGUST 2011 ------------------------

Football's public health tab is not all concussions and it's not all death. Last month a CBS News report estimated that there are 140,000 annual "mild to severe spinal injuries" in high school football, with 10 resulting in paralysis.[5] I suspect alternative methodologies might set the former number lower and the latter higher. Whatever the statistical sweet spot, the existence of a substantial and unacknowledged subsidy is clear, as catastrophic medical costs for spinal injuries can run to $500,000 for just the first six months.

As I post this item, I know of at least two young football players who lie comatose from early season brain (not spinal) injuries: Adrian Padilla in California and Tucker Montgomery in Tennessee.

Rasul "Rocky" Clark — who was left paraplegic by an injury in a high school game 11 years ago and recently had to downgrade his care under changes in Illinois Medicaid policies — was the focus of the CBS story. The Clark case was also covered by the *Chicago Tribune*.[6]

This is about more than health insurance reform. Clark's now-inadequate Medicaid coverage itself only kicked in after his suburban Chicago school district's $5 million catastrophic health insurance policy benefits dried up.

You say that playing football is a "personal choice and risk"? Indeed it is: a personal choice and risk for which all American are paying through the nose — both daily and for as far into the future as the mind's eye can see.

3 OCTOBER 2011 --------------------------

Today I had a long telephone conversation with Burl Ingle, father of Adam Ingle, a 17-year-old high school player in Kansas, whose near-fatal traumatic brain injury was reported by Anthony Powell of KSN (NBC 3) in Wichita.

My immediate interest was confirming the story, not yet fully reported in the media, that the incident in the Valley Center–Andover game was actually Adam's second head injury in four days — he was also concussed, and briefly lost consciousness, in practice the previous Tuesday. I'll get to that. But I also want to tell the whole story from Mr. Ingle's perspective. He and I appreciate that we have a difference of opinion on the viability of youth football. Where we agree is that our disagreement is respectful and that it sheds light on the issue's cultural fault line.

The earlier injury at Tuesday's practice indeed happened. Burl Ingle said the first he knew of it was when Adam told doctors and nurses at the emergency room Friday night. Adam — who used to get up at 5 a.m. to lift weights, and who prided himself on playing hurt — never informed coaches or trainers, who didn't witness the blackout. After thoroughly looking into everything, Mr. Ingle is convinced that there was no negligence on anyone's part. It was just one of those things that happen in football. His takeaway is that the sport simply needs better communication among players, parents, and coaches, and a less macho ethic.

Mr. Ingle accepts the bigger picture. He has other sons who have played college ball, one at Clemson, as well as a brother who played briefly for the Dallas Cowboys. "We're a football family," Mr. Ingle said. "And Adam is in God's hands."

When Adam collapsed on the field in the third quarter against Andover, he turned blue, obviously suffering from a brain bleed that required emergency surgery. The doctors saved his life, and now he is the midst of a long, slow recovery. Home after a week of hospitalization, he has little stamina. (When I spoke with his father, the neuropsychologist had just paid a visit, but they had to cut it off after 15 minutes.) He can't yet hold down any food. But he can walk, and he expects to attend this Friday's game. He has been nominated for homecoming king.

I wouldn't want to be the campaign manager for anyone else on the ballot.

Adam's dream of a football career is over. However, Butler County Junior College has already stepped up to offer him a full scholarship to be the football team's equipment manager. Mr. Ingle said that when this normally stoic young man got the news, he smiled from ear to ear, then cried for the first time since all this happened.

So . . . does this add up to another cautionary tale of the insanity of football? Or another thread of the American tapestry?

You decide.

4 OCTOBER 2011 -------------------------

Yesterday on Twitter, the NFL's public relations chief, Brian McCarthy, wrote, "Standing ovation for @nflcommish at Congress of Neurosurgeons re: player safety." Roger Goodell was a speaker at yesterday's session of the professional group's meeting in Washington.

Though McCarthy went on to say that the Goodell speech was posted at the NFL communications website, that does not appear to have happened yet. Last night McCarthy provided me with the text of the speech, which is unremarkable, in my reading: a restatement of the league's already familiar talking points.

The idea that the Congress of Neurological Surgeons gave the commissioner a standing ovation — whether before or after the speech I didn't clarify with McCarthy — is appalling. A polite reception for an invited guest? Of course. A standing O? Completely out of line for a professional association holding itself up as a gatekeeper of public health. Like President Obama's crusade against college football's Bowl Championship Series while saying absolutely nothing about the national concussion crisis, this is a measure of how juvenile and football-centric American culture has become at all levels.

Crude but fair analogy: the CEO of a tobacco company gets a standing ovation at a convention of oncologists and pulmonary and heart specialists in the 1960s for a review of the company's research and development on filtered cigarettes.

This unprofessional professional group, whose journal *Neurosurgery* already was at the NFL's beck and call, has definitively KO'd its own credibility.

As Goodell suggested in his speech, the league's best and worst practices filter down to the amateur levels. At Yukon High School in Oklahoma, quarterback Corben Jones suffered a concussion at a game on September 23, yet played the next game a week later. Even many of those advocating different protocols for the professional sport agree that youngsters should *never* rush back to action.

Yet the *Oklahoman* newspaper quoted Corben Jones' coach, Todd Wilson, saying he "never worried that his quarterback would miss the game. 'You never know with a head injury, but knowing Corben, it would have had to been pretty bad to keep him off the field Friday,' Wilson said. 'It didn't surprise me that he performed pretty well.'" The *Oklahoman* named Jones "City-Area Player of the Week."[7]

By Matt Chaney's count, critical-care brain injury No. 8 in 2011 prep football was sustained last Friday in Chandler, Arizona, by Valley Christian High School's Dillon Lackhan. He had emergency surgery for a subdural hematoma.

14 OCTOBER 2011 -------------------------
What sports reform still lacks is its equivalent of MADD — Mothers Against Drunk Driving. We can call it PUNT — Parents Under Neurological Trauma. But first our own public health agencies have to get on our side.

The NFL has partnered up with Centers for Disease Control to publish an educational toolkit for school trainers and medical personnel for the treatment of concussions. A CDC spokeswoman admitted to me that the NFL's $150,000 grant for "Heads Up" marked "the first time the CDC Foundation has received external funding to help support" this initiative, which had a decade's history encompassing various outreach to health care professionals and patients, school professionals, sports coaches, parents, and kids and teens. CDC's own funding for this program has averaged around $200,000 a year.

11 NOVEMBER 2011 -------------------------
While criminal investigations and civil lawsuits begin burying Pennsylvania State University and Joe Paterno, the deposed iconic football coach, over their harboring for at least nine years (and probably 17 or more) of Jerry Sandusky, a serial child rapist assistant coach and ex-coach and pillar of the community, I suggest we all turn our attention to the last remaining myth undergirding the JoePa statue in front of Beaver Stadium and sanitizing the JoePa name on the campus library building. I also suggest we don't stop there as we proceed to bring the Penn State scandal home, where it belongs, to our own

schools and communities and mass insanity.

The myth goes like this: as a cautionary tale of the temptations of big-time football, Penn State is especially "ironic." For, you see, the program over which Paterno ruled for nearly half a century, in polished insularity, was exceptionally "clean."

BS, PSU.

I wonder how many people reading this piece have heard of a former Nittany Lions defensive end named LaVon Chisley. He is serving a life sentence for murder, which gives fresh meaning to the sour joke, "Penn State? They're going to wind up in state pen." In 2006, PSU student Langston Carraway — whose family had invited Chisley to live with them after his life spiraled into drug abuse and Paterno dumped him — was stabbed 93 times by Chisley.

Blogging for the *Baltimore Sun*, Chris Korman, who wrote a decade ago for the campus newspaper the *Daily Collegian*, said he was as disgusted as every other sentient person over the unchecked crimes against humanity by Jerry Sandusky through his associations with Penn State and the Second Mile Foundation for at-risk kids. But Korman was not shocked. An extended excerpt below — but first a program note: The most aggressive and prescient Pennsylvania journalist on the Paterno scandal has been a sometimes wacky Pittsburgh-based sports-talk host, Mark Madden, who cut his teeth reporting on (you guessed it) pro wrestling.

Here's Korman:

> [Paterno] wasn't the same cerebral intellectual-as-football-coach that I'd read about and admired as a kid. . . . He seemed entirely comfortable with the idea that he'd made his bones decades ago, and that was that. The culture surrounding him supported that notion, of course. It was almost impossible to question the tenets of his virtue without being labeled nothing more than a

rabble-rouser. Yet his players ran amok and left us constantly reading through police reports and court documents, and Paterno too often dismissed their transgressions as boys being boys. He was lenient in exactly the way Joe Paterno was not supposed to be.

[. . .] Penn State has long operated in a bubble; major newspapers from Philadelphia and Pittsburgh did not insist on covering the football program thoroughly, and the townspeople in State College had it in their best interest to make sure the football team, the heartbeat of their little city (and economy), had few obstacles (i.e., players who aren't academically eligible, or who get arrested).[8]

Though the football team is something less than the economic heartbeat of my city, Berkeley, the DNA is familiar. You can't have lived here for as long as I have and not be familiar with hushed-up police-blotter stories involving Cal football players. (I do not refer to the well-publicized cases, such as that of current National Football Leaguer Marshawn Lynch.) To the extent coach Jeff Tedford is held accountable, it is only for his ongoing failure to recruit and develop quarterbacks as good as Andrew Luck. Tedford's program, too, is one of the "clean" ones. We all know that, because that's what we're told.

There is a sickness in our society, and it has a name: football worship. The symptoms are evident in red and blue states alike, in rural provinces and urban strongholds, in honkytonks and ivory towers, in profit-hungry enterprises and in the vicarious fantasy projections of paying fans and unpaid volunteer coaches.

This is not a problem that will be solved by bringing the National Collegiate Athletic Association to its antitrust knees, or by paying de facto professional college players something closer to their market value. And it won't be solved by saying that it exists at Pisspot

Polytechnic or USC or Miami or Ohio State . . . or Penn State . . . yet somehow not here, right here, where each and every one of us lives. We are all Penn State.

15 NOVEMBER 2011 -----------------------
Many have remarked that a key to the unraveling in State College, Pennsylvania, was its insularity — a corollary to Penn State football's lack of accountability. I agree, and I am struck by how that most heinous of criminal patterns — systematic child sexual abuse — seems to attach itself to putative nonprofit institutions (Penn State, the Second Mile Foundation, the Catholic Church) more readily than to for-profit companies. There is plenty of corruption, plenty of ugly practices in the upper reaches of corporate America, but not so much *this*.

In that spirit, I sent a message with the text below yesterday morning to Bob Ladouceur, the legendary football coach at De La Salle High School in Concord, California, with copies to Leo Lopoz, the school's athletic director, and John Gray, the director of communications (for the athletic department, I believe, not the school, though I could be wrong about that). When none of those gentleman replied, I followed up today with the school's principal, Brother Robert J. Wickman, F.S.C. I will publish any response I receive from anyone at De La Salle.

> To be transparent from the outset, I am a critic of the football system at all levels. I seek your responses to the questions below. . . .
>
> By way of background, I know nothing about you or the De Le Salle High School program other than what I have read and heard as a general sports fan and as a consumer of Bay Area news media. I am familiar with your proud record of national-class athletic suc-

cess, which includes alums such as current National Football League star Maurice Jones-Drew. I recall the tragic story of Terrance Kelly, the De La Salle standout who became an innocent-bystander murder victim in his hometown of Richmond, California, on the eve of embarking on a student-athlete career at the University of Oregon. By far my single biggest source of information is the very long and nice profile of you by reporter Rusty Simmons, which was published on the front page of the *San Francisco Chronicle* on October 16 of this year.

I thought Mr. Simmons' piece was a weak piece of journalism, and I told him so directly at the time in a polite email exchange. In the course of thousands of words of praise (whose sincerity I do not doubt), he quoted and cited the post–De La Salle life of only one of your ex-players — and that was Patrick Walsh, who has gone on to assume the same job you hold, but at Serra High School in San Mateo. Mr. Simmons replied to my criticism by saying he could have quoted enough Ladouceur protégés to fill a book.

Here are my questions to you:

1. Browsing your website, I was stunned to encounter first these words at the top of the home page: "The public's perception of what we do or what we stand for is drastically different than what actually takes place. I can imagine that this is probably true for many organizations. This is especially true for our football team. People are constantly writing the local papers questioning the integrity of our program. It's upsetting in so much that it questions the integrity of school officials and coaches sworn to uphold the ideals of our founder St. La Salle. What's

worse, it completely nullifies the hard work, sheer grit, and determination of our student athletes at De La Salle High School." What motivated you to say this? (Certainly not, I would think, coverage like that of the *Chronicle*.)

2. In his profile, reporter Simmons wrote that your own playing career had been ended by two serious injuries. I have no idea why he either did not ask you or he chose not to specify your injuries. Can you please do so for me?

3. Would you release publicly the budgets of the De La Salle High School Athletic Department and football program?

4. As you will see, the focus of my blog is the concussion crisis in football. Please share with my readers the complete record of the Spartans, during your tenure, in the area of traumatic brain injuries. Please also tell us the specifics of how your program has evolved in diagnosing and treating concussions and in formulating return-to-play procedures.

21 DECEMBER 2011 -----------------------

Chris Mortensen of *ESPN* reports that the NFL will employ independent athletic trainers to spot concussions from the press box level and alert the folks at field level. Nice step, comments Mike Florio of NBC Sports' *Pro Football Talk*, but they need independent neurologists on the sidelines.

Excuse me while I refrain from doing handsprings. Professional football players are pros and they have a union. A lousy and corrupt union, maybe, but the jockocrats can do whatever they'll do. For all I care, they can assign certified morticians to every game.

The point is that "concussion awareness" steps, such as this latest one, are not reproducible at the feeder levels of American football mania: public high schools and peewee leagues. Most of the participants there shouldn't be playing Russian roulette with lifelong mental disability in the first place. And those worthies don't have the dough for independent trainers and independent neurologists. Most of them don't even have press box levels. Only the morticians, plus the lawsuits flowing therefrom.

We need a national sports concussion policy. Until we get one, we'll have an affirmative action program for the billable professionals, both the earnest and the cynical, of Concussion Inc.

24 JANUARY 2012 -----------------------

This week I came across the most heartwarming quote I've seen in some time. It was from Dr. Howard Derman, co-director of Houston's Methodist Hospital Concussion Center. Just as UPMC is the official sports medicine provider for the Pittsburgh Steelers of the NFL and the Pittsburgh Penguins of the National Hockey League — doctors-to-team paid endorsement contracts and all — the Derman group in Houston serves the same function for the NFL's Texans, Major League Baseball's Astros, and Major League Soccer's Dynamo. Methodist Hospital offers young athletes ImPACT baseline tests for $5 a pop, and freely circulates materials on such topics as "Return to Play Defensive Back," "Return to Play Wide Receiver," and "Return to the Classroom After a Sport-Related Concussion."

Discussing the youth tackle football leagues of greater Houston, in which more than 1,000 kids as young as five play every year, Derman told the *Houston Chronicle*, "I'm not saying it's safer to play football as a child [than other activities], but the plasticity — flexibility, in layman's terms — in the brain is greater in a child, and it has more room to swell. So things we see in adult football players are slightly less of a concern in children."[9]

This might be the most exotic argument I've heard yet from the "concussion awareness" crowd: it's better, not worse, for little kids to get their brains bashed . . . precisely because they're still growing!

Through an intermediary, Dr. Derman has complained. Since Derman marked at the top of his email that it was not for publication, I have emailed him my request for permission to publish it.

In the meantime, here is my own reply to the substance of Derman's comments:

> My fundamental response to you is: you gave the quote to the *Houston Chronicle*; you own it.
>
> The point of the *Chronicle* story is that football is safer than cheerleading. Beyond preposterous.
>
> It is good to hear that you are paid $0.00 by the Texans. Is Methodist Hospital likewise paid $0.00? Or maybe the better question: does Methodist Hospital pay the Texans $0.00? The team's logo and association are right there on your center's website (which, incidentally, has no non-patient contact info, and no telephone number for media inquiries, that I can see).
>
> My article did not claim that $5 was an unfair market price for what I have long opined is the unreliable ImPACT test. That the true cost is more does not surprise me and merely reinforces the argument that football concussion "solutions" will bankrupt our public schools. There is no way every high school football program in the country can successfully execute all the "football safety" mandates of new state-by-state legislation.
>
> Please call me anytime. I also invite you to email your and Methodist Hospital's contracts with the Texans, for both medical services and sponsorship.

24 JANUARY 2012 ------------------------

Stefan Fatsis, with whom I haven't always agreed, has a hell of a strong post in his latest contribution to the Slate-Deadspin NFL Roundtable — a smart fan's gasfest that I sometimes poke fun at, but not this time.

> [T]he NFL's chief marketing officer, Mark Waller, [tells the *New York Times*] player safety is "probably one of the most important topics for casual fans, *particularly mothers*." I added the italics, because if Mom thinks football is crazy dangerous, she's not going to let her son play, and if enough sons don't play, football loses popularity, and if football loses popularity — you get the picture. Mom may not be reading websites that track catastrophic football injuries, but she will be watching the Super Bowl.[10]

I'm also amused by the news that the NFL is about to unveil yet another new safety website, this one focused on the evolution of football rules. I wonder if it will juxtapose contemporary commentary with observations by Dr. Joe Maroon on how you just need to make sure you lead with your shoulder pads when executing the flying wedge. (And maybe Dr. Joe and WWE can lend John Cena, Rey Mysterio, and others to do "don't try this at home" public service spots.)

24 JANUARY 2012 ------------------------

In college we used to joke, "If I were smart, I'd get good grades." And if I could write as well as Robert Lipsyte — author, commentator, former *New York Times* sports columnist — I'd be Robert Lipsyte. Since I can't, I'm not, but I'm a Lipsyte reader and admirer, which is good enough today.

Writing for TomDispatch.com in a piece headlined "Four Reasons to Watch the Super Bowl," Lipsyte neatly straddles disgust and sympathy. The essay isn't perfect (the take on class warfare seems to me more Jello-like than lucid, and Tim Tebow was not a rookie in 2011), but the takeaway is a gem. It comes right after Lipsyte tap-dances on the Joe Paterno legacy and breaks down how football's "little insults to the brain" begin early and "add up to catastrophe in middle age":

> So if you believe in taking responsibility for "every other kid," go organize in your community against helmet-wearing tackle football — at the very least until high-school age. (If you let your own kid play peewee football, you should be charged with child abuse.) It's hard to go up against Jock Culture, which you'll be watching in its full power and glory on Sunday. Then again, it's hard to go up against the banks and the war machine, too. It's time, in other words, to occupy football.[11]

3 FEBRUARY 2012 -------------------------

Comes now the NFL with a PR blitz out of the school holding that the best defense is a good offense. Sunday's Super Bowl telecast will include a 60-second NFL "public service announcement" recapping the history of its bold efforts to make football safer.

Credit the *Business Insider* website with noting that the NFL last year *censored* a Super Bowl commercial from Toyota that tried to address the concussion issue. The abrupt U-turn "shows the NFL is worried about losing the ethical debate over whether it is right to allow youngsters to play a game that requires them to hit each other with their heads."

These are heavy-duty days for my trusty barf bucket. The last edition of CBS's *60 Minutes* had correspondent Steve Kroft lionizing

Roger Goodell, the NFL commissioner. Quite obviously, full access to Goodell was a booby prize to one of the league's broadcast partners in its off-year in the Super Bowl rotation. This year, the big game lands on NBC, where we can look forward to seeing whether the ace announcing team of Al Michaels, Chris Collinsworth, and sideline reporter Michele "Scoops" Tafoya can again distinguish themselves as possibly the last viewers in the country to call a concussion a concussion — as they were back in September on the Sunday night of Michael Vick's "neck injury."

Last week we had several New York Giants caught bragging that they had targeted Kyle Williams, the goat of the 49ers' loss to the Giants in the conference championship game, because they were aware of his history of concussions. That was an example of a gaffe — classically defined as the misdemeanor of openly stating a truth that was supposed to remain tacit.

The question I want to ask is why we have a society in which the son of a major league sports executive, Chicago White Sox general manager Ken Williams, continues to risk lifelong brain injury, early dementia, and death-in-life. I think the answer has something to do with the glory and folly of the American sports dream machine, which refuses to discriminate on the grounds of race, creed, or color, so long as you're willing to have your cerebral neurons stomped into seaweed. This also helps explain why our current president, also African American, has made his No. 1 sports policy priority the abolition of the Bowl Championship Series, evidently on the grounds that the descendants of slaves, along with the rest of us, don't have enough college football games in December and January. Ah yes, "American exceptionalism."

The most important non-football subplot of Super Bowl hype week has been the organized labor demonstrations in Indianapolis protesting Indiana Governor Mitch Daniels' signing of union-busting "right to work" legislation.

"War on workers is the real Super Bowl in America," Harvey Araton, a *New York Times* sports columnist, wrote on Twitter. Nice piece of pith. I doubt that Araton's bosses would deem fit to print an 800-word development of this theme.

Though '60s nostalgia and its supporting demographic bulge still take up a lot of sentimental space, we may be living through even more momentous times today; as part of that package, Sunday's spectacle warrants more than a strong sniff. I wonder what will become remembered as the American empire's Masada? When will be our equivalent of the Edict of Milan?

One thing's for sure: the Coliseum is alive and well, and that ain't no flabby metaphor. It's a phenomenon playing out in real time right in front of our eyes . . . with Al, Chris, and Michele as our cheerful guides.

11 MARCH 2012 --------------------------
Gregg Doyel of CBSSports.com has one of those death-of-football contemplations. "What would be the tipping point?" Doyel writes. "I can imagine it."

> A popular player — I'm thinking of a particular guy, but don't want to name him — gets destroyed by a hit to the head and has to retire, then lives his death right before our eyes. You think it can't happen? It already has, with Webster and Mackey and more, too many more. And it will happen again.
>
> I can imagine the day when a U.S. politician makes like John McCain in 1996, when McCain took on the UFC, only this time the politician decries football as "human cockfighting." I can imagine the day when a handful of high schools stop offering football for safety reasons, liability reasons, even lack-of-interest reasons.

I can't imagine the death of football, no.

But give me another decade or two. Ask me again.

Here's how I put it in the introduction to my ebook *UPMC: Concussion Scandal Ground Zero*:

> As footballers of all ages, and at all levels of in-formed consent, continue to get maimed and killed for our uninterrupted *panem et circenses*, the problem with high-minded commentary is that it is all too high-minded. Sure, we don't know what the concussion tipping point will be. But I, for one, have a vision of what it *could* be: for example, a three-time champion quarterback murdering his supermodel wife on the 50-yard line at halftime of the Super Bowl — and taking out the intermission song-and-dance act along with her.
>
> Of course, just to ruminate in such a fashion is deemed in extremely poor taste. By contrast, one presumes, the natural ebb and flow of today's violent sports spectacles combine the visual splendor of Rembrandt, the wit of Molière, and the compositional brilliance of Shostakovich.

Now cue the song "Dueling Banjos" from the movie *Deliverance*.

12 MARCH 2012 ----------------------------

While the mass and class actions of disabled NFL veterans grab the headlines, the keys to chop-blocking Football America's out-of-control popularity and participation will happen in the youth and high school leagues. The sweet spot is the coming cluster of cases on behalf of victims of death and catastrophic injuries in games sanctioned by public school districts. It won't take many of them before the stewards of these taxpayer-supported institutions take a hard look at the viability of this particular "enrichment program."

I've pointed to the Ryne Dougherty case in New Jersey, since that one zeroes in on one of the most important fault lines of "concussion awareness": death from a second traumatic brain injury following a return-to-play decision involving the use of the vaunted but criminally overemphasized ImPACT "concussion management system." But a case in my state, California, may have beaten the Dougherty suit to the edge, as they like to say in this sport.

The family of Scott Eveland, 22, has settled with the San Marcos Unified School District for close to $4.4 million. As a result of a head injury sustained during a Mission Hills High School game in 2007, Eveland is permanently confined to a wheelchair. He can communicate only by having someone support his elbow while he types on an iPad.

As part of the settlement, the district admits no responsibility, yadda yadda yadda.

14 MARCH 2012 ---------------------------

Last Saturday, the *San Francisco Chronicle*'s Bruce Jenkins wrote a column that I would describe as consistent with his philosophy of "Football is war — get over it."[12]

The exchange below followed. I give Jenkins credit for responding honestly, though I believe mistakenly. Too many of his sportswriting brethren either don't think about the subject at all, or, when they do, try to have it both ways.

> [Muchnick to Jenkins]
> I would like you to reflect on the concussion crisis
> and tell my blog's readers why you believe football at

the youth and public high school levels remains medically, financially, legally, and morally sustainable in light
of what we have learned about traumatic brain injury.

Your column is useful in several ways: as a piece
of nostalgia, as a deflation of the PR-driven hypocrisy
of the NFL regime, and as a description of football's
essence. I am not, however, asking you whether professional head-hunting linebackers or bounty-bearing
defensive coordinators should be disciplined by the
commissioner. I am asking you whether this sport can
continue on its present course of participation and
popularity. My own view is that it cannot. Middle-class
kids, by and large, no longer box, and as awareness and
lawsuits penetrate, neither will they play football.

In a previous exchange, you first responded, essentially, that nothing would change because football
prowess has always been a chick magnet (I paraphrase
only slightly). Then, when pressed, you said you'd have
to think about it more.

Have you thought about it more? And what do
you think? Some sports columnists prefer not to get
involved in social issues, and I appreciate that. But this
is not about the playing of "God Bless America" during
the seventh-inning stretch, or the meaning of Pat Tillman. It is about the direct impact of your commentary
beat on public health.

[Jenkins to Muchnick]

I believe the increasing awareness will reduce participation to a degree, largely through parents' input,
and I have no problem with that. I was a decent athlete
growing up, and I played just about every sport BUT

football. It's a crazy way to go unless you're fully committed to the nature of the game. The sport will not die,
however, and I'm not sure it will even suffer a significant loss in participation. As I follow youth sports in my
area (Half Moon Bay), I see countless boys who either
play the game or wish they were good enough to make
the team. As my wife put it so well, "Men go to war"
(she was talking about the A's-Giants territorial-rights
issue), and an awful lot of boys seek out contact sports.
For years, it was widely believed that boxing would die
out as a sport, but it won't, for the rest of time, because
there will always be guys who want to beat the hell out
of each other — because it's fun, because they have
nothing else going in life, because they want to take out
frustration. I'm on the side of common decency, but I
don't see major changes in the game of football down
the line, as far as popularity or participation.

I have never argued that football "would die out as a sport." With
that in mind, the way boxing has not become extinct — but rather,
and significantly, declined — seems to make my point, not Jenkins'.
Everything about his boxing model (most especially the way it skews
by class) reinforces this.

Football as a brutal spectacle of undeniable primal fascination?
Yes, of course. Football as the national hearth? No possible way, once
the seeds of concussion awareness finally get around to sprouting a
full-fledged "Mothers Against Drunk Football."

A taxpayer-funded school system on the outskirts of San Diego is
out nearly four and a half million bucks. This is dough that could have
gone to football safety or to a new line of cheerleader uniforms or to
swimming or girls' lacrosse or the jazz band or the dance troupe . . . or
even (gasp!) to teachers and libraries.

We also know that there's a lot more litigation where the Eveland case came from, and that these heavily lawyered tussles at the Pop Warner and prep levels — and more important, the circulation of their underlying narratives — are what will drive American sports reform. As a football nation, we can bathe only so long in bathos and war games and maimed linebackers and running backs being wheeled out to the 50-yard line at halftime of the homecoming game to drink in the affection of the crowd.

26 MARCH 2012 ---------------------------

In a better world, the news media would show a hundredth as much interest in the killing and maiming of kid athletes as they do in whether the New Orleans Saints can still compete for next year's Super Bowl despite the suspension of their bounty-busted coach, Sean Payton.

Alas, Scott Eveland, the Southern California teenager who was paralyzed for life four years ago — leading to a recent $4.4 million settlement between his family and the San Marcos Unified School District — isn't on anyone's fantasy team. The only place Eveland belongs is in the dystopian literary vision of *The Hunger Games*.

So let's move the courtroom chains from disability to death, and let's take the parameters beyond pedestrian ambiguities in medical advice and administrative oversight. The next frontier of football litigation involves specific issues surrounding the ImPACT "concussion management system."

Call it legal fig leafs and their discontents.

In September 2008, Ryne Dougherty, a linebacker for Montclair High School in New Jersey, suffered concussions in back-to-back games, yet was cleared to return to play. The next month, another hit caused a fatal brain hemorrhage. He was 17. In 2009, the Dougherty family sued both their son's personal physician and the Montclair school district in state superior court. That lawsuit is still in the pre-trial and discovery phases.

Though the Dougherty story touches on ImPACT, it does not neatly fit what I believe may become a classic fact pattern of these cases: an athlete who is explicitly cleared through the use of a second ImPACT neurocognitive test and goes on to suffer a disabling or fatal further injury.

Of course, even when that happens — I consider it a matter of when, not if — we can be confident that if ImPACT is named as a defendant or if a defendant school district tries to draw it into the case to share liabilities, the company will mount a defense that the software was not to blame, but rather the imperfect way it was applied.

Even so, *Dougherty v. Montclair* is an interesting opening volley for this coming flurry of multimillion-dollar litigation. I believe "avalanche" is not a hyperbolic predictive word. For all we know, there are many such underreported cases already in the pipeline.

When young Ryne was first concussed, the Montclair High School program was just beginning to use ImPACT, and he was among the first group of football players there to take a "baseline" examination of their cognitive functions. Discovery may clarify some of these facts and whether ImPACT played substantially into the return-to-play recommendation of the Doughertys' physician, Michelle Nitti.

There are so many open questions here, it's hard to know where to start. Since Ryne had already suffered two concussions, a baseline test at that point made no sense. Indeed, even those with a kinder assessment than I of ImPACT's value would be forced to agree that a *midseason* baseline test for Dougherty's teammates was oxymoronic, as well. In any case, school officials said Ryne's particular test was considered invalid at the time because one of the kids in the room during the session was behaving disruptively . . . whatever that means.

My tentative takeaway is that this episode illustrates not the potential of ImPACT, fully installed and used precisely as designed, but rather the never-ending pitfalls, loopholes, fine print, and literally deadly caveats associated with a product aggressively marketed to high schools as a solution, if not *the* solution, to prevention of "second concussion syndrome." Not to mention the legal exposure associated therewith.

I further contend that the ultimate lesson of all these cases will be the tail-chasing, bottomless-budget-pit inanity that is "concussion awareness." You can mandate the staffing of an athletic trainer. You can mandate the purchase of ImPACT. You can mandate contracting all the paraprofessionals and support personnel — real or phony, certified or simply earnest — to interpret the data. But who makes the call to send the kid back out there to get head-banged again?

And when the worst happens — as it inevitably will, time and again, despite layer upon new layer of expensive, unproven, ass-covering measures — who will foot *that* bill?

The taxpaying public doesn't yet seem terribly exercised by the ramifications of turning teenagers into human cannon fodder for Friday night lay religious services. But one diligently spotlighted narrative at a time, the rationalizations let loose by "concussion awareness" are destined to send the dollars flowing in a different direction.

9 MAY 2012 -------------------------------------

During the 1981 Major League Baseball players' strike, I traveled to Norfolk, Virginia, to watch the New York Mets' top farm club at the time, the Tidewater Tides. As I would confirm over the years in attendance at more minor league games at all levels, there are only a handful of genuine prospects on the field at any given time, even in Triple A. The overall skill level is such that routine relays, rundowns, and double-play balls get bungled, and baserunning is atrocious. Why, the '81 Tides even had a first baseman named Ronald McDonald!

In the developmental product, a good 80 to 90 percent of the roster consists of filler: guys either chasing delusions or playing for the love of it, who are under professional contract only because every team needs 25 players. They're cogs in the machine. They're part of the cost of refining those one or two or three diamonds in the rough.

This principle — the meritocratic bell curve of God-given talent — applies to all sports. But as we are now learning with accelerated alarm, only in football does it have profound public health implications.

Football is more than a game — and in case you're wondering, that is not a compliment in this context. Football is a kind of lifelong lifestyle, burdening its enthusiasts with the unintended dead weight of long-term mental disease. It is a game meting out not just wins and losses, but life and death.

And that is why I say, with gathering conviction supported by crystallizing science, that any fellow parent who lets his son play public high school tackle football, at an age clearly before both his brain has developed and he has agency to decide for himself, should have his own head examined.

In a recent radio interview, I was accused of advocating a "nuclear option" when I reject the idea that youth football can be saved from itself through a combination of better helmets, new rules, more careful coaching, and abracadabra state laws, which will force public school systems to turn their sports fields into triage centers and their locker rooms into neurocognitive testing laboratories. But the only thing I'm really calling for is the dissemination of better information in support of better choices.

The toothpaste of "concussion awareness" is out of the tube, oozing like spinal fluid. When all the solutions have been implemented and (mostly not) paid for, more or less the same critical mass of bad outcomes will happen anyway. These include, silently, insidiously, the killing of brain tissue over time. And if I happen to be exaggerating a tad, who among us really want to volunteer their sons for the next generation of guinea pigs in the "control groups" of NFL-underwritten "peer-reviewed literature"?

Yes, football promotes some good values, such as teamwork and community. So does the marching band. So does the school drama group. So do basketball, volleyball, and crew, not to mention math study gangs. (Oops, that last example was a rhetorical mistake — it exposes me, once and for all, as a "pussy.") Let's seek our bonding opportunities elsewhere, and let's leave the risks and astronomical preventive and medical costs to private clubs catering to the genuinely elite, the unambiguously professionally tracked jocks.

Last week I got a call from Tom Farrey, the fine investigative reporter for ESPN's *Outside the Lines*. We spent some time picking each other's brains, so to speak, on concussions. But as the conversation moved along, I told Tom that I thought he'd already spotlighted much of the problem in his book *Game On: The All-American Race to Make Champions of Our Children*.

A lot of people believe the trouble with youth sports is that they aren't *professional* enough, in the sense that too many of the coaches don't know what the hell they're doing, in terms of both athletic technique and sports medicine and safety. For my money, these activities are, instead, too *professionalized*: rather than pushing the bodies and minds of our young people toward some larger purpose, they become obsessed with the mannerisms, recklessness, and brass-ring-grasping of the one-dimensional superjocks, the celebrity wannabes.

In every healthy society, there's a mix of elements of patriarchy and matriarchy. Only in Football America, it seems, have our mothers been reduced to enablers. If these voices of pragmatism and safety have not been drowned out altogether, they've been channeled into the cottage industries of Concussion Inc.: desperately trying to make an untenable state of affairs just a little less untenable.

Meanwhile, the national male football death and disability toll mounts.

On Tuesday's *Outside the Lines* on ESPN, Matt Chaney, a good friend of this blog, debated Merril Hoge, the network commentator whose own NFL career was aborted by concussions.

Hoge's setup was boilerplate apologia, though I must say somewhat more coherently articulated than his despicable attack a few days earlier on Kurt Warner for the corporate sin of thinking out loud in public about whether football was really a desirable activity for his own kids.

In his *OTL* confrontation with Hoge, Chaney lucidly cited the views on brain trauma by such distinguished doctor-researchers as Ann McKee and Bennet Omalu, and forcefully made the case that promises of future prevention and reform are the same-old, same-old in football history, and this time doomed by both a public health tipping point and sheer marketplace economics.

Hoge thereupon called Chaney "uneducated" and "ignorant" — two of the more inaccurate epithets one could pull out of one's anus to defame this courageous heat-seeking loose cannon. A cable talk shoutfest broke out.

I've also had a chance to view the ballyhooed *Intelligence Squared* debate over whether college football should be banned. It pitted writers Buzz Bissinger and Malcolm Gladwell against former players and current media types Tim Green and Jason Whitlock.

The debate was a hash, because this overbroad prompt, with its specter of prohibition, sucked everything but the kitchen sink into its vortex: not only the concussion crisis but also general sports and higher education corruption, the challenge of American competitiveness in the global economy, and, from the proponents of the measure, some fierce moralizing that might not have taken its own prescriptions entirely seriously. But, what the hell, that's the polarized format of these things.

Green and Whitlock, for their part, were reduced to simply citing football's powerful mystique, over and over and over, like subconcussive blows. Whitlock, in particular, kept returning to the theme that you had to be there, in the trenches, in the locker room, and in the great bootstrapping experience of the American melting pot, which had handsomely rewarded him. He appeared to have done no preparation beyond rehearsing this burly persona and wishing everyone else would lighten up and indulge the excesses of our cherished freedom — which he parsed as "free-dumb," the right to choose consumption of tobacco, pornography, football, what have you. This blaze of intellectualism nearly blinded me.

Green touted the ritual of playing the national anthem as evidence that spectacled sports entertainment fosters community and nation-building. Playing defense with a more amiable, yet somehow even more shocking, dose of denial than even Merril Hoge, Green pooh-poohed the drumbeat of the past decade of TBI findings as hyperbolic neurosis, analogous to the concern that cell phone usage might cause brain cancer.

I don't know whether college football should be "banned." But if Green is the best his side can produce, football at all levels is in big trouble. Compared to him, Dave Duerson was Stephen Hawking.

8 SEPTEMBER 2012 ----------------------

If the NFL is serious about paying its fair share for the public health carnage wrought by its $10-billion-a-year global marketing colossus, the league can offer to underwrite catastrophic insurance for every amateur youth program that persists in enrolling kids in an activity of unavoidable fast or slow brain death — despite growing and widely accepted evidence that no one under the age of, at most, 14 should be doing this.

Instead, Roger Goodell and the NFL decided to take Congress and the news media out to dinner and a movie, in the form of a $30 million grant to the Foundation for the National Institutes of Health.

Congressman Chaka Fattah, the Pennsylvania Democrat who is Mr. Brain Research in Washington, couldn't be happier that the NFL has turned the federal government into an honest woman.

> Advancing our knowledge and treatment in neuroscience requires a mix of public-private resources and partnerships. The National Football League is showing the way with today's generous, well-placed gift. This $30 million grant provides a model for significant public-private research partnership to learn more about how our brains function, develop, and misfire. The NFL and the FNIH are to be commended for joining up on this major step. I look forward to working with our federal science agencies and with private/nonprofit partners including the pharmaceutical industry, other businesses, sports, academic and research institutions, the military, the National Science Foundation, and other government research agencies to assure that we advance brain science in a cooperative fashion.

Meanwhile, what passes for healthy skepticism in consensus news commentary can be summarized as follows: "Great step. Of course it's just PR on the part of the NFL, and of course they've got to give a lot more. But let's hope this money enables valuable new research on traumatic brain injury."

Excuse me — but since when did public health agencies become middlemen for private interests? Where did I miss that step in my civics classes?

The idea of the feds laundering a tax-deductible check from the Tobacco Institute for "further study" of the harmful effects of teen smoking would be ridiculed into oblivion. Yet that is precisely what is going on here with the NFL's "model of public-private partnership."

I always thought the National Institutes of Health relied on tax-payer funding, from which it was supposed to help prioritize and fund medical research. I didn't know its mission included brokering a particular industry's calculated largesse.

The NFL already has funded the Centers for Disease Control's "Heads Up" campaign of "concussion education." By definition, this had the arbitrary effect of framing concussion education as something less urgent than "just say no to football."

Now the NFL owns NIH, too. And few citizens are even talking about what that means. Congressman Fattah is among those who are *bragging* about it.

1 NOVEMBER 2012 ------------------------

A case in Texas continues the litigation trend we've been discussing. Since 2008, Oscar Cordova III has been disabled after surgery for a fractured skull and brain clot sustained in a junior varsity game. The family sued not just the Mission Consolidated Independent School District, but also Pittsburgh-based ImPACT Applications, Inc., for the software that allegedly informed a school athletic trainer's decision to clear Cordova to resume exercise.

Like the Dougherty suit in New Jersey, the Cordova case does not appear to include slam-dunk evidence of a premature ImPACT-based return-to-play recommendation following a concussion. The New Jersey facts are ambiguous on the ImPACT-based part of the equation: the extent to which those who authorized return to play in fact relied on this new school district tool. The Texas facts leave open questions on the return-to-play part of the equation: it appears the youngster might not have gone back into a game, where a second collision episode ensued. (Possibly, "return to exercise" will prove to have included hard drills and hitting in team practices.)

Though this factor could end up being a hurdle for the Cordova plaintiffs, their scenario does mark another step in the growing exposure of ImPACT and those who point to it as a solution. The most recent amended petition in Hildalgo County district court calls ImPACT's marketing, I believe accurately, "fraudulent and misleading" because it "claims, suggests, or implies its product can detect traumatic brain injury without proper medical diagnosis, lulling consumers into a false sense of security."[13]

Thanks to Nate Rau of Nashville's *Tennessean* for reporting on the existence of the Cordova case and for passing along the document.

5 NOVEMBER 2012 ------------------------

Paul Anderson, whose *Concussion Litigation Reporter* is easily the most comprehensive resource in its field, informs me that the Cordova family's case against the Mission School District in Texas, and ImPACT Applications, Inc., has settled. The terms are confidential.

In his full analysis, which can be accessed only by subscribers, Anderson writes:

> ImPACT has drawn fire from the scientific community for failing to identify concussions and prematurely allowing athletes to return-to-play. According to recent media reports, a series of studies concluded, "the false positive rate appears to be 30 percent to 40 percent of subjects of ImPACT . . . [it] may even increase th[e] risk" of returning to play too soon.[14]

24 NOVEMBER 2012 ------------------------

The fat is in the fire. The NFL claims to be fighting obesity in our kids. But obesity is fighting the NFL.

If the NFL is right and I am wrong, I wonder why the league's retirement system has been reduced to weight-baiting as a tactic to resist paying disability benefits to former players. This has come up most recently in the litigation by Jimmie Giles, a tight end for Tampa Bay and others in the '70s and '80s.

Independent Football Veterans organizer and blogger Dave Pear chronicles Giles' win over the league in federal court in Maryland. Judge Ellen Hollander's ruling is a thorough demolition of the illogic of the NFL retirement board (on which Players Association appointees, such as the late Dave Duerson, sit alongside management reps).[15]

Pear writes that at one point the balky benefits dispensers of the Bert Bell/Pete Rozelle Retirement Plan "even tried to use the fact that Jimmie was 'overweight' and it was pointed out to them that Jimmie's teams had certainly never considered him overweight in his position as a tight end during his entire career!"

Tight ends are an interesting test of the obesity hypothesis, for both sides of this argument: these guys are part interior linemen, part "skill position" pass receivers. As every casual fan knows, the real career fatsos are the defensive tackles and offensive guards, who fling their girth, free-range and steroid-fattened alike, into the trenches on every play. Orlando Brown, who died last year at 40, is a good example. I don't think their families care whether they suffered from brain trauma or drug abuse or obesity — they're all prematurely disabled or dead just the same.

By the same token, I don't believe the parents of America require a single-bullet scientific theory before resisting sending their kids, head-first or heads-up, into the NFL's particular public-spirited division of the conveniently urgent war on obesity.

Meet the new "Dr. No" of CTE — Kevin Guskiewicz.

In the community of dissident retired NFL players, Dr. Ira Casson has gone down in infamy as "Dr. No." He is the league medical consultant who denied to everyone, even Congress, the link between football head-banging and skull-swiveling, and the phenomenon now clearly identified by researchers as chronic traumatic encephalopathy.

I nominate Guskiewicz as successor to the Casson Endowed Chair in Industry-Induced Denial. This one has some added kick, since Guskiewicz — chair of the Department of Exercise and Sport Science at the University of North Carolina — was a recipient last year of a MacArthur Foundation "genius fellowship."

It is one of the agonies of this story that many so-called experts are really just politicians in white lab coats. Not satisfied with faculty tenure, intra-disciplinary renown, and other perks of minor celebrity, they go for powerbroker status. In the process, they sell themselves on the idea that fame and access — their particular coin of the realm — are not only good for others as well, but also public-spirited even in excess.

Here and there, I've criticized Boston's Sports Legacy Institute and the Boston University Center on CTE for succumbing to these temptations. But nearly three years after unwisely accepting a $1 million NFL grant, the Boston folks are showing signs of finding their sea legs in this crucial public health fight. This may be because the NFL has moved on to bigger game — including subsidies of the National Institutes of Health and Centers for Disease Control, and co-opting female youth sports bloggers into promoting the oxymoron of "safe football" — but I don't care about what might motivate them. What I do care about is that Dr. Ann McKee (who was always uniquely outspoken) is blasting the equivocations of the recent international "concussion summit" in Zurich. Chris Nowinski is ripping the NFL's latest pawn of a concussion committee co-chair, Dr. Richard Ellenbogen. And Dr. Robert Cantu is no longer speaking with forked tongue about the need to eliminate tackle football for kids under 14.

But then there's Guskiewicz.

Guskiewicz told Joe Nocera of the *Times*, "My 16-year-old and my 12-year-old played football this year. They had a great experience." He added that studies like those of the Boston group "clearly show that CTE exists in players without a history of concussions, but they haven't completely connected the dots."[16]

Imagine the intellectual timidity of having a forum like the *Times* and using it to emphasize that *they haven't completely connected the dots*. Queue up the tobacco company executives!

Guskiewicz, being of sound, indeed genius-level, mind, also told ESPN, "The vast majority of the neuroscience community does not believe that research has yet identified a causal relationship linking repetitive head trauma in football and CTE; I include myself in that."

This is all part of what Congresswoman Linda Sánchez, in House Judiciary Committee hearings in 2009, called the "slow walk" of the football industry and its hangers-on regarding the discretionary assessment of injured pinkies . . . oh, excuse me, the progressively damaged brain tissue of a significant slice of our male children.

Parents who wait for the experts' "consensus" to coalesce in peer-reviewed, theoretically perfected, non-conflicted research are playing what Chris Nowinski has aptly termed "a gambler's game" with their sons' mental health. America's parents, instead, need to be voting with their instincts — and their feet.

And with no thanks to Kevin "Dr. No" Guskiewicz.

13 JANUARY 2013 ---------------------------

Robert Griffin III is a marvelous athlete, an electrifying performer. Let's hope the mishandling of his knee injury only temporarily detains him, and his fans' enjoyment of him on the field.

But I'm a little bored by the controversial apportioning of blame for the fiasco that allowed him to continue in a Washington Redskins playoff game past the point where sidelining him would have been the competitively prudent, not to mention the humane, thing to do. Does the lion's shame of the responsibility go to the heartless coach? To the stubbornly persistent player? To the dangerously unmanicured turf?

How about to the culture of football? In case you're wondering, that's a fancy way of saying "all of the above."

In a piece today on ex–Miami Dolphin Jason Taylor, the *Miami Herald*'s Dan Le Batard fills in some blood-curdling novelistic detail on the real life of a National Football League gladiator.[17] As I will explain below, even this powerful article misses what I think is the public health punchline. Le Batard writes, "[A]s the rules change but the culture really doesn't . . . we think we know this forever-growing monster we are cheering on Sundays. But we don't. We have no earthly idea."

And here's Taylor's poetically graphic answer to The Question: "Would I do do it all again? I would. If I had to sleep on the steps standing up for 15 years, I would do it."

The few readers of this blog and other viewpoints like it, and the many who refuse to face the factory-processed ingredients of their obsessive entertainment sausage, believe the conveniently unreflective Taylor solves their moral dilemma — that the ongoing commitment of national resources to the development of thousands of Jason Taylors a year, on NFL and college football rosters, is just the way it is, a human inevitability, a social contract for metaphorical mustard gas and neutron bombs.

But there is another way, other than the catchall "choice," of looking at this version of certified American virility and the death-and-disability sentence it imposes on our population's health, happiness, and productivity. For too long, football-think has dominated, even monopolized, soulcraft in our sports literature. It does not have to be so forever.

After taking note of Taylor's self-image and that of the world he inhabits ("His mentor, Dan Marino, has a quote up on one of the walls in [the injury treatment section of the team facility], something about how being in the training room doesn't make you part of the team"), let's take inventory:

Painkiller shots on the bottom of the foot — more than one before every game if the first one misses the sweet spot and simply causes more pain. (Not so much as to completely numb the foot — otherwise you couldn't run on it — but enough to enable you to play on it "better than my backup would have.")

Regular epidurals for a herniated back disk. (Wait! I thought only "weak" women, not manly men, subjected themselves to epidurals, and only when they were giving birth . . .)

Pre-game hits of Toradol. ('Cause you have to mask the pain from the injury, and from the injection to mask the pain of the injury. Le Batard notes that the types of painkillers Taylor used are linked to causing injuries he didn't know he had, or simply knew about and doubled-down on masking, such as the compounding foot injury plantar fascitis.)

Surgery for "compartment syndrome." (Nerve damage and a life-threatening blood-pressure jump followed an unfelt kick to the calf. Could have required amputation of the leg if the operation had not been done on an emergency basis. But it was — happy ending!)

Post-surgery staph infection requiring the insertion of a catheter in armpit. (And infecting and endangering the skin surface where the catheter resided for a half-hour each day by practicing and playing through the condition.)

Sideline neurologists? Sideline neurologists?? SIDELINE NEUROLOGISTS??? (Where is Jim Mora Senior when you need him?)

The crisis in the feeder circuits of our football system — peewee leagues and public high schools — won't be solved with more medical personnel, with more ImPACT tests for phony return-to-play decisions following concussions, with more EMR units diverted to this game's calculated and ongoing emergencies, and away from all the spontaneous ones in our daily private lives.

No, the football crisis will be solved when every single league and team, at every level, is sufficiently funded to replicate the measures of the $10-billion-a-year NFL. Hand out as many painkillers, oral and needle variety, as it takes. Provide as many epidurals and catheters as the traffic will bear. Let no space-age helmet technology at the top not be subsidized in bulk at the bottom.

Maybe then the parents of youth football — not the adults of pro football who were programmed from an early age to skew the definition of manhood into Jason Taylorism — will tote up the real human and economic bill of their way of life. Maybe then they will exercise their . . . ahem . . . "choice."

30 JANUARY 2013 ------------------------

The queenpin of Super Bowl hype week will be officially announced tomorrow. The National Football League Players Association, with funding enabled by the recent collective bargaining agreement with the league, is throwing $100 million — a hundred mil! — at Harvard University. The purpose is to study a few guys across time for . . . God knows what. The outcome, presumably, will be to make us all feel better about the football industry's top-to-bottom *prima facie* batter-ing of the American male brain.

The stenographers of the news media — mesmerized by the Harvard brand, dazzled by the round numbers, and impressed by the activism of one of the nation's most corrupt unions — will take it all down at the New Orleans press conference and add, "Amen."

Unraveling the scientific speciousness, public relations dissem-bling, and audacious money-changing of this do-nothing project requires an entire series of articles. Let's get started.

The study announcement is premised on a big lie, and it goes downhill from there. The lie is that "the NFLPA is alarmed that its members die nearly 20 years earlier on average than other American men." In fact, life expectancy is not the issue — the preponderance of evidence is that pro football players live more or less as long as the general pop-ulation. And the NFLPA full well knows it. This is what Hitchcock would call a MacGuffin: a non sequitur plot swerve of no relevance. The scandalous gross national product of football is its robbery of *quality of life* — plus all the associated and unaccounted-for public health costs. The phenomenon includes a constellation of discrete pathologies, to be sure. But the hub-and-spoke of the whole system is brain trauma.

This leads to our next point about Harvard's impending "land-mark study": it is no such thing. Rather, it is a game of running out the clock. The announcement will emphasize how our growing focus on chronic traumatic encephalopathy has made the public forget such equally urgent matters as "searing joint pain" and "heart disorders linked to extreme strength training."

(There is not a word about Toradol, the addictive drug that has been criminally over-prescribed by NFL doctors so as to mask both orthopedic and neurological injuries.)

Harvard's kitchen-sink methodology, with a cohort of 1,000 guinea pigs at exorbitant cost, has the rest of the research community not only steaming with envy, but also howling with derision. According to the *Boston Globe*, a matched control study of the 100 healthiest and 100 sickest participants will be carried out at 26 sites — approximately *eight patients per site*. This pencils out to an annual cost-per-patient of nearly $50,000. Maybe lab technicians and tenure-pimping assistant professors will be getting two-way taxi fare every day.

The NFLPA isn't stupid. Well, it is stupid in the sense that its definition of members' best interests is crabbed and thoroughly private-spirited. But DeMaurice Smith, executive director of an empire of collusion, knows where his nest is feathered. If you're keeping the temperature of the football public, you can tell that there was more real outrage over Robert Griffin III's knee injury than there was over Jovan Belcher's murder-suicide.

The Harvard study announcement, however, comes at a moment of hopeful counter-signs. With measured words and good timing, President Obama has finally said out loud a few words that might persuade some of America's parents to begin the process of commencing to think about the possibility of considering whether they should weigh discouraging their sons from eliminating extracurricular options outside of football. (In response, Alex Boone of the San Francisco 49ers, who must be on everyone's short list for NFL father of the year, told Scott Ostler of the *San Francisco Chronicle*, "If my son wants to play, he can do whatever he wants. He's his own man.")

Also in the past week, the Centers for Disease Control's National Institute for Occupational Health and Safety sent letters and fact sheets to all former NFLers who played for at least five years during the period 1959 through 1988. The CDC reported brain and nervous system disorders at three times the rate of the general population. (Lou Gehrig's disease and Alzheimer's were individually four times higher; Parkinson's was about the same.)

Who will carry the day? The slick elites at Harvard who just fleeced dumb jocks out of $100 million to build a bridge to nowhere? Or the creaking wheels of government in its role of protecting public health and safety during Obama's second term?

31 JANUARY 2013 ----------------------

A hundred million bucks! Folks, that's not a research grant — it's a line item in the budget of a sovereign nation with designs on developing its own hydrogen bomb. It reminds me of the Corleone family's nine-figure gift to the Catholic Church in *Godfather III*.

"Scorcher," said Paul Anderson, editor of the *Concussion Litigation Reporter*, commenting on my commentary. Thanks, Paul. You and others know that I always try to execute Mother Nature's grand plan for burning away old forest growth.

We've all come a long way, baby, since Chris Nowinski and his Boston University Center for the Study of Chronic Traumatic Encephalopathy three years ago got panned in some circles, including this one, for accepting $1 million from the National Football League. Frankly, there are lots of people who have worked longer and more effectively than me on this issue, and Nowinski is near the top of that list. With some additional perspective, we should concede that he was savvy enough to pocket some of Roger Goodell's loose change, but persistent and resilient enough to stay on the attack in his own way. Though still dissatisfied with the strength and consistency of the statements emanating from Nowinski, Dr. Robert Cantu, and their sister Sports Legacy Institute, I have no question that, in speaking out against pre-teen tackle football, they're going a lot deeper than most similarly invested critics. These include, most especially and disappointingly, the female sports blogger community, which continues to nibble at the "NFL Evolution" carrot instead of mobilizing a principled Mothers Against Drunk Football movement.

Nowinski and some journalists, notably Patrick Hruby, are also putting traumatic brain injury at the center of the debate over the unpaid mercenaries who stock the rosters of college football — the NFL's zero-cost farm system.

Over the past 24 hours, I have been bombarded with requests to target this or that conflict in the NFLPA's heavy petting with the prettiest girl in academia. (If the players' union is A.J. McCarron, then Harvard is Katherine Webb in tweed.) For the most part, I decline such invitations. Yes, NFLPA president Domonique Foxworth is enrolling in the Harvard Business School, and his wife, Ashley Manning Foxworth, went to Harvard Law. And as retired Chicago Bears quarterback Bob Avellini points out, Bears owner Michael McCaskey taught for a while at a certain well-known institution of higher education in Cambridge ("Our Fair City"), MA. None of this establishes anything more than we already know about Harvard's enormous influence on Wall Street and Main Street; it is the same reason the bestselling book in China is a primer on how to groom your kid to get accepted there for undergraduation admission. How many U.S. Supreme Court justices didn't come out of Harvard, Yale, or Columbia law?

Did I forget to mention that Chris Nowinski is both a Harvard alum and a former WWE wrestler? Chris didn't. But before anyone gets started — no, Domonique and Ashley's wedding planner, Sara Muchnick, is not related to me, so far as I know. (Though who can say precisely what went down in those 19th-century Pale of Settlement shtetls . . .)

The far more interesting story on Foxworth (who himself is rehabbing an ACL knee injury, the better to underscore the point that Harvard is expected to use its windfall to dilute any swift and purposeful study of traumatic brain injury) is the one of his dashed hope to succeed the disastrous DeMaurice Smith as executive director of the NFLPA. Smith has spent the past year with his mind barely on the store as he hobnobbed in the nation's capital in search of landing a new job, before the growing evidence emerged of the incompetence and corruption at the union, on his watch and for his gain.

As that great academician-satirist Tom Lehrer sang in his composition "Fight Fiercely, Harvard": "Impress them with our prowess, do!"

6 FEBRUARY 2013 ------------------------

Kevin Guskiewicz — MacArthur genius fellow to the world, "Dr. No Junior" to us — has pulled out the culture war/gun control rhetoric.

Despite being a MacArthur GF, or maybe because of it, Guskiewicz can't stop making embarrassing statements in defense of football. In a new quote in *Education Week*, this intellectual titan stoops to the rhetorical level of "football doesn't kill people; it's people who pull the trigger on football who kill people."

Well, OK, let's not put words in the mouth of "Dr. No Junior":

> Guskiewicz cited recent comments made by President Obama regarding the safety of football, but respectfully disagreed with the president. He expressed optimism that "we can find a way to make the game [of football] safe," noting that two of his three children participated in football this past fall.
>
> "There's no evidence that football makes people stupid," Guskiewicz said. "There is evidence, however, that people make football stupid."

I think this passes for wit in Guskiewicz World. Someone at the University of North Carolina public relations office should take this dude aside and explain that it's not words that make people appear stupid. There is evidence, however, that words stupidly strung together sure do.

One of the tactical conundrums of the future-of-football debate is whether to play the culture-war card. The idea, supposedly, is that you present the most neutral, clinical, non-ideological facts in support of the proposition that we shouldn't devote so many public resources to the spectacle of kids beating each other's brains in, and let them speak for themselves. The celebrated obstructionism of "geniuses" like Guskiewicz, who plays to the grandstands and the yahoos, shows just how hard that is.

31 MARCH 2013 --------------------------

Now that the NFL and its trickle-down entities are in limited hang-out mode — to borrow the Nixonian term — official authorities like Dr. Richard Ellenbogen, co-chair of the league's Head, Neck and Spine Injury Committee, are sustaining verbal hernias in public. The litigation deluge means they have to disclose. But *defensive* litigation mode means they have to qualify, question, play to the inner skeptic in us all. And hope that no one applies that skepticism to the messenger as well as the message.

Last week the *New York Times* reported on the fact sheet, covering epidemiological findings with regard to various neurological disorders in the ex-player population, which was mailed out by the National Institute for Occupational Safety and Health. The newspaper leaked the nugget that an unnamed doctor-expert affiliated with the NFL had advocated removing chronic traumatic encephalopathy from the fact sheet, on the grounds that the phenomenon was "not fully understood." Thus, Lou Gehrig's disease, Alzheimer's, and Parkinson's made the cut; CTE did not.

Ellenbogen, plowing upfield to his right — always to his right! — and with his head up — always with his head up! — endorsed this approach. "We've got to be careful because CTE is a pathological diagnosis," he said. "We know that exists. That's been proven forever. What's important about this study is, if I played sports and had concussions, what's my chance of getting these?"

Note the rhetorical stutter-step: CTE has "been proven forever." But that was just health talk. Now we're talking about the real stuff: risk management. What are the numbers and at what threshold are those numbers actionable?

The NFL, enabled by the people my friend Matt Chaney calls "yaks," would like us all to forget, thanks to collective spiritual memory disorder, how recently and grudgingly it has conceded the existence of "proven forever" CTE. The question of research focus "was surely discussed by every football official with a clue by 1986, whether of league, union, or NCAA, then inexplicably dropped from a Johns Hopkins University study that initially planned a control group of college football players," says Chaney.

And nearly two years ago, Chaney was still hammering at the carefully circumscribed parameters of epidemiological studies of footballers.[18]

Soon the banks for study of the effects of traumatic brain injury–heavy occupations will have bigger surpluses than our national petroleum reserves, and Harvard University will be $10 million into its $100-million fleece of the National Football League Players Association to tell us what we already know, what has "been proven forever" — just not yet in Harvardese.

Football's golden age is over. Yaks like Ellenbogen remind us that golden ages end at the height of their popularity, revenue, television ratings, national obsession; and when smartly managed, they don't plummet. Those numbers can hold, desperately, conterintuitively, self-deceivingly, for quite a while. Silver ages have long shelf lives.

8 AUGUST 2013 -----------------------------

Public health takedowns of the football industry are in the works, both on film and in print. Maybe some day, and if we're lucky maybe very soon, American sports culture will be blessed with anti-football movement spearheaded by Christian Rightists and headquartered in one of the states of the Old Confederacy, or at least one of the counties of Pennsylvania somewhere between Philadelphia and Pittsburgh. "You may say I'm a dreamer . . ."

Ah, but Concussion Inc. is a world of ever-shifting alliances and treacheries. A neurologist at Loyola University in Chicago, Christopher Randolph, is out with a study casting doubt that football players show mental decline distinguishable from the general population: "We still do not know if NFL players have an increased risk of late-life neurodegenerative disorders. If there is a risk, it probably is not a great risk. And there is essentially no evidence to support the existence of any unique clinical disorder such as CTE."

One of the contributors to the study is the University of North Carolina's football-first Kevin Guskiewicz, whom I have taken to mocking as "Dr. No Junior." The MacArthur Foundation, inexplicably, gave Guskiewicz one of its "genius" awards — which in this case must be a genius for simultaneously homing in on the zeitgeist while propounding research that gives comfort to the already comfortable.

By contrast, previously I've spoken highly of Randolph for tearing to shreds the quackery (my word, not his) of Dr. Joseph Maroon, neurosurgeon to the Pittsburgh Steelers and the superstars of WWE, and his fellow witch doctors at the University of Pittsburgh Medical Center, who have foisted on public school districts and parents of youth athletes across the country the for-profit ImPACT "concussion management system."

See what I mean about alliances? I ask you not to hold Randolph's current lunacy against his previous bullseye on ImPACT and its cousin "How many fingers am I holding up? What day of the week is it?" software "solutions."

Paul Anderson, the sharp attorney who edits the *Concussion Litigation Reporter*, has noted the extent to which mere dubiousness, no matter how reasonable or reckless, becomes an exalted scientific and rhetorical commodity as the football industry manages what shapes up as its long, slow decline.

"Let the manufacture of doubt begin in earnest," Anderson tweeted in response to the Randolph-Guskiewicz news.

18 AUGUST 2013 ------------------------

It's time for more than left-handed compliments to ESPN's *Outside the Lines* on the football traumatic brain injury story. Today the investigative unit's Steve Fainaru, John Barr, Mark Fainaru-Wada, and Greg Amante have the down-low on the National Football League's founding concussion guru Dr. Elliot Pellman — a quack with an offshore medical degree and no neurology credentials, whose renewed and continuing prominence in NFL advisory circles can't be killed with a helmet-to-helmet hit.[19]

*The New York Time*s busted Pellman for résumé hype years ago. Earlier this year, Patrick Hruby of Sports on Earth updated the new-and-improved Pellman[20] — though Patrick held off on using the line I fed to him about Pellman via LBJ: "The NFL would rather have Pellman inside the tent pissing out than outside the tent pissing in."

One of the new facts in ESPN's excellent piece is that Pellman had a doctor-patient relationship with then–NFL commissioner Paul Tagliabue.

Choose your favorite mallard on the NFL pond. With my pro wrestling pedigree, I'll always be partial to Dr. ImPACT Dr. Resveratrol Dr. Sports Brain Guard Supplements, Joe Maroon, and his fellow Anatidae at the University of Pittsburgh Medical Center (at least one of whom is a convicted growth hormone trafficker).

21 AUGUST 2013

The tyranny of football-think is evident everywhere: in the passive solutions of parents who should know enough to "just say no," and now in the intellectual backlash of writers who ain't going to jump on no anti-football bandwagon.

Alexander Nazaryan of *Atlantic Wire* has an overview of the newest examples in "The Culture War Over Football."[21]

The antidote for this new round of counter-attacks on behalf of the savage wars of peace, domestic variety, at the expense of our sons' health, and the gross national mental product, is Matt Chaney, the Cassandra of football harm. Chaney, author of the overlooked book *Spiral of Denial*, is readying a new article for ChaneysBlog.com; he uncovers 35 cases of football fatalities in 2012 that didn't make the cut of the not-so-authoritative, though widely cited, list compiled by Dr. Fred Mueller at the University of North Carolina.

A dose of Chaney from his article-in-progress is the cure for the common football-is-good backlash.

> A teen football player dies suddenly in America, for reasons unrelated to collisions on the field, and the postmortem investigation produces more questions than answers — particularly whether the sport contributed mortally.
>
> And so it goes for too many fatal cases of active football players, mostly juveniles, with the game's possible link neither verified nor nullified because of two prime areas of limitation:
>
> First, the reputedly "deficient" state of autopsy in America, especially for children, as part of the death-investigations system that a government report[22] characterizes as "fragmented" and "hodgepodge."
>
> And, secondly, the equally challenged research field

of football fatalities, funded in present form by game organizations and led by two men lacking medical doctorates and certifications, Fred Mueller and Bob Colgate, a professor and a sports administrator, respectively, who largely troll news reports for gathering incomplete data.

Thus the mortality rate of American football remains incalculable, despite those long-standing Mueller-Colgate statistics widely cited as epidemiology, including by the CDC.

Such holes in football-injury tracking are "known for years," says Charles Yesalis, ScD, retired epidemiologist. "You have the problems articulated [regarding death investigations], but it goes beyond that. It's often based on whether an autopsy is done. And even if an autopsy is performed on the athlete, there are a lot of times that it's just not nailed down, particularly, regarding what's the cause of death and the like. So there's that issue."

Meanwhile, the researchers aiming to quantify football's risk and casualty face their own obstacles.

Beyond the few cases of collision fatalities tied directly to the sport, injury researchers typically rely on minimal data for judging whether a case was "indirectly" game-related, such as a cardiac death.

Anecdotal information and subjectivity can influence the record-keeping process, like coaches' quotes and other bits from news items. In many cardiac cases that kill players, grieving parents declare football was not a factor; some families refuse to cooperate with researchers.

For player deaths involving autopsy, researchers Mueller and Colgate value official rulings, but local coroners or medical examiners, elected to the job in many jurisdictions, often do not go far in probing cause or link to football. Many coroners are incapable themselves and lack funds for contracting specialized follow-up that could shed light.

"You really have to start digging through the medical charts," Yesalis suggests for strengthening a Mueller-Colgate study, although "the variability of [medical records] is scary when it comes to producing really solid research."

"All this variability, of how the medical record [of a casualty] is written, how it is accessed or not by the researchers, and whether it's clear that this event was precipitated and related to some sport activity — football, track and field, whatever — anybody who thinks the process is precise is very naive and hasn't done a lot of work with medical records, examining them for research purposes."

This review of 35 players who died during 2012 — see annotated cases below — demonstrates the problem. Determining death risk and casualty in vast American football remains a lofty goal, mere talk, despite the contemporary clamor for accurate injury reporting as part of establishing a "safer" game.

Indeed, Mueller and Colgate, funded by football and publishing from the University of North Carolina, qualify merely 15 of these fatalities as game-related for their 2012 report.

25 AUGUST 2013 --------------------------------

We've finally found the writer who puts the "foot" in football stupidity. It is Max Boot. We recently brushed off his ill-researched *Wall Street Journal* essay, "In Defense of Football," on the grounds that it would be a waste of bandwidth.

But as a Blog of Record, we are duty-bound to inform you that a plagiarism controversy has erupted inside the conservative community over the provenance of Boot's 2,000 poorly chosen words. *Politico* has the story[23] of the rejection by *WSJ* of freelance journalist Daniel Flynn's article "In Defense of Football" — quickly followed, as fourth down follows third, by the newspaper's soliciting of Boot to write a piece under the same (admittedly hackneyed) headline.

Boot is a think-tank expert whose special expertise is being wrong about America's benevolently imperial wars. The *Journal* editor who solicited Boot noted that he has a "football obsession." Perhaps what he most loves about football is that it is such a faithful metaphor for America's benevolently imperial wars.

Anyway, let me hold the principals' coats while they duel amongst themselves over originality, credit, and filthy lucre (the newspaper paid Boot $4,000 after he accepted the assurance of sports editor Sam Walker that "This thing will write itself!").

30 AUGUST 2013 --------------------------------

Yesterday a mediator announced a $765 million settlement in a lawsuit against the National Football League by 4,000 retired players. It will come as no surprise to followers of this space that I think the NFL settlement is a dud. It settles nothing. Like Big Tobacco, the $10-billion-a-year NFL has written a check to make the first round of claims go away for pennies on the dollar. There are many screwed-over retired players who have opted out or not yet filed.

But more important, the league's very omnipotent act has

demonstrated more acutely than ever that public high school football is a dead man walking, a zombie, a cultural obsession with no sustainable model. Cash-strapped public school districts scrambling for the resources to pay a reading recovery instructor can't afford the tiniest fraction of the NFL's litigation load.

Further, this shows how the NFL, for a cool three-quarters-of-a-bil, continues to default on the subsidized public health costs of its profiteering. More adroitly than RG3 slipping a tackle, NFL lobbyists have simply shifted these costs to schools in the form of "concussion awareness" state-by-state legislative measures that don't work — or at least don't work nearly well enough for their outlay and leap of faith: sideline neurologists, local ambulance services on call, "ImPACT" neurocognitive tests to line the pockets of WWE medical director Joe Maroon and his fellow witch doctors at the University of Pittsburgh Medical Center.

Let the maniac parents who feel otherwise continue to push their kids into this brain-busting extracurricular activity . . . in private clubs. Let's get our public institutions out of it.

2 SEPTEMBER 2013 ----------------------

We've made the point that the National Football League's $765 million settlement with retired players will not calm the ferment in the football industry's feeder systems. On Monday's *Good Morning America* on ABC, the parents of Derek Sheely talked about their lawsuit over his 2011 death while playing football at Frostburg State University in Maryland.[24]

The Sheely case also has drawn the interest of Maryland parent and advocate Tom Hearn, whose guest column we are pleased to publish below. In a nine-page fully footnoted letter,[25] Hearn asked Maryland's university regents to discuss Sheely's death and sports safety issues. By law, Governor O'Malley is invited to each regents' meeting, and Hearn urged the governor to attend the next one.

Hearn's piece raises questions every university governing board in the country should be asking about their athletic programs:

- Have you discussed sports concussions and other sports injuries at your meetings?
- Have you abdicated your responsibility on football head trauma by delegating decisions on limiting contacts to the NCAA rather than following the leads of the Ivy League and the Pac-12 Conference?
- For public universities, does limited sovereign immunity for coaches, administrators, and even regents create perverse incentives that make sports more dangerous for students?

by Tom Hearn

Last Friday, the Maryland Board of Regents, which oversees the state's university system, met by conference call. The day before, I emailed the regents a letter, asking them to add to their agenda a discussion of Derek Sheely, the Frostburg State University student who died two years ago of head trauma sustained in football practice with the school's team.

On August 22, Sheely's family filed a complaint in which they allege that his death stemmed from misconduct by Frostburg's football coaches and an athletic trainer.

The day after I sent my letter — the day of the regents' meeting — the university's chancellor explained that the regents' bylaws did not allow them to discuss Sheely's death at Friday's meeting. He committed that he and the regents would review my letter carefully and follow up with me.

The most pressing question is whether Frostburg football is currently safe. According to the Sheely lawsuit, the football coaches conducted dangerous helmet-to-helmet "Oklahoma-style" tackling drills over three days that caused Sheely to sustain a bleeding gash on his forehead and that the two football coaches and athletic trainers named in the suit ignored concussion signs that he displayed before collapsing unconscious on the field. Each of these staff currently serves in these positions at Frostburg.

It is not clear that the regents are aware of Sheely's death, of the suit his family has filed, or of the broader issues of concussions in college football and other sports. A review of the minutes of the regents' public meetings since August 2011 reflect no discussion of Sheely's death. The minutes also reflect no discussion of concussions in intercollegiate football.

There is no discussion in the regents' minutes of the long-term risk that repetitive head blows in football may lead to chronic traumatic encephalopathy (CTE) not only in retired NFL players but also in college football players, for example, Owen Thomas, a University of Pennsylvania football player who committed suicide in April 2010.

There is also no discussion in the regents' minutes of the short-term risks that repetitive head blows in football can lead to altered brain function, even in players who are not diagnosed to have sustained a concussion, and that such altered brain function can take months to return to baseline.

Further, on September 28, 2012, 13 months after Sheely's death, the regents adopted Policy V 2.10,

University System of Maryland Policy on Intercollegiate Athletics. The policy requires a university president to report to the regents' information about a school's intercollegiate athletics program such as student participants' academic performance and financial aspects of the program.

The regents' policy, however, requires no reporting on concussions or other injuries that students sustain from participating in intercollegiate athletics. The report filed by Frostburg State University for the 2010–2011 school year contains no information about concussions or other injuries. (No report by Frostburg State University is available at the Board of Regents website for the 2011–2012 school year, the year in which Sheely died.)

By law, the regents are required to invite Governor O'Malley, Treasurer Nancy Kopp, and Comptroller Peter Franchot to attend each of its meetings. If you will recall, in 2011 Pennsylvania's Governor Tom Corbett exercised a similar role to lead the Board of Trustees for Penn State University to address the child abuse scandal related to Penn State football coach Jerry Sandusky.

I respectfully urge Governor O'Malley, Treasurer Kopp, and Comptroller Franchot to attend the regents' next meeting and play a similar leadership role on the issue of the safety of students when they participate in intercollegiate athletics within the University System of Maryland.

At their next meeting, the regents needs to get a report from staff of whether football at Frostburg is being conducted safely and whether football at other Maryland Schools is being conducted safely.

At their next meeting, the regents should also adopt limits on full contact football practices similar to those adopted by the Ivy League, the Pac-12 Conference, and the NFL. The NCAA has not adopted such limits and appears to be committed to studying the issue. The regents' deference to the NCAA amount to an abdication of their responsibility to keep Maryland students safe when they participate in interscholastic sports.

Finally, regents need to evaluate whether it is appropriate for football and other sports programs to be covered by the limited immunity from tort liability that Maryland law provides to state institutions and their personnel. Under Maryland law, the liability of a state agency such as the Board of Regents for tort damages is up to $200,000.

School personnel, that is, coaches, athletic directors, university presidents, the chancellor, and even regents are only liable for torts — like a student dying in a school-organized football practice — if their conduct is malicious or grossly negligent. For negligence, these school personnel get a free pass.

The regents need to ask whether the limited immunity has created perverse financial incentives for the universities it supervises. Football and other sports programs represent significant revenue source and an opportunity to market a school's "brand." If liability for a tragedy like Derek Sheely's death is capped at $200,000, in a perverse Ford Pinto–like cost benefit analysis, does this represent a small operating cost with no financial incentive for a university to correct dangerous conditions?

One private sector discipline that gets lost by

intercollegiate athletics being conducted by state employees is the discipline of liability insurance. If the
University System of Maryland had to obtain insurance on the private market for the football program at
Frostburg, would an insurer be willing to provide coverage? If so, would the premiums be affordable?

Would a private insurer condition coverage on the
regents banning dangerous football tackling drills,
like the Oklahoma drills that the Sheely family allege
caused their son's death?

These serious issues may be beyond the regents'
willingness to address. That is why Governor O'Malley
needs to step in.

*Tom Hearn is a parent from Montgomery. Last year, after
his son sustained a concussion playing JV football, he advocated to the Maryland State Board of Education that they
take steps to address concussions in high school sports. Hearn
is @ConcussionMCPS on Twitter.*

10 SEPTEMBER 2013 ----------------------

"The family of a Montclair High School football player who died two
days after collapsing in a 2008 junior varsity game agreed Monday
to settle its lawsuit against the school and the township's Board of
Education for $2.8 million, the family's lawyer said."[26]

Though the National Football League's recent $765 million set-
tlement with thousands of retired players hogs the headlines, the resolution of the Ryne Dougherty case is a much more telling harbinger
of football's future.

Not mentioned in the news account cited above is that this case
involved more than the liability of a public school system for wrongful
death. It also exposed the expensive futility of newfangled "concussion

awareness" measures, such as the quack ImPACT "concussion management system."

21 SEPTEMBER 2013 ----------------------

We're happy to report that yesterday the regents of the Maryland state university system invited Tom Hearn to address them at their board meeting. An adaptation of Hearn's article here on September 2, also has run in online versions of both the *Baltimore Sun* and its sister *Chicago Tribune*.

Way to go, Tom. Again — these kinds of places are where the debate over the future of football is headed.

2 OCTOBER 2013 ---------------------------

Appropriately, corrupt doctors are front and center in separate excerpts of the book *League of Denial*, by Mark Fainaru-Wada and Steve Fainaru, which are published today by *Sports Illustrated* and *ESPN: The Magazine*.

Other than Joe Maroon and the Pittsburgh neurology quack pond, what jumps out at me most in the *ESPN* excerpt by the Fainarus is the role of Kevin Guskiewicz, the MacArthur fellow I now mockingly call "Dr. No Junior" — after the original "Dr. No" Ira Casson, whose repeated *nyet* negativity at a Congressional hearing grilling him about traumatic brain injury is lampooned on YouTube as the ultimate in tobacconist defensiveness.

In the Fainarus' account, Guskiewicz, who attended a 2006 NFL doctors' concussion summit organized by new commissioner Roger Goodell, felt the event "had the makings of a *Saturday Night Live* skit, with Casson as the parody of a man in denial":

Oh, my gosh, as long as I live I'll never forget that day. I use that as a teaching point with my students. I'm like, 'The day that you have to stand up in front of a group and tell them that you're a man or woman of science, your credibility is shot, especially when you have nothing to put in front of people to convince them.' That was a bad, ugly, ugly day for the NFL.

But ugliness is as ugliness does. Today Guskiewicz himself shills for the football establishment as a promoter of "safe football" — a position with all the public health conscientiousness of a marketer of filtered cigarettes.

The story, as told by me, isn't about all these great men, who it turns out aren't so great but simply stiffs like you and me, but with advanced degrees allowing them to peddle selective expertise to the highest bidder.

No, the story is about the power of a brand and the money behind it. The shill docs come and go, through the revolving door of PR hard denial to the revolving door of PR soft denial. Ending the systematic braining of young American males for mass entertainment isn't in their hands. It's in the hands of parents and the public.

13 NOVEMBER 2013 ----------------------

The most revealing quote in *League of Denial: The NFL, Concussions, and the Battle for Truth* — Mark Fainaru-Wada and Steve Fainaru's page-turning game-changer of a book — comes early on from Dr. Ann McKee, the central casting blonde-bombshell laboratory coat face of chronic traumatic encephalopathy. She replaced Dr. Bennet Omalu, the original sprightly African lab coat face of CTE.

Musing aloud to the Fainarus a year ago, McKee says, "[H]ow come I just don't say, 'Let's ban football immediately'?" She answers her own question: "I think I would lose my audience."

Yes, *League of Denial* is a book about science in the sense that, along the way, CTE earns classification as a discrete pathology. This is because, under a microscope, a dead brain that was impaired by the disease exhibits the strangling tau protein accumulations also found in Alzheimer's, but in different parts of the brain and without the beta-amyloid residue also attendant to Alzheimer's. The Fainarus explain it all concisely, brilliantly, for a general readership.

It's important to bear in mind, however, that *League of Denial* is not only, or even primarily, about science. For whenever public health collides with ingrained, commercially successful social customs, hard science gets you only so far. Moreover, what the world recognizes as pure science is often only slightly less elusive than art.

And that problem is the tangled web the Fainarus weave: a chaotic, improvisational dance of academic egotists, corporate butt-coverers, bad timing, and juicy intrigue, all with an unmistakable overlay of inevitability. Anyone who hasn't been playing football without a Riddell Revolution helmet knows how this story will end . . . at some indeterminate point in the future, with a whimper, after all the books have been written and read. What remains to be known are just a couple of details — how long it will take to get there and precisely what will constitute the tipping point.

With its bickering ensemble, mixing crude politicos and earnest pointy-heads, and its long, truth-bending narrative arc, *League of Denial* is in the tradition of *The Best and the Brightest*, David Halberstam's 1972 opus on how Team McNamara came — if I may be permitted to exploit a gridiron term — to "put the ball on the ground" in Southeast Asia. From my perspective, the Fainarus' final product has foibles, and I'll get to some of them. But don't let those cloud what, in the round, is a huge achievement in sports journalism. In journalism journalism.

In coming years, literature will further concentrate the American mind on the gross national cognitive product–decimating insanity that our billion-upon-billion-dollar football industry has become. These forays have to combine good writing, good reporting, good analysis, and, finally, "bona fides"; like Ann McKee said, you mustn't lose your audience! The authors of *League of Denial*, who work at ESPN, have delivered on their end. They found Goldilocks' sweet spot: their verbal porridge is not too hot, not too cold, just right.

In a few places, the book tips its cap to ConcussionInc.net, for which I am grateful. *League of Denial* goes deep with the tragedy of Dave Duerson, a retired defensive back and fallen business tycoon who joined in stonewalling old colleagues' brain injury claims on the Bert Bell/Pete Rozelle NFL Retirement Plan board — virtually up to the moment Duerson shot himself to death while admitting that he, too, was a victim of the syndrome. In the wake of that 2011 episode, Rick Telander and Paul Solotaroff wrote a fine article for *Men's Journal* chronicling Duerson's tormented last days, and Alan Schwarz of the *New York Times* raised the question of whether the deluded Duerson's presence on the disability review board tainted its body of work. But so far as I know, only Alex Marvez of FoxSports.com and I have persisted in digging into the Duerson case files with an eye toward correcting injustices.

League of Denial also quotes my friend, Missouri-based writer Matt Chaney, calling Kevin Guskiewicz "Gus Genius" (a jab at that worthy's MacArthur Fellowship), plus me tagging him "Dr. No Junior" (a reference to the senior "Dr. No," Ira Casson, who once chaired the NFL's Mild Traumatic Brain Injury Committee). These sallies appear in the epilogue, where the Fainarus ably bring their story home.

Heretofore, Guskiewicz had been part of a group of researchers the authors refer to as "The Dissenters," since they pecked away at stubborn denial in the higher councils of the league and even in the scientific research the league's well-connected consultants manufactured for publication in the most prestigious "peer-reviewed journals." But like just about everyone in *League of Denial* at one time or another,

Guskie shows his own ass once he becomes an ultimate insider, apologizing for the health toll of the football system and nitpicking at others' more aggressive extrapolations of concussion-related findings.

In contrast, other figures in the book come off better at the end than in the middle. One is Dr. Robert Cantu, who had signed off on corrupt NFL research and bizarrely lax editorial standards when he was sports section editor of the journal *Neurosurgery* (whose jocksniffing editor-in-chief, Dr. Michael Apuzzo, was also a team physician for the New York Giants). At least Cantu came around to clearly opining that no one under age 14 should play tackle football, period.

Still others intersperse good deeds with manipulative self-promotion, such as the formidable activist and ex-WWE performer, Chris Nowinski, sometimes in concert with the *Times'* Schwarz, his veritable amanuensis.

Without the spadework and high-end media access of the troika of Cantu and Nowinski in Boston, and Schwarz in New York, no tome as powerful as *League of Denial* would have had any hope of coming to light from a major publisher in 2013. Yet the Fainarus call out the vanity of these haughty Northeasterners, too. The climax of the process was a million-dollar NFL grant to the Boston University Center for the Study of CTE, which was accompanied by — and this is strictly my interpretation — a year or more of the Gray Lady's compromised coverage of the age of "concussion awareness." Dutifully, in the wake of the uncontrollable Omalu's split from the Boston group, the *Times* and others blacked out this native Nigerian, who didn't give a rat's rear about football, in favor of the mediagenic McKee, a rabid Green Bay Packers fan.

Commenting on the sister PBS documentary *League of Denial*, some have said the NFL Players Association is a missing character. After reading the more fully developed book (whose review here supersedes further comment on the television production), I agree. As noted, the

Duerson angle is there, but not the dissenting work of disillusioned union activist Sean Morey. *League of Denial* doesn't deal with the fault line between pre-1993 retirees and beneficiaries of the more recent collective bargaining improvements, or with the corruption and cronyism of the late NFLPA executive director Gene Upshaw. I suspect the authors were just making economical storytelling choices.

The same might be said of another missing character: government at all levels. When the battle of the buzzards was on, between Nowinski's Boston research group and Omalu's, for the right to examine the CTE evidence in another celebrity suicide, Junior Seau, the NFL maneuvered the family to donate the brain, instead, to the National Institutes of Health. This was quickly followed by a $30 million donation to NIH, the largest charity check in league history. The Fainarus don't bother pausing to underscore that NIH is an agency of the federal government, whose pursuit of the public interest gets warped by such levels of supposed corporate largesse.

League of Denial doesn't get around at all to the NFL's parallel eight-figure underwriting of a "public education" campaign under the auspices of another federal agency, the Centers for Disease Control. A pity, as this would have fit neatly into the too-short chapter so tastefully entitled "Concussion, Inc." (And, guys, you know where to send the royalty checks.)

The Fainarus only briefly touch on the regime of state statutes known as "Zackery Lystedt Laws," which add to the expensive and untenable "safety mandate" burdens of public high school football. *League of Denial* seems mostly uninterested in our theme, at least in this context, of how concussion awareness got vacuumed up by the NFL and its retinue — especially the developers of the ImPACT concussion recovery testing program — in ways that would not only protect Big Football's interests, but also isolate new profiteering opportunities from them.

Which, of course, brings me to this blog's bête noire and favorite punching bag: Dr. Joe Maroon of the Pittsburgh Steelers, the NFL, the

University of Pittsburgh Medical Center, and ImPACT Applications, Inc. I could fill an ebook with Maroon material not covered in *League of Denial*. Come to think of it, I already did.

But Maroon does get his, too, when he lies about the concussion history of ex-Steeler suicide Terry Long; when he feuds unproductively with pioneer researcher Omalu; when he issues a dingbat endorsement of a supplement called Sports Brain Guard; and when he co-authors the UPMC study that got hyped by the Riddell helmet company and drew the ire of Senator Tom Udall. (Curiously, and unreported by the book, Udall's Senate Commerce Committee hearing on the subject didn't name Maroon — one of many examples of the good doc's Teflon treatment in government investigations and media accounts.)

League of Denial doesn't mention Maroon's position as WWE medical director, though it recounts the Chris Benoit double murder-suicide and has an extended passage on the meeting at the West Virginia Brain Injury Institute, arranged by Maroon, at which an independent researcher, Peter Davies, examined Omalu's brain tissue slides and, much to the NFL's chagrin, confirmed Omalu's breakthrough findings.

I am perplexed by the Fainarus' decision to bestow on Maroon a quote bearing the moral of the whole shootin' match: "If only 10 percent of mothers in America begin to conceive of football as a dangerous game, that is the end of football." Any of a dozen other folks, all with demonstrably superior sincerity, surely said something similar at one time or another, and, worse, Maroon to this day sticks with an outlandish sound byte about how more people die in automobile accidents than on football fields. Oh well. The Fainarus seem less convinced than I am of the centrality of Dr. Joe in concussion cover-up and opportunism, and they have a right to their own conclusions.

Generally, I would describe *League of Denial* as the definitive work on the top-down generation-long strangulation of pertinent brain injury data emanating from the NFL's Park Avenue headquarters. If the worst things I can say about this book are in the mild dissents above — along with disappointment in *League of Denial's* poorly done index — then that is very high praise. As we move forward, other writers will stand on the Fainarus' shoulders and execute the next definitive work, on this sport's bottom-up toxic culture.

----

1   For a good analysis of Ellenbogen's flawed stance, see "For the NFL, Is More Protection Really the Answer to Its Concussion Quandary?" by Mike Seely of Seattle Weekly, blogs.seattleweekly.com/dailyweekly/2011/05/for_the_nfl_is_more_protection.php.

2   www.nytimes.com/2010/06/30/sports/football/30concussions.html.

3   www.sfgate.com/cgi-bin/blogs/ninerinsider/detail?entry_id=92054.

4   host.madison.com/ct/sports/football/professional/article_20a7a8f2-280b-11e0-aca5-001cc4c03286.html#ixzz1VbY5XaoE.

5   www.cbsnews.com/video/watch/?id=7376583n&tag=mncol;lst;1.

6   articles.chicagotribune.com/2011-08-31/news/ct-met-rocky-clark-insurance-0831-20110831_1_medicaid-program-hmo-style-new-doctors#.TnjzC5mJFhE.email.

7   newsok.com/city-area-player-of-the-week-corben-jones-defense-gets-yukon-back-on-winning-track/article/3610037.

8   This is from a blog at BaltimoreSun.com. The post is no longer accessible online.

9   This Houston Chronicle article is no longer accessible at the newspaper's website.

10 See "Why Are Ray Lewis And 'Friday Night Lights"s Peter Berg Shilling For The NFL On Player Safety?," deadspin.com/5880953/why-are-ray-lewis-and-friday-night-lights-peter-berg-shilling-for-the-nfl-on-player-safety.

11 www.cbssports.com/nfl/story/17423602/death-of-football-thats-crazy-until-you-start-thinking-about-it.

12 See "Bounties, crushing hits long a part of NFL," www.sfgate.com/cgi-bin/article.cgi?f=/c/a/2012/03/10/SPH51NIKRH.DTL.

13 The full 10-page brief is viewable at muchnick.net/impactfraudclaim.pdf.

14 concussionpolicyandthelaw.com/2012/11/02/impacts-reliability-challenged-in-court/.

15 See "Jimmie Giles: Legally Eligible for FULL Disability Benefits," davepear.com/blog/2012/11/jimmie-giles-legally-eligible-for-full-disability-benefits/.

16 www.nytimes.com/2012/12/15/opinion/should-kids-play-football.html.

17 Le Batard: "Jason Taylor's pain shows NFL's world of hurt," www.miamiherald.com/2013/01/13/3179926/dan-le-batard-jason-taylors-pain.html.

18 See blog.4wallspublishing.com/2011/06/23/research-for-nfl-brain-trauma-sputters-along.aspx.

19 See espn.go.com/espn/otl/story/_/id/9561661/central-figure-nfl-concussion-crisis-appointed-years-ago-league-position-commissioner-paul-tagliabue-patient.

20 (www.sportsonearth.com/article/47668524/.)

21 www.theatlanticwire.com/entertainment/2013/08/culture-war-over-football/68464/.

22 www.ncjrs.gov/pdffiles1/nij/233287.pdf.

23 See "Plagiarism or coincidence? Writer, Wall Street Journal square off," www.politico.com/story/2013/08/daniel-flynn-wall-street-journal-plagiarism-95865.html#ixzz2crLRYvY2.

24 See the video at www.wjla.com/articles/2013/08/derek-sheely-s-parents-sue-frostburg-state-university-over-son-s-death-93210.html.

25 muchnick.net/hearnletter.pdf.

26 www.nj.com/essex/index.ssf/2013/09/family_of_montclair_high_school_football_player_ryne_dougherty_who_died_in_2008_settles_lawsuit_for.html.

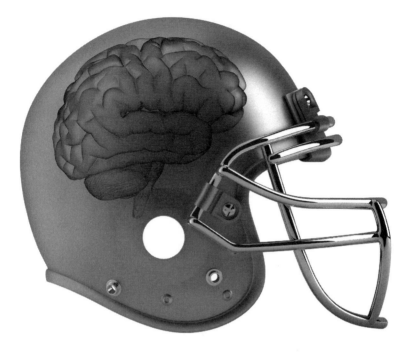

JOVAN BELCHER, BOB COSTAS, AND ME

Kansas City Chiefs linebacker Jovan Belcher, 25, murdered his girlfriend, Kasandra Perkins, 22 (mother of their two-month-old daughter), this morning at home in front of her mother, then drove to the team's Arrowhead Stadium facility, scuffled with personnel there, and shot himself to death.

Even those who did not know Belcher as either a player or a person extend sympathy to the families and friends of the two dead, and the many traumatized.

In 2009, I wrote the book *Chris & Nancy: The True Story of the Benoit Murder-Suicide and Pro Wrestling's Cocktail of Death*, about the

2007 incident in which WWE's Chris Benoit murdered his wife and their seven-year-old son before taking his own life.

In my short ebook *UPMC: Concussion Scandal Ground Zero,* published earlier this year, I wrote: "Sure, we don't know what the concussion tipping point will be. But I, for one, have a vision of what it *could* be: for example, a three-time champion quarterback murdering his supermodel wife on the 50-yard line at halftime of the Super Bowl — and taking out the intermission song-and-dance act along with her."

In a little more than a month, the Notre Dame football team taking the field for the national college championship game will include a player who, two years ago, was cleared of criminal charges and campus discipline after the suicide of a woman who said he had raped her. The athletic director at Notre Dame, Jack Swarbrick, was previously a practicing lawyer and is a long-time business associate and friend of USA Swimming executive director Chuck Wielgus. In a deposition and to this blog, Swarbrick refused to discuss his advice to Wielgus on how USA Swimming should handle its long-standing coach sexual abuse scandal, on the grounds that such conversations were attorney-client-privileged.

The malignancies of our sports system are metastasizing. The fanboys and girls can continue to make excuses, rationalize, deny this state of affairs. That is what they do best.

The rest of us will face it and do something about it.

2 DECEMBER 2012

The No. 1 question I'm being asked is whether Jovan Belcher had a known concussion history. The short answer: no. The long answer: it doesn't matter. The "known" part would be ambiguous, anyway. The "concussion" part wouldn't reveal the damage caused by the thousands of subconcussive blows endured throughout his football career (and in his high school wrestling career, it must be added).

Only postmortem examination of Belcher's brain tissue could reveal whether chronic traumatic encephalopathy played a part in the murder of Kasandra Perkins, the mother of their infant daughter, followed by his own suicide.

But unlike, for example, Dave Duerson and Junior Seau, Belcher pointed the gun at his head rather than his chest before pulling the trigger. (Chris Benoit, the WWE star who was the subject of my 2009 book, hanged himself on his exercise machine pulley.)

So I don't know how much useful brain tissue the technicians at the crime scene and the coroner in Kansas City were able to preserve. I'm guessing that the leading light of the CTE field, Dr. Bennet Omalu, who is also the chief medical examiner of San Joaquin County, California, might have a chance, if he has access, to make at least tentative findings in this area, but they would be controversial. (Omalu tells me by email: "The answer is a bold yes [in the hands of a] skilled forensic pathologist who has vast experience with cases like that. We have been able to perform autopsies on individuals buried for two to three years, and still we were able to examine their brains and derive definitive diagnoses. A gunshot wound to the head, or shotgun wound to the head, should not preclude CTE analyses and/or diagnoses.")

And now on to what I consider the nitty-gritty, which is not TV show forensic heroics. It's what I call "the cocktail of death" and what Matt Chaney calls "the spiral of denial." Football's profiteers and their fanboys are playing the old tobacco-style shell game here. As the dramatic anecdotes, buttressing epidemiological data, emerge and accumulate, does it matter whether an individual died of lung cancer, emphysema, or heart disease? By the same token, the Belcher baby and the society that picks up the pieces — literally — of her father's brain and consequences don't much care if her father died of CTE, drug abuse, inchoate mental imbalance, or toxic levels of DirecTV. She's just as orphaned regardless. How about "all of the above"?

The thing about football is that it disables and kills in so many ways that you can't possibly codify all of them, much less produce a consensus pie chart. You just have to exercise some common sense and downsize the industry . . . excuse me, the *sport* . . . starting with kids. Let the last holdout child-abusing parents send their little boys out to slaughter in the name of glory, spectacle, and character-building. But not on the public dime.

A further exchange on Twitter, with Dave "@EdgeOfSports" Zirin about corporate media sports murder self-censorship.

Zirin: "Neither Fox nor CBS mentioned the words 'murder,' 'Kasandra Perkins' or even 'Jovan Belcher' in halftime shows. League directives?"

Muchnick: "I can do better than that. NYT's 2300-word profile in 2010 of Senate candidate Linda McMahon didn't include 'Benoit' or 'death.'"

3 DECEMBER 2012 ------------------------

Tracking the slow or fast decline of American football, as driven by public health concerns, involves following the science, of course — in addition to following the deaths, the money, and the sound bytes. Bob Costas went all lofty on us last night at halftime of NBC's *Sunday Night Football* while addressing the Jovan Belcher murder-suicide. As Costas would have it, football safety is the background of this story. The foreground is *gun control*. I disagree.

With good timing, a new chronic traumatic encephalopathy study by the Boston research group makes the publicity rounds today. This one has numerosity, 85 donor brains, and Dr. Robert Cantu correctly observes that anyone who still doubts the discrete pathology of CTE no longer should.

When it comes to the risk thing, Chris Nowinski reminds us that predictions are "a gambler's game." This layman would like to pursue that line for a moment, and again advance the idea that the two interconnected components of traumatic brain-injury study tend to get glibly atomized, when they should be integrated.

One component is the sports injury known as concussion. This is now understood to come in both detected and undetected varieties: observable loss of consciousness as well as less easily identified symptoms. One of the costs of the new concussion awareness has been the evolution of the term "concussion" into virtual catchall status.

The other component of football TBI is *subconcussive accumulation*, with CTE-associated long-term effects. At the far end of this scale, we find dementia and cognitive impairment in ex-athletes who were much too young.

"The dots are really about total head trauma," Cantu tells the *New York Times*. This leads him to emphasize such things as reduced contact in practices, hit-sensor technology in helmets, and — to be fair to his boldest and most admirable point — recently articulated support of the camp advocating elimination of tackle football below age 14.

But what I'd like to ask is whether the football safety debate properly stops at "total head trauma." Cantu's colleague, Dr. Ann McKee, summarizes the same study similarly but differently, saying, "If individuals play football — *especially if they have concussions that aren't properly managed* — they can develop areas of brain damage." The italics are my own, underlining what I think these hard-working researchers themselves might not fully appreciate about the dissonance of their message.

For it seems to me that football serves up more than one TBI problem. There's a "total" problem, in the form of concussions-cum-subconcussions. And there's an entirely "random" but nonetheless systematic problem, in the form of reported catastrophic injuries and unreported chronic ones. The latter problem is less conducive to hard science. It suggests that this subject is, at root, social — non-disciplinary, or at least "multi-disciplinary." No one is lining up to hand out grants for *that*.

The "dots," in my view, are not some still-undeveloped quotient of hits-per-brain-cell-per-age, as the Cantu crowd maintains. Take a look at the recent interview by *USA Today* of Dr. Richard Ellenbogen, the National Football League's brain-injury co-chair. Ellenbogen spent most of his energy warning against snap visual diagnoses by press box–level consultants or even ad hoc sideline neurologists. He argued that the team medical and training staffs, those with the most knowledge of individual players' baselines and histories, are still the best equipped to manage the fallout of in-game collisions.

Ellenbogen may be right, but my point is that the whole discussion shows how much more artistic than scientific the concussion-management game is. It leads to the question of whether America's parents are truly, *consciously* prepared to put their son's futures, and broader national male mental health, in the hands of people who, for all intents and purposes, are making up the rules as they go along.

Last night NBC, an NFL broadcast partner, in a halftime segment Dan Patrick had hyped as "must-see TV" (not that he or his bosses care about ratings or anything, mind you), made sure not to go there. Costas firewalled his Belcher civics lesson at gun control. Speaking as someone who has never owned or even fired a gun, I don't think that approach moved the chains. Indeed, it may have had the effect of shortening the shelf life of the tragic weekend news, rather than extending our collective memory of it.

4 DECEMBER 2012 -------------------------------

On Monday night, Washington Redskins quarterback Robert Griffin III dazzled ESPN's football nation with his ball-handling. But Griffin had nothing on the verbal wizardry of NBC's Bob Costas, who a night earlier, during his halftime commentary on the Jovan Belcher murder-suicide, quoted columnist Jason Whitlock's call for gun control reform.

In the culture-war fishbowl that is the New York media world (and to mangle a metaphor), Costas became a lightning rod. As new details emerged in the Belcher investigation, the focus was on how Fox News was calling Costas the most horrible person in the world for seeking to trample the Second Amendment and how MSNBC was calling Fox News the most horrible network in the world for calling Costas the most horrible person in the world.

And the NFL band played on.

Costas told the *New York Times* that "the criticisms of his commentary 'hold no weight with me' because the same people saying that that was an inappropriate time and place to talk about the gun issue 'would have thought it was fine if they agreed with what I was saying.'"[1]

Well, actually, I agreed with what Costas was saying but I don't think his commentary was fine — because it was a diversion from encouraging his audience, in a football broadcast, to think about the likelier far larger role of football in the murder of Kasandra Perkins and suicide of Jovan Belcher.

Even Dave Zirin, the sports editor of the *Nation*, who praised Costas to the skies for having a smidgen of substance (in contrast with Fox and CBS on Sunday football), is saying today on Twitter, "Terrible indictment of media that story of Kasandra Perkins & Jovan Belcher is now a debate about Bob Costas. NFL breathes sigh of relief."

As Costas's fellow gun control proponent, but one disappointed that he chose the easy and somewhat self-aggrandizing culture war instead of the truly instructive one right in front of his nose, I want to make another point: the Belcher case seems to me a pretty flabby prop for the gun control argument.

I wrote a book about the 2007 double murder-suicide of WWE's Chris Benoit; no gun was involved there. Further, the Belcher reports show that he fired nine shots into his girlfriend, then tenderly kissed her. This was no 10-year-old kid pulling a firearm from the mantle and accidentally discharging it.

All in all, we need fewer reenactments of hardened cable-news crossfire on gun control, and more non-trivial discussion about the elephant in the room: the pistol that went off inside Belcher's brain.

4 DECEMBER 2012 ------------------------

In the past couple of days I've taken some new swings at my friend Bob Costas. I don't want to exaggerate or grandstand by implying that we're close pals. But we are fellow St. Louis sports mafiosi, he has done me some nice turns, and I have great respect for his body of work. On the latter, how could I not? Even if this is prettiest-lady-in-Siberia territory, it bears repeating that Costas, in terms of communicated intelligence about the world at large, is head and shoulders above his contemporaries in sports broadcasting.

As I've written, right-wingers went after Costas for talking about guns in his Jovan Belcher commentary on NBC Sunday night. Meanwhile, I and some others expressed disappointment that Costas, by his emphases, had put the ever-polarized gun debate at the center of the public conversation in the Belcher postmortem, and football's more consensus-friendly pathologies (brain injury, painkiller abuse, celebration of violence, etc.) on the margin.

In a just-concluded phone conversation, Costas explained that he believes he did no such thing. Bob doesn't want me to quote him, but I'll try to transcribe his train of thought faithfully, in the hope that those of us who feel more or less the same way about the excesses of football in our society can keep the right target in the cross-hairs going forward.

Sorry, bad metaphor . . .

In Bob's mind, he was delivering the absolutely strongest and most responsible editorial possible at that moment of known and verified information about the Belcher–Kasandra Perkins tragedy — within the all of 60 seconds of air time he was allotted. In the ensuing 36 hours, considerably more Belcher info has surfaced, and we will be hearing what Costas has to say about it — perhaps as soon as his Thursday show on the NBC Sports cable network.

Notwithstanding the attacks on him by yahoos, Bob does not even see himself, in this context, as advocating gun control per se. Rather, he was reflecting on the gun *culture* so prevalent in America, perhaps especially among athletes, and perhaps especially, especially among football players.

Finally, Bob points out that he explicitly concluded his commentary with an observation extraneous to the Jason Whitlock column he was quoting about guns. Costas said that in the next days, "Jovan Belcher's actions, and their possible connection to football, will be analyzed. And who knows?"

Fair enough. I think I've made my point and I think Bob has made his. Onward.

7 DECEMBER 2012 -------------------------

Matt Chaney, author of the superb but barely noticed 2009 book *Spiral of Denial: Muscle Doping in American Football*, is our most fearless historian of football's harm. In a post at his blog last year, Chaney writes about the 1980 murder-suicide of retired Kansas Chiefs offensive tackle Jim Tyrer. Chaney calls Tyrer "one of the greatest offensive tackles in history," who remains shut out of the Pro Football Hall of Fame only because "the league and media suddenly wanted to forget him."[2]

1   mediadecoder.blogs.nytimes.com/2012/12/03/at-halftime-costas-put-spotlight-on-guns-by-morning-the-spotlight-was-on-him/.

2   "Football Brain Trauma Can Twist Personality, Spur Violence," blog.4wallspublishing.com/2011/06/16/football-brain-trauma-can-change-personality-spur-violence.aspx.

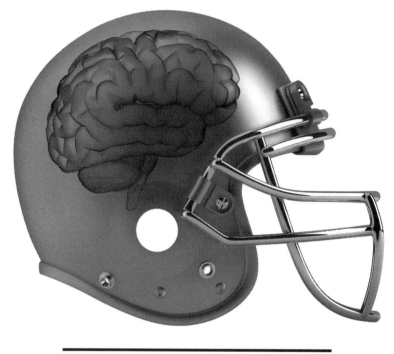

MY FRIEND GEORGE VISGER

24 JUNE 2011 ----------------------------

Former San Francisco 49er George Visger comments on my criticism of Dr. Richard Ellenbogen, co-chair of the NFL concussion committee:

> I agree with you, but think Ellenbogen is trying to do the right thing. I played DT for the 49ers in '80 and '81 when I developed hydrocephalus from numerous concussions, and underwent emergency VP shunt brain surgery at age 22. My shunt failed (in Mexico fishing) just four months after we won Super Bowl XVI and my

brother brought me home in a coma. I underwent two more brain surgeries 10 hours apart and was given last rites. I was also given the hospital bills, and had creditors on me for nearly five years till I successfully sued the 49ers for WORKERS COMP! I am now on brain surgery No. 9, multiple gran mal seizures and currently taking my sixth different seizure med since starting on them over 25 years ago. The side effects have been catastrophic on my everyday life.

Ellenbogen called me ~ 1 1/2 years ago when I called him out on Dave Pear's blog immediately after he was hired. He and I correspond regularly now. He asked I submit suggested rule changes which he would present to the NFL Rules Committee. Many of my suggestions have been implemented today (much to the chagrin of players). Only difference I had was I wanted all fines for head-to-head hits levied at the owners, not the players.

I was one of four ex players and five NFL Hall of Fame players asked to speak at a press conference in Washington, DC, last Monday, prior to the Carl Eller vs. NFL lawsuit.

We need more folks like you not afraid to air the NFL's dirty laundry.

George Visger

SF 49ers '80 and '81

Survivor of Nine NFL Caused Emergency VP Shunt Brain Surgeries

Benefactor of ZERO NFL Benefits

24 JUNE 2011 ----------------------------

There are a million concussion stories in the Naked City, and this blog can't possibly tell more than a tiny fraction of them. But it is worth repeating over and over again the story of George Visger, whose football brain injury turned him into a real-life version of the protagonist of the 2000 cult movie *Memento* — someone robbed of the basic human function of short-term memory. Fortunately for all of us, Visger attacks his plight with grace, zest, and educational meticulousness.

Visger isn't hunting for the murderer of his wife — he just seeks a scrap of justice for himself. So far, going on 30 years, there has been none from the $10-billion-a-year National Football League. (I think it's safe to upgrade from the "$9-billion-a-year NFL" after yesterday's announcement of a 10-year extension of ESPN broadcast rights at a *raise* of nearly $1 billion annually.)

I originally referenced Visger's case after he posted a long comment in response to a blog item. Yesterday Dave Pear's Independent Football Veterans blog republished my report on confronting DeMaurice Smith, executive director of the NFL Players Association, at the Santa Clara University Sports Law Symposium.

John Hogan, the wise and indefatigable attorney for disabled players, added in a comment under my post that Smith also had failed to answer the specific question in Hogan's own talk at the symposium about crater-sized loopholes in the new "neurocognitive benefit" the union is hyping in its collective bargaining agreement with the league. Hogan: "I don't see it helping many guys. You have to be vested, under 55, and not on Line-of-Duty or Total and Permanent. That pretty much leaves out all guys who are working. But how do you perform sustained, competitive work if you have a significant neurocognitive impairment?"

That's when George Visger jumped in again. The floor belongs to him:

John,

To answer your question, "But how do you perform sustained, competitive work if you have a significant neurocognitive impairment?"

I developed hydrocephalus (water on the brain) while playing DT with the '81 SF 49ers, and underwent emergency VP shunt brain surgery. Four months after we won Super Bowl XVI, my shunt failed and I had two more brain surgeries 10 hours apart and was given last rites. Virtually no memory for nearly a year after. My first recollection was of receiving bills for the brain surgeries from the 49ers front office with the total circled "YOU OWE THIS AMOUNT." (I was hoping for at least flowers and a cheesy card.)

After fighting off creditors for four years, the 49ers counsel forced me to take the stand while he grilled me at my Workers Comp hearing on what I did my last day of practice (we're not talking malpractice or liability claim, just a simple Work Comp claim like ANY injured employee is entitled to). I won my case in '86 and they offered me $35K to disappear. It sounded appealing as I was living in a dirt-bag apartment, swinging a hammer for $12/hour and bouncing at nights for $10k to survive. I told them to keep their money and I kept my medical claim open AND asked to finish my biology degree through Vocational Rehab. All injured employees are entitled to Voc Rehab. I had four years of bio at Colorado before being drafted in '80 and wanted to finish. Thank God I kept the medical open and didn't take the cash.

I completed my degree in biological conservation in 1990 while surviving four more brain surgeries (in

'87) and multiple gran mal seizures. During the four-and-a-half years it took to complete my degree, the 49ers Work Comp was responsible for every bill associated with my being retrained (books, tuition, mileage to school each day, mileage to doctors' appointments, doctors, meds, counseling), and I received disability while I was in school full time or recovering from my surgeries. I had two additional knee surgeries during this time, including a Gore Tex ACL transplant, repairing the sloppy job the 49ers did in '81. Everything covered but still not worth the price my family continues to pay for my having played two years in the NFL.

Twenty nine years later, I have now survived nine emergency VP shunt brain surgeries, multiple gran mal seizures, suffer from major short-term memory deficits, and have been diagnosed by Dr. Amen and Dr. Claydon as suffering from early onset dementia. I was on four different dementia medicines at once last year, to help me continue functioning as a self-employed environmental consultant. The side effects were worse than the treatment so I upped my hyperbarics and Omega 3's and only take two Arricept/day to increase my neurotransmitters. I am functioning better than I have in years.

How to Survive with an NFL Caused
Traumatic Brain Injury

1. I literally write down everything in my Rite-In-The Rain notebooks. Waterproof, fit in your back pocket. I have 30 years of these, 12–15 pgs/day. Each phone call, conversation, etc., goes in with time, who, what we spoke about, what I did at each

project, when I left the office, mileage when left, time.

Here's an example from today. I'm on a Caltrans project I have been working on 14–19 hrs/day out of town the last two months.

9/9/11 Spent nite at Copelands. 267,092 (mileage) left @ 5:42

6:21 Site T-7A. 267,111. Traffic crew setting out signs, data

7:09 7A bell hole dug, contact ETIC for BMPs (DI protection)

7:21 7D 267,112 Done, no paint

7:29 7E 267,113 by Chevron, almost complete.

7:31 Called ARB – Clay sched?

7:33 Called Reynoldo vm

7:34 – 7:42 Called Phil Woltze – Arch. Survey L & M during const, spot check A & D, pre con survey F & I before exca. CALL PHIL BEFORE BREAK GROUND F 09/10

7:52 Site 7 F 267,118- started box, PGE onsite

8:08 Site 7 G 267,220- saw cut, exca. Dump, front load.

8:14 called Jeff E, Snelson Con Cord. T 44 not theirs. Thinks ARB

8:16 called Clay con cord Snel. rec'd Carlile.

8:17 Carlile, onsite in pm with backhoe, ex if USA'd.

8:20 – 8:47 Called Chris P – ARB super. Moving tanks in am T44 to 7/9. Need arborist at 44, cultural at 7/9. Discharge @ 100 gpm 9-5, 50gpm 5 – 9. Coord Lauren/Clay – ARB. Brkdwn tanks now. Need RTC, Encroach permit, discharge permit. Have ETIC install DI protect prior to mobe. Traffic control?? CONDUCT ENVIRO TRAIN- ING FOR CREWS AT 7A TOMORROW 7:00. GET MIKE P FOR CULTURAL, REYNAL- DO, KEITH FOR SWPPP TRAINING.

You get the picture. Some days I have 22-plus pages of notes to read through before doing my data reports.

Every couple nights I read through the pri- or week's work/life. After reading what I did last week 3–4 times I know what I did, even if I don't really remember doing it. I will highlight import- ant items with various colored pens I need to come back to (red = work, yellow = home, blue = other). This eliminates wasted time reading unimportant information.

2. For appointments I use Post-Its on my dash, my bathroom mirror, desk and screen of computer. When done, crumple up and toss on floor (very ca- thartic). Computer alarms go off at 14, 7, 4, 3, 2, 1 day intervals prior to appointments. The day of the appointment at 5, 4, 3, 2, 1 hour intervals, then at 15, 10, 5 minute intervals prior. Despite all this, I will get busy on a report and even with 5 minute reminders, still miss meetings.

3. Tell people you work with or for to remind you of things. Everyone who works with me (clients included) knows to ask, "Do you have your note- book handy?" when they call.

I'm not shy about letting people know what I'm

dealing with (as you all can tell by now). Clients who are hesitant to use my services will quickly learn I plain and simply outwork others and cover their tails with my detailed notes. I have been subpoenaed for lawsuits years later, brought out minute-by-minute detailed information that even the regulatory agencies don't have. No one remembers like they think they do. My notebooks are my memory banks.

4. Investigate anti-seizure/psychotic or other meds you may be on. My experience has been the side effects are usually worse than the symptoms. Many doctors will prescribe drugs as a "cover your ass" rather than what is best for the patient. If the drug is "standard of care" and you have problems, it relieves them of liability. Be proactive, don't rely totally on professionals; doctors and attorneys (sorry John) are humans (at least some are). They're not God and make mistakes. Look out for yourself or your loved one.

5. Hyperbaric oxygen treatments (HBOT). No drugs involved, just oxygen. I'm into my 90-plus treatments at one or more hour treatments, and began remembering things on my daily schedule after seven to nine treatments. I am a firm believer in HBOT — best thing to happen to me in 30 years regarding my TBI.

6. Mega doses of Omega-3 fish oils and anti-oxidant fruit juices. I use Dr. Barry Sears Omega-3s as they are industrial-grade purified and his SeaHealth

Plus anti-oxidant. Two capsules of the anti-oxidant/day reduces inflammation in all your tissues, especially neurons in your brain. Inflammation of neurons due to repeated head trauma (not just concussions but the 1,000s of subconcussive hits) causes early death of the neurons = dementia.

With Omega fish oil, make sure they are purified. Fatty fish store heavy metals and toxins in their oil. Ensure it's been cleaned.

7. Work your brain. We worked our bodies to keep in shape and you need to do the same for your brain. New buzz word: NEURO-PLASTICITY. Old school was once brain damaged, that's it. Recent research has proven by working your brain you can literally grow new neurons into areas of your brain we don't use and are not damaged. Humans only use 5% of our brains. Exercises such as using your left hand if right handed, changing your routines, and playing kids' memory games causes you to concentrate more, which stresses your brain and causes it to grow new neurons or activate existing neurons that aren't being used.

There are ways to function with TBI. The NFL certainly doesn't want to take responsibility for putting their ex-employees in these situations, as it's not only bad PR but costly.

Think what we could do if we all functioned at the capacity we are capable of. I hate to say it, but the last thing the NFL wants to see is a bunch of highly motivated players and families operating at optimum levels, calling them on their criminal handling of their injured employees.

Those of you in my situation and those family members dealing with a TBI survivor try these techniques. It's the only way I have learned how to function.

We need to take control of our lives again.

FYI: I have cc'd De Smith on this and will request he send his response to me via Dave Pears' blog. The man works for the players (though we are no longer considered a player even though we pay dues). There's no reason he didn't address questions at the Symposium. I am looking forward to your comments, De.

George Visger

SF 49ers '80 and '81

Survivor of Nine NFL Caused Emergency VP Shunt Brain Surgeries

Benefactor of ZERO NFL Benefits

15 OCTOBER 2011 ------------------------

It's not nice to speak ill of the dead, and to be sure, Al Davis — the Oakland Raiders' owner who died Saturday at 82 — was a colorful figure whose dark side is easy to gloss over for the media types who too often serve as ruling-class stenographers. At the peak of his powers, he had a brilliant football mind, and he raised business ruthlessness to an art form. He also was intermittently droll, a quality that should not be devalued.

The *San Francisco Chronicle*'s Scott Ostler quoted Howie Long, the Raiders' Hall of Famer who is now a television analyst, about the time he failed to get his grandmother, who had cancer, into the right hospital in Boston for treatment — until he enlisted Davis, who called back "20 minutes later" to say he'd secured the bed.

Yeah, right, not a second more than 1,200. The story recited house history about how everyone considered "a true Raider" had Davis's "absolute loyalty." Apparently Dave Pear, a member of the 1980 Raiders Super Bowl champions who now leads the community of retired players who were screwed by the National Football League's penurious pension and disability plan, didn't make the cut.

(Of course, the Raiders hardly enjoy a Bay Area monopoly on pro football executive callous. The 49ers never paid one dime of the seven-figure medical bills of George Visger, a member of the 1981 champs who had emergency brain surgery shortly after the Super Bowl, followed by dozens of other operations and ongoing health issues in the decades since.)

In 1995, as the Raiders prepared to play their first game back here after a 13-year absence, my then second-grade son and I were at a barbecue at the home of a school friend in another part of Berkeley. All the other adults, perhaps half of whom were career civil servants in the governments of Berkeley and the neighboring Oakland, were uniformly enthusiastic about the return of the NFL. My contribution to cocktail chatter was an observation that taxpayers of a beleaguered city shouldn't be in the business of subsidizing a football team. I might as well have been advocating the abolition of rent control and the quadrupling of DMV fees.

Three years later, I took both my young sons to Jon Gruden's first home game as the Raiders' coach. The walk-up ticket windows were woefully understaffed, and as we waited in the single long line we could hear the roar of the crowd reacting to Napoleon Kaufman's long touchdown run on the first play from scrimmage. By the time we were settled in our seats, the first quarter was over. The crowd's notorious rowdiness further ensured that it would be the last pro football game I have attended in person.

As is well known, the Raiders broke the hearts of their Northern California fans by moving to the Los Angeles Coliseum (and registering the most recent of their three Super Bowl wins while there), and at the time of his death Davis was still claiming territorial rights in the Southland for an actual or threatened second exodus. Sportswriters and columnists respectfully emphasized his persona as the Tiresias of the gridiron, but were not nearly as diligent in noting that he was arguably the biggest civic thief in East Bay history.

The "improvements" to the Oakland Coliseum to get Davis to reverse his original jilting turned a multi-purpose stadium already suffering from a deficit in baseball atmosphere into a rock-bottom mausoleum. The city and Alameda County got fleeced to the tune of scores of millions, a corporate and individual-income base in no position to support it faced one of the pioneering models of the scam now familiarly known as PSLs ("personal seat licenses"). Enough low-lives, however, regularly dug deep enough for individual game tickets to lower the quality of the Raider fan experience, both in the parking lot and inside the stadium (though not enough to prevent one of the NFL's lowest rates of home sellouts, and thus highest rates of local TV blackouts of games).

For all this on-again, off-again pseudo-fealty, Davis and his Raiders sold the myth that their franchise was some kind of community treasure.

Davis, who owned a mansion in Piedmont, died of "undisclosed causes" at his home of late, "a hotel near the Oakland airport," the *Chronicle* said. Tom FitzGerald, the lead byline on the obit, told me, "I agree readers would like to know the cause of death. If we get anything on that, we'll report it. But, as you know, the Raiders are a very secretive organization. I'm not holding my breath that they will disclose that information."

29 MARCH 2012 ---------------------------

Thursday is a big day for George Visger, author of our ebook *Out of My Head: My Life In and Out of Football*.

First, he and his old San Francisco 49ers teammate Dan Bunz will be honored on the floor of the California State Senate. After the

Senate votes on a concurrent resolution proclaiming March "Brain Injury Awareness Month," Visger and Bunz will be presented certificates of recognition by Senator Ted Gaines of Sacramento.

Then George heads straight to his home-away-from-home, the Hyperbaric Oxygen Clinic of Sacramento, for one of the treatments he credits for his recent improvements in memory and general cognition. While inside the oxygen chamber, Visger will be interviewed by Vernon Glenn of KRON4 News in San Francisco.

The entire crack staff of ConcussionInc.Net LLP is proud of George Visger.

17 DECEMBER 2012 -----------------------

Last week I drove up to Sacramento for dinner with my friend and ebook author, the unsinkable George Visger. I was supposed to meet him at 7 p.m. at the Hyperbaric Oxygen Clinic near the UC Davis Medical Center. George is basically sleeping on the floor of the clinic these days while he tries, again, to get back on his feet financially. His last contract as a wildlife biology consultant on a construction project ended in February, which was also the last time I saw him in person.

Another friend of mine, Patrick Hruby, has a big text-and-video package on Visger coming out next month at ESPN.com. Hruby understands how emblematic George's dire straits are of a generation of brain-wounded National Football League veterans. Patrick is a brilliant writer with a wonderful human touch, and I can't wait to read and view what he produced.

But I'm also here to tell you that Visger is not in despair. Even in a hyperbaric chamber, his relentless sense of humor leaves no oxygen for self-pity.

When I made plans to drive to Sacto, I asked George whether I should bring in some Popeye's Chicken, or if he had a key to the clinic and in-and-out capability.

He emailed back: "They actually let me out of the clinic on occasion, as long I'm with a responsible adult so I won't wander off. Can you bring one?"

But when I arrived, guess what? There was no George, nor any response to my texts and voicemails. Fortunately, the clinic's co-owner and manager, Mike Greenhalgh — who lives right next door — was still inside with another patient, and we hung out and traded notes on the latest concussion developments. Eventually George called. He had been visiting with his indestructible 5-foot-1, 89-year-old Lebanese mother, "Big Rita," and his phone had frozen. Despite a mess of yellow Post-It notes and memory notebook entries, our dinner engagement had slipped his agile mind. No harm, no foul.

Over dinner, Visger told me about the progress he's making with his brain-injury awareness message. He's an engaging and charismatic public speaker — all defensive lineman's shrunken hulk, combined with those kinetic Mediterranean gesticulations and eyebrows — and he is in demand for conferences and school groups. Some even pay honoraria, which in his rent-free condition will help build a bridge back to a normal family life until he lands a new consulting gig. Right now, his wife, Kristi, and their two kids at home, Jack and Amanda, are making a ridiculous 90-minute commute every day from the in-laws' in Sacramento to their school and sports in Grass Valley.

Our dinner wasn't all business. I described for George my eight-year-old daughter's Chinese dance performance at the Richmond Senior Center. In turn, he related the story of how, shortly after meeting Kristi, he got instantly "harpooned" by Stefani, her then two-year-old, blue-eyed, blonde-haired daughter.

At that point I could have busted George's chops by reminding him that he'd told me that anecdote a dozen times already. *Check your goddamn Post-It notes, Visger!* But why bother? It's still a great story in every retelling.

Driving back home late that night, I started thinking about all the George Visgers out there: ex-NFLers, some stars, many more journeymen, who are disabled far too young, in ways small or large, and whose resourcefulness and support networks vary widely. And an idea formed for something I'd first pondered more than a year earlier. After a story on this blog about a retired player in distress (not Visger), a reader began underwriting monthly shipments of high-end Omega-3 supplements to the player. Many believe fish oils hold hope for reversing brain decay and sharpening mental acuity. The reader-donor insisted on anonymity; all he requested was that the recipient report back to him periodically on his progress.

The larger idea goes like this. We all know the ultimate political and legal solutions for the plight of NFL veterans lie in the future. As a nation, we haven't gotten our arms around this football problem; hell, we can't even get our arms around the assault-rifle problem. It appears that future benefits for damaged professionals will be resolved in some combination of collective bargaining and litigation. Meanwhile, reducing the national mental-health toll on what are now the millions of American male youths whose parents foolishly launch them into Pop Warner and high school football lies even further on the horizon.

But that doesn't mean the United States of Football — to borrow the title of Sean Pamphilon's new documentary — can't take some interim humanitarian steps. By the US of F, I mean Fan Nation: the millions of NFL spectators who every week blithely shell out $20 for parking and $12 for stadium beer, or whatever the traffic will bear these days, not to mention the price of tickets and premium cable packages. The entertainment they . . . we . . . derive from watching men destroy each other's brains is a guilty pleasure, and it's an increasingly *conscious* guilty pleasure.

So I think it's time for fans, whether on an organized or an ad hoc basis, to take action on behalf of taking care of their fallen former heroes. They can start by imposing a simple self-tax — the price of one lousy six-pack a month at a tailgate party, for example. Pooled and well distributed, these funds would offer substantial collective relief for the scattered and isolated men and their families throughout the land who, like the ex-player cited above, could use an over-the-counter mental aid, or just some food or rent money. Perhaps the new so-called fan lobbies, League of Fans (leagueoffans.org) and Sports Fans Coalition (sportsfans.org) — which so far are concentrating on issues like public stadium subsidies and TV blackout rules — could step up to coordinate these efforts.

Just a little something to reflect on at the cusp of Week 16, the college bowl season, the NFL playoffs, and Beyoncé's halftime show on February 3, 2013.

A happy holiday season to all.

8 FEBRUARY 2013 ----------------------

Two years ago the Concussion Inc. ebook imprint published a kind of *Reader's Digest* autobiography by George Visger. Today ESPN.com published a long profile of Visger by Patrick Hruby, one of the country's most brilliant writers on sports or anything else.[1]

Hruby has it all: Visger's bone-crunching ethos; his full medical history; the battles with football authorities — including the supposedly irreproachable Bill Walsh — over being made whole for his sport-induced brain injuries; how it all fits into the chronic traumatic encephalopathy research of Dr. Bennet Omalu; and, most painfully, the toll on Visger's marriage with his wife, Kristi, who has had to protect herself and their children from a gentle giant who can fly into rages, even though they have never had an estrangement of the heart.

I did not pretend that George's ebook short was anything like a comprehensive account of his life story, which can turn so abruptly from warm to chilling. Hruby's article shows that the Kristi aspect might be the most telling omission, both in terms of personal pain and in terms of illustrating the range and fallout of Visger's challenged memory.

Last January, as we were going to press, George called me to make sure the ebook hadn't neglected to document his deep debt to Kristi and his relentless campaign to make things right for her and their family. I assured George that we had indeed included this note:

> The stress on Kristi from living with me — not know-ing who was coming home from one day to the next — blew us apart. Kristi once told me she hates what football has done to her life. Others tell me I had anger-management problems and scared my own fam-ily. The thought of this absolutely kills me, and I am determined to win Kristi's trust again. As I write this, Kristi and the kids are with her parents, and I'm at Mo-tel 6 the few days I am not on the road working as an environmental inspector and biologist.

---

1   "The Damage Done," es.pn/12z0kbJ.

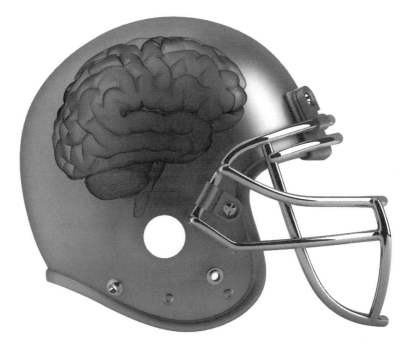

THE MICHAEL VICK AND KRIS DIELMAN FOLLIES

Al Michaels, Chris Collinsorth, and everyone involved in the production of last night's NBC telecast of the Philadelphia Eagles–Atlanta
Falcons game have to be questioning their professional pride today —
if they have any.

Michael Vick got blown up and clearly suffered a concussion.
Michaels and Collinsworth babbled about a "neck injury." Ace sideline
reporter Michele "Scoops" Tafoya told scores of millions of viewers
that Vick was spitting up blood because he "bit his tongue." And as
Vick departed for the locker room — with no visible support for his
"neck injury," by the way — the network completely whiffed on the

prime-time opportunity to educate its audience on the use of the new, supposedly John Madden–inspired, edict to remove concussed players to a quiet space.

What a disgrace.

20 SEPTEMBER 2011 ----------------------

What becomes most clear from a quick survey of the coverage of Michael Vick's concussion in Sunday night's nationally televised game is that sports journalists have little interest in reflecting on the world beyond sports. The most common thread of sociological insight by the boys in the green eyeshades is the relation between football and *fantasy football* — the internet-facilitated game-within-the-game by which fans build teams with the interchangeable parts of athletes' statistics. In the process, they "objectify" jocks, in the words of the sternest commentators. This we are supposed to take as a bad thing.

The lesson, however, does not extend to projecting the NFL's allegedly changed culture on concussion management to a broader understanding of public health.

Last September, when a Fox telecast showed Philadelphia linebacker Stewart Bradley wobbling from a concussion but going back into the game, *New York Times* concussion writer Alan Schwarz excoriated the NFL's unenforced return-to-play protocols in a news analysis.

But the problem then was the league, not how we all perceived the league. This September, Schwarz is no longer writing about traumatic brain injuries. And today's *Times* story from Philadelphia, by Mark Viera, is football-centric: "As Fans Fret, Eagles Assess Vick's Injury."

At the thinking fan's forum, the Slate-Deadspin NFL Roundtable, Josh Levin tried and failed to engage Barry Petchesky.[1] Levin began with some pointed comments on the essential un-governability of football's violence:

Roger Goodell has futzed with the league's rule-book in an attempt to ratchet down the game's most-frightening-looking injuries: hits to the quarterback's head, kill shots on defenseless receivers, blows to kamikaze special-teamers. Vick's concussion, caused when an Atlanta Falcon knocked the quarterback backward into his beefy Eagles offensive lineman Todd Herremans, reveals the limitations of this exercise. For the NFL, this was the worst kind of head injury — one it's impossible to spin as a consequence of rule-breaking.

Levin then asked Petchesky whether he agreed "with the *Concussion Blog*'s Dustin Fink that NBC was spinning for the NFL in saying that the obviously woozy Vick had a 'neck injury.'"

Petchesky didn't bite. He dismissed NBC's inaccurate reporting as football "gamesmanship, the equivalent of saying a hockey player has an 'upper body injury' to avoid putting a target on a guy who might return to the game." That Vick didn't return proved the NFL guidelines "worked to perfection."

21 SEPTEMBER 2011 ---------------------

After dropping off my son at UCLA last week, I took the 101 back north. In Westlake Village, at the tip of Los Angeles County, I passed by the Oaks Christian School, the football factory that has attracted the sons of jockocratic celebrities, including Will Smith and Joe Montana. Soon I was driving through the Ventura County city of Oxnard, which I used to know mostly from the references to it by James Garner's dad on *The Rockford Files*.

Today, Oxnard is on the map as yet another grim capital of the sky-rocketing youth disability and death wrought by our culture's insane obsession with football.

Last Friday, Adrian Padilla, a safety for the Oxnard High School team, suffered a serious concussion in the game at San Luis Obispo. After walking off the field, he collapsed on the sidelines. Padilla, 17, underwent emergency brain surgery at Sierra Vista Regional Medical Center, where he remains in critical condition.

A week earlier, at the opening game at Sacramento's John F. Kennedy High School, tight end Reginald Wilson "went up for a pass, was hit in the back, and then hit his head on the ground. Paramedics took him to the hospital and he stayed through the weekend," reports Hugh Biggar of the *Sacramento News & Review*. Coach Chris Palumbo told Biggar that Wilson "lost feeling in his legs and had memory loss," but is making a "remarkable recovery" and will soon return to school.

The day before the Sacramento incident, 17-year-old Kainen Boring sustained a traumatic brain injury from a helmet-to-helmet collision on the practice field of Bledsoe County High School in Tennessee. He was declared brain-dead a week later, and on Sunday his family took him off life support.

Young Boring's "personal trainer," Houston Thomas, told the media, "They said it was a perfect form tackle. But for whatever reason it made just a freak accident."

At last word, a second high school player in Tennessee, Tucker Montgomery, still lay in a coma.

Unless I've lost count of the necrology maintained by author/ blogger Matt Chaney, there are already 14 American football fatalities this year, including 13 kids, three of them from athletic collisions. (The other head-trauma victim was a college player, 22-year-old Derek Sheely. Most of this year's deaths seem to be heat- or heart-related, not from contact, though the disclaimer is hardly reassuring about the overall phenomenon.)

On this Sunday's NBC prime-time football game, the lions and the Christians forged on. America's poster child for glory, demonizing, and redemption, Michael Vick, got concussed in front of 24 million viewers. Announcers Al Michaels, Chris Collinsworth, and Michele Tafoya blabbed misleadingly about a "neck injury" and how Vick was spitting up blood because he "bit his tongue." Even when the trainer for Vick's Philadelphia Eagles did the right thing and led him to the locker room, per new National Football League protocols, the opportunity to speak the truth about traumatic brain injuries was lost.

In half a century of watching televised sports, this may have been the most disgraceful display by commentators I have ever seen. And that's saying a lot, since I was also in front of the tube when the same NBC wildly speculated as to the identity of the 1996 Centennial Olympic Park bomber, which fueled a witch-hunt of a wrongfully accused man.

By Monday morning, all was back to normal for the NFL and its fans ... sort of. For those who have Vick on their fantasy league teams, the main question was whether he would be good to go *next* Sunday.

25 SEPTEMBER 2011 ----------------------
In two emails yesterday to the media relations staff, I asked the Philadelphia Eagles the identity of the "independent neurologist" who cleared Michael Vick to play today. I later forwarded the message to their counterparts at the National Football League office.

There has been no response.

The NFL's return-to-play protocols following concussions, which were promulgated in 2009, state that a player "should not be considered for return-to-football activities until he is fully asymptomatic, both at rest and after exertion, has a normal neurological examination, normal neuropsychological testing, and has been cleared to return by both his team physician(s) and the independent neurological consultant."

This morning's *Philadelphia Inquirer* does not name the "independent neurologist" on the Vick case. Nor does anyone else appear to have done this. The *Inquirer* does quote Vernon Williams, medical director of the Kerlan-Jobe Center for Sports Neurology in Los Angeles, saying, "There is some evidence — and this isn't completely worked out — of what we call injury-induced vulnerability. Once the brain has been concussed, in many people it is easier for them to suffer a second concussion." Williams adds, "As you increase physical exertion and demand on the brain and body there's a risk you have in a return of symptoms. Think about the differences in your exertion level, your adrenaline between practice and a game — there's a pretty significant difference there."[2]

Chris Nowinski, of the Sports Legacy Institute and Boston University's Center for the Study of Chronic Traumatic Encephalopathy, continues his rhetorical tiptoe through the tulips, saying some of the right things while coming off more like an NFL bureaucrat than an independent public health advocate. Nowinski told *Newsday* he would have been happier to see Vick "err on the side of caution" and not play. According to *Newsday*, "Nowinski thinks the NFL is doing 'a much better job' of determining when it's safe to play. But as the NFL notes in its policy, a critical element of managing concussions is 'candid reporting of players of their symptoms.'"

My interpretation here is that Nowinski's overarching theme from the Vick controversy is the league's potential liability for a player's disability or death. And such liability is mitigated by the double-reverse protocols of consulting an unnamed "independent neurologist." The NFL is further protected if Vick did not "candidly report" his symptoms.

I would much rather have seen Nowinski say something on behalf of the millions of people who will watch today's Eagles–New York Giants game, and the millions of families of youth football players who are being misled by the opaque baloney at the NFLHealthandSafety. com website. Some of that nonsense spews from Dr. Joseph Maroon, neurosurgeon for the Pittsburgh Steelers and medical director for World Wrestling Entertainment; Maroon's University of Pittsburgh

Medical Center was involved in the review of Vick's neurocognitive tests, according to ESPN's Sal Paolantonio.

If Nowinski anywhere has joined me in calling for public disclosure of Vick's "independent neurologist," I missed it.

26 SEPTEMBER 2011 --------------------

One of the wisest observers of the Michael Vick scenario is a coach and trainer named Sal Marinello. Though not well known to readers of this blog, he is a fine example of what I call the fatalistic wing of the concussion debate — honorable sports industry professionals who don't deny the magnitude of traumatic brain injury but who, in my view, need a nudge toward recognizing that their fatalism is neither pragmatic nor acceptable when it comes to tackle football funded and promoted by, for example, public high schools.

Marinello's credentials include USA Weightlifting certified coach; president of the Millburn-Short Hills (New Jersey) Athletic Club; assistant men's basketball coach at Montclair State University; and head athletic development coach for both Mercy College (New York) men's lacrosse and Chatham (New Jersey) High School.

Here's his take, via email, on Vick: "Despite the post-game comments, anyone who watched the Eagle game could see that a) Vick certainly was not OK and b) the Eagle game plan reflected this. He also took several shots to the head that seemed to affect him. Since he broke his hand and will be out three to four weeks, he will get the 'rest' he needs."

More important, there's a longer essay on Marinello's blog entitled "There Is No Such Thing as Safer Football"; the money paragraph:

> Tobacco will never be outlawed, and neither will football. Education has resulted in fewer people smoking, and the attention paid to the risks and dangers will

probably have the same effect on football. Will fewer
kids play? Probably. Is this a bad thing? Probably not,
and for a variety of reasons.[3]

You have to appreciate Sal's candor — three days after he posted
this piece, his own son broke his arm playing football.

But you also have to wonder whether he's asking the right question.
Sure, tobacco will never be outlawed. But do high school recreation
centers include cigarette vending machines? (Sal disagrees with my
analogy. He retorts, "What would you say when parents and residents
of a town do not complain about having — or want — the machine in
the school? This scenario more aptly describes the current situation.")

Another smart observer in the fatalistic camp is Buzz Bissinger,
author of *Friday Night Lights*. I am not trying to put words in
Bissinger's mouth, but my sense is that — like Marinello and unlike,
for example, Alan Schwarz, Chris Nowinski, and Dr. Robert Cantu
— Bissinger isn't searching for an imaginary sweet spot in football
safety. Though he recognizes that the game can be improved around
the margins, he also understands that its blood sport essence is ath-
letically unalterable.

The Marinellos and Bissingers have to be careful, though, because
their positions get appropriated by yahoos and libertarian wackos. In
Bissinger's case, he has written movingly about the passion play of
football in places like Texas; if he is saying that elites are acting drastically when they seek to tamper with popular mass entertainment on
the basis of intellectual abstractions, he has a point.

But I don't think the evidence of epidemic health damage to
American youth is any more an abstraction. At the very least, the fatal-
ists and the idealists need to join forces to remove the blinders from
the deniers.

Here's your Michael Vick medical report, Version 2.2:

> Today Philadelphia Eagles coach Andy Reid said Michael Vick "has a hand contusion — not a break."
> What Vick has for sure is bruised feelings.

What he might also have is another concussion, days after being cleared by an "independent neurologist" whom neither the Eagles nor the NFL will name.

30 SEPTEMBER 2011 ----------------------
Michael Vick medical reports are subject to further review, like Vietnam War body counts. But as this article was being written, he was assuring one and all of the "100 percent chance" that he will start Sunday's game at quarterback for the Philadelphia Eagles. Since the 49ers are the Eagles' opponent, Bay Area television viewers will be complicit in the next rubber-necking twist of the increasingly grotesque Vick saga.

Reformed criminal, repentant canine abuser, astonishingly gifted athlete . . . Vick brings the whole package to the uniquely American story of industrial death and disability in sports. An unsound mind in an unsound body.

Two weeks ago, he got knocked silly when he was thrown into his own lineman in a nationally televised game. However, the NFL's cowardly partners at NBC didn't dare call it a concussion. The "C" word, you see, is nearly as taboo as "Voldemort" was for Harry Potter's friends.

After an "independent neurologist" cleared him, Vick got rushed back to the starting lineup last Sunday. My pleas to the Eagles and the NFL to provide the name of this vigilant descendant of Hippocrates went unheeded. Where did the "independent neurologist" get his medical degree, I wonder — a correspondence course in the Bahamas?

Perhaps the "independent neurologist" will apply for a position on the panel of experts soon to be appointed by the federal Centers for Disease Control and Prevention, and charged with developing national guidelines for management of concussions in school sports programs. If he's not available, then I'm sure Joseph Maroon of the Pittsburgh Steelers, the University of Pittsburgh Medical Center, and World Wrestling Entertainment — whose team carefully reviewed Vick's neurocognitive results last week against his "baseline" tests — will be glad to buckle up his chinstrap.

Even before Vick got knocked out of the game with the New York Giants by a hand injury, he was fuzzy and ineffective. "Not right today," "just didn't seem like he was 100 percent," "something was off," Fox professor of footballogy Howie Long mumbled.

Vick first complained that NFL referees weren't giving him his fair share of roughing-the-passer penalties. Then he took it back.

The Eagles first said Vick's right (non-throwing) hand was broken. On Monday, they said nah, it was just a boo-boo. Darn that ancient and unreliable X-ray technology!

So the next installment of the Vick soap opera, *As the Stomach Turns*, resumes on schedule. "From where we sit — contusion or break — Michael Vick must sit this week. He needs to get his mind and hand right," Philadelphia blogger-columnist Frank Ward wrote. From where *we* sit, in front of our TV screens, he has to play. There are NFL standings and fan-league fantasy standings at stake. I wish Vick no ill, but if more comes his way, the opportunity to educate should not be missed.

Tony Basilio, a radio sports-talk host in Knoxville, Tennessee, who has interviewed me about pro wrestling, encouraged me to keep it up. "What Philly did with Vick disgraceful," Basilio wrote on Twitter. "Somebody's going to die on an NFL field soon."

3 OCTOBER 2011 ----------------------------

Michael Vick, at the Philadelphia Eagles' news conference yesterday after his team lost for the third time in four games: "I heard Steve Young a couple of weeks ago mention when he played it was a sense that came over him and the sense was 'Over my dead body — I will not lose this game. I will not let this guy in front of me beat me.' It's just that 'over my dead body' perspective you have to take."

Metaphorically speaking only, of course.

I think.

17 OCTOBER 2011 ---------------------------

Will Carroll, @InjuryExpert on Twitter, writes the "Fantasy Football Expert" column for the *Sports Illustrated* website. His new one, as he puts it, wonders whether the National Football League's concussion policy is failing.[4]

To review the latest installment of the Michael Vick traumatic brain-injury saga, Vick returned to play yesterday just a few plays after taking a blow to the head that obviously left him groggy. (My post earlier today wrongly said Vick sat out a single play; I am correcting that.)

"If the players on the field and the announcer in the stands all thought that Vick had symptoms of a concussion," Carrol writes dryly, "it has to make one wonder what the medical staff saw that took it the other way. Perhaps it was dirt in Vick's eyes, but it's more likely that they were just blowing smoke in ours."

I care very little whether the NFL's concussion policy is working. But the national concussion policy, based on the NFL's model and representations? That's another matter. If the league's titular policy committee chairs, Drs. Richard Ellenbogen and Hunt Batjer, don't speak up about the Vick follies, they're not only over their heads — they're out of the game.

The recent concussion developments involving, in particular, Michael Vick of the Philadelphia Eagles and Jahvid Best of the Detroit Lions have reminded even the most football-centric journalists of a distressing truth: there are no independent neurologists — independent of the National Football League teams of these injured players, that is — assisting, much less being given final authority, in return-to-play decisions. Certainly not within games.

(The Eagles asserted that an "independent neurologist" cleared Vick before the game against the New York Giants, but refuse to name him or her. As for the "dirt in the eye" and "wind knocked out of him" incident last Sunday in the game against the Washington Redskins . . . forget about it.)

But there's an even more fundamental NFL medical issue that is well known but not widely or clearly reported: a number of team physicians, or the institutions employing them, have tangled financial relationships with their clubs. These call into question their ability to provide down-the-middle player diagnoses and return-to-play advice.

For example, the University of Pittsburgh Medical Center is a corporate sponsor of the Pittsburgh Steelers, in addition to being its preferred health care and sports medicine provider. (UPMC has the same relationships with Pitt sports teams, but those are intra-institutional and more intuitive.)

NFL spokesman Greg Aiello told me that sponsorships do not compromise medical care: "League policy is that team hospital, medical facility, or physician group sponsorship cannot involve a commitment to provide medical services by team physicians." Aiello also pointed out that Article 39 of the new collective bargaining agreement with the NFL Players Association details "Players' Right to Medical Care and Treatment," stating: "The cost of medical services rendered by Club physicians will be the responsibility of the respective Clubs, but each Club physicians' primary duty in providing player medical care shall be not to the Club but instead to the player-patient."

The CBA does seem to attempt to tighten the principle that a team physician's primary duty is the care of the player, regardless of contractual relationships with teams outside the four corners of the medical-services contract itself. As a pro football beat writer put it to me, "All players are allowed to choose their own surgeons for surgeries, but clearly teams like when players use the teams' docs."

The NFL's position is that there is no linkage between sponsorship contracts and medical services. But as the breaches of the league's professed new culture of "concussion awareness" and extra caution reach farcical levels — and I am far from the only one saying as much — it is worth underscoring that the NFL's heavily lawyered verbiage of doctor independence and true Hippocratic independence are not one and the same.

28 OCTOBER 2011 ------------------------------

Kris Dielman, an offensive guard for the San Diego Chargers, suffered a "violent" and "scary" grand mal seizure on the team plane returning from Sunday's game against the New York Jets, in which Dielman had returned to play following an in-game concussion.

Mike Florio of NBC Sports' *Pro Football Talk* comments:

> Here's hoping that the NFL decides in the wake of this incident to implement meaningful procedures aimed at spotting concussions and getting players who have suffered concussions out of games — and that every lower level of the sport eventually will follow suit. Anyone who has been paying any attention to high school football lately knows that the culture has not yet changed, and that as a result players are staying in games when they simply shouldn't be.

It's time for the NFL to provide real leadership on this issue, not lip service aimed at placating Congress and/or CYA memos intended to satisfy the lawyers.[5]

Hope away. Dielman told the San Diego reporters, "I just banged my head a little bit. Now I gotta deal with it."

30 OCTOBER 2011 ------------------------

The NFL is "investigating" the Kris Dielman incident. But the league can't investigate itself on the question of whether it even gives a damn. For all its outrageousness, the fact that Dielman continued on the field is just another manifestation of the ultra-competitiveness of pro football. They can all say they'll take measures to ensure that it doesn't happen again, but inevitably it will.

That Dielman was on a cross-country flight hours later, however, is something else entirely. Even I know that you don't get on an airplane in the immediate aftermath of a head injury, and I have none of the medical degrees amassed by such NFL experts as Ira "Dr. No" Casson and Joe "Sports Brain Guard" Maroon.

Does the NFL care even a little bit about the health of its players? Does anyone else care that the NFL doesn't care?

What the general public has yet to grasp is that the pro game is both better and worse on safety than the amateur game. Worse, of course — because it is competitive and dollar-driven to the exclusion of all else. But also better — because it has resources. At lower levels of football, the NFL can only be aped, less competently . . . by definition, less *professionally* . . . off the field as well as on it.

And that is why youth football is doomed. Having-it-both-ways good intentions will not save lives and protect public health.

29 FEBRUARY 2012 -----------------------

Kris Dielman retires.

---

1   deadspin.com/5841793/michael-vicks-head-injury-is-the-nfls-worst-nightmare.

2   "Vick's return comes with risks," Philadelphia Inquirer, September 25, 2011.

3   www.healthandfitnessadvice.com/the-healthy-skeptic/there-is-no-such-thing-as-safer-football.html.

4   See sportsillustrated.cnn.com/2011/writers/will_carroll/10/17/michael-vick-concussion2/index.html.

5   profootballtalk.nbcsports.com/2011/10/27/report-kris-dielman-had-seizure-on-plane-after-concussion/.

RITALIN — THE NEW GROWTH HORMONE

18 APRIL 2011 -------------------------

Here's a story you'll be hearing a lot more about in six months or six years: National Football Leaguers — followed by college, high school, and youth league football players — soon will be gaming corrupt Pittsburgh Steelers/World Wrestling Entertainment doctor Joseph Maroon's "ImPACT" concussion management software system by taking the amphetamine-family drug Ritalin before being retested to assess their recovery from head injuries.

According to one concussion expert I've spoken with, this has already started happening at the NFL level. And of course it makes perfect sense. Ritalin is the medication prescribed most notoriously for "hyperactive" kids and sufferers from ADD (attention deficit disorder), with the goal of improving mental focus. Inevitably, professional athletes and their handlers would seize on Ritalin's ability to mask the fact that they hadn't entirely "cleared the cobwebs" from recent blows to the brain. (The phrase in quotes was used last week in an admirably candid interview by Fox TV commentator Terry Bradshaw, 62, discussing how concussions during his own Hall of Fame career have proceeded to impair his quality of life.)

With the assistance of a doc with a promiscuous prescription pad — if not simply a friendly pharmacist who doesn't need to get too rigorous about the whole script thing — a player who "got his bell rung" can ease the process of identifying whether the diagnostician in front of him is holding up three fingers or four. Which, in more technologically sophisticated form, basically describes the ImPACT program that Maroon and University of Pittsburgh Medical Center colleagues have successfully pushed on the sports establishment — aided by authoritative-sounding articles in journals such as *Neurosurgery*.

Yet somehow this same class of esteemed researchers went 74 years between the 1928 discovery of dementia pugilistica ("punch-drunk syndrome" in boxers) and that of chronic traumatic encephalopathy in athletes in other contact sports. It took a Nigerian-born forensic pathologist, Dr. Bennet Omalu, to come across the latter almost inadvertently in autopsies of retired Steeler Mike Webster and others. Since Omalu wasn't well connected or sufficiently coached in how far he was supposed to go in his scientific conclusions, his follow-up articles on CTE got unofficially blacklisted from *Neurosurgery* until very recently.

Meanwhile, Dr. Maroon — pillar of the community, 70-year-old ironman competitor, supplement huckster — forges on.

Though I'm hard on Maroon, I am somewhat sympathetic about the shortcomings of ImPACT. People who know a lot more about the subject than I do say it can be a decent tool. "I use it to scare players and their parents when they get complacent about a concussion," a high school trainer explained to me. "ImPACT does establish a baseline of certain neurological functions, and it has value. But concussion management is still a subjective thing."

The problem with ImPACT is that it was overhyped as a solution, at the expense of attention that should have been paid to more central considerations: prevention and unbiased, non-commercialized basic research.

The result, I fear, is that medical paraprofessionals like this trainer, and all of amateur sports in America, will find themselves in the same pickle with concussions that we already face with steroid abuse. (That's assuming there is any more such a thing as an amateur sport — which anyone who last week viewed the PBS *Frontline* documentary on high school football might be led to question.) In recent decades, elaborate specialized cat-and-mouse protocols were set up to test athletes' urine, but the most ambitious and resourceful among them simply moved on to human growth hormone, which doesn't show up in their pee-pee.

Ritalin potentially is the HGH of concussion testing. I didn't expect ever to find myself typing the words "I feel for Roger Goodell," but the NFL commissioner has a point when he jawbones for HGH blood testing during collective bargaining with the Players Association. Now, in order to demonstrate responsibility for the health of its athletes and, more importantly, the overall gross national mental health, the league will have to do more than cite the very limited ImPACT system, along with the very limited and inaccurately targeted $20 million in research the league has spent — mostly to bolster the clinical-corporate yes men epitomized by Joseph Maroon.

20 APRIL 2011 ----------------------------

One of the seminal national magazine articles on chronic traumatic encephalopathy — "Game Brain" by Jeanne Marie Laskas in the October 2009 issue of *GQ* — suggests that the Ritalin trail also extends to the post-career agony of brain-damaged football players.

"Game Brain" tells the story of the late Pittsburgh Steelers Hall of Famer Mike Webster's descent into mental illness and homelessness, and the postmortem discovery of his CTE by Dr. Bennet Omalu. In 1997, Laskas writes, Webster met Bob Fitzsimmons, a lawyer who is now on the board of directors of West Virginia University's Brain Injury Research Institute: "Mike Webster sat down and told Fitzsimmons what he could remember about his life. He had been to perhaps dozens of lawyers and dozens of doctors. He really couldn't remember whom he'd seen or when. He couldn't remember if he was married or not. He had a vague memory of divorce court. And Ritalin. Lots of Ritalin."[1]

21 APRIL 2011 -------------------------------
Today's column by Alex Marvez, FoxSports.com's lead NFL writer, confirms our story earlier this week on how Dr. Joseph Maroon's ImPACT concussion test can be manipulated by taking the drug Ritalin and by other means.[2]

The Marvez piece draws from interviews he and former quarterback, and NFL most valuable player, Rich Gannon conducted on their Sirius radio show with brain imaging expert Dr. Daniel Amen and with Ronnie Barnes, the New York Giants' vice president of medical services. The FoxSports link also embeds Marvez's earlier video report on Dr. Amen's work.

Writes Marvez: "Baseline testing is the crux of the NFL's new 'go/no-go' concussion policy. Any player who suffers a head injury must now pass a six- to eight-minute test that measures such elements as cognitive thinking, memory, concentration, and balance. Those results are then compared to how the player scored in the preseason to determine clearance for an in-game return."

But Amen told him that a number of his player patients have said "they purposely do bad on the testing to start, so if they get a concussion it doesn't affect them." Amen also verifies that using Ritalin is another potential form of cheating. "Ritalin will work," Amen said. "It helps boost activity to the front part of the brain. In my mind, it's not the first thing I would do to rehabilitate a concussion, but it would be on the list of things to do." The doctor underscored that this practice is "not approved or a smart thing to do."

----

1   www.gq.com/sports/profiles/200909/nfl-players-brain-dementia-study-memory-concussions.

2   See "Players could try to beat concussion tests," msn.foxsports.com/nfl/story/NFL-players-could-try-to-beat-concussion-tests-042111.

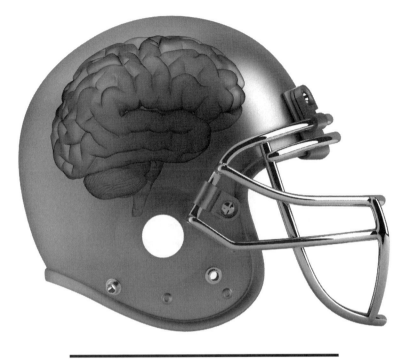

OBAMA THE KITSCH KING

This is what happens when the president-elect goes on *60 Minutes* to promote the creation of a college football national championship playoff. Last week Congressman Joe Barton, a Texas Republican, held a hearing of the House Subcommittee on Commerce, Trade and Consumer Protection on this urgent issue, questioning Bowl Championship Series coordinator and Atlantic Coast Conference commissioner John Swofford in the opening volley for what Barton is calling the College Football Playoff Act of 2009.

Among Barton's pearls of statecraft was this quote: "They keep trying to tinker with the current system and to me it's like — and I don't mean this directly — it's like communism. You can't fix it. I think they should change the name to the BES — Bowl Exhibition Series — or just drop the C and call it the BS system because it isn't about determining a champion on the field."

There was no word on whether the bill would get stuffed with such pork-barrel measures as improved health and safety standards for "student-athlete" gladiators who are pushed to the limit and beyond in 12-month-a-year training regimens, leading one to croak every couple of years.

Let's not even get into whether these unpaid mercenaries are entitled to a fair share of the profits that their prime-time spectacles produce for the National Collegiate Athletic Association and its members. No, the revenues are reserved for the "educators," the coaches, and their shoe sponsors. To operate otherwise would be too much like — and I do mean this directly — communism.

As it turns out, your correspondent knows a thing or two about the ways of the House Subcommittee on Commerce, Trade and Consumer Protection. Two years ago, the then-ranking minority member, Florida Republican Cliff Stearns, weaseled into the wall-to-wall cable TV news coverage of the murder-suicide of pro wrestler Chris Benoit by proposing legislation to force the wrestling industry to adopt Olympics-level testing for steroids.

Stearns acted after Mark Kriegel, a columnist for FoxSports.com, called for Congressional involvement in wrestling's pandemic of occupation-related deaths. Kriegel quoted my just-published book *Wrestling Babylon*, whose appendix listed 89 deaths of pro wrestlers under age 50 from 1985 through 2006 — a list *Wrestling Observer Newsletter* publisher Dave Meltzer called understated. In his press release and media shots, Stearns cited the numbers from my book, without attribution.

The crusading congressman soon lost interest in the subject and moved on to the telecommunications subcommittee, though not before making a televised appearance at a show at the Funking Conservatory, a wrestling school run by retired great Dory Funk Jr. in Stearns' Ocala district. Funk gave Stearns a signed pair of wrestling boots.

The reformist baton was passed to the chair of the Commerce, Trade and Consumer Protection Subcommittee, Illinois Democrat Bobby Rush. Coincidentally, Rush is the only politician ever to defeat Obama, who challenged Rush's reelection in the 2000 primary.

Rush huffed and puffed. In November 2007, the congressman promised hearings combining the wrestling issue with the findings in major league baseball's just-released Mitchell Report. In February 2008, the subcommittee grilled the heads of all the legit major sports leagues and their players' union chiefs — but not World Wrestling Entertainment chair Vince McMahon, who claimed his lawyer had a scheduling conflict.

"I am exceptionally and extremely disappointed," Rush said. "I want to assure Mr. McMahon that this committee fully intends to deal with the illegal steroid abuse in professional wrestling. And we hope he will be part of the solution and not part of the problem."

It was a bigger sham than WrestleMania. Though the public didn't yet know, Rush himself had to know that McMahon had already given testimony to another Congressional committee — in a closed-door interview two months earlier with staffers of Congressman Henry Waxman's House Committee on Oversight and Government Reform.

At the time, the lead investigator for Waxman, Brian Cohen, reviewed the ground rules that had been negotiated. "Our intention was that you were able to come in here without having a media circus," Cohen purred.

Never one to foster media circuses, Congressman Waxman proceeded a few weeks later to stage an internationally televised hearing to probe, among other things, whether an abscess on baseball pitcher Roger Clemens' ass cheek was caused by repeated injections of human growth hormone by his estranged personal trainer, Brian McNamee.

Clemens heatedly denied this but acknowledged that McNamee had given HGH to Clemens' wife, Debbie, prior to a *Sports Illustrated* swimsuit shoot. And the Republic survived the revelation, even if Clemens' reputation didn't.

Getting back to Obama and his high-priority war on the BCS, one of the questions arising from his first 100 days is exactly when, if ever, he will be held to account for his descents into frivolousness and bad taste. He certainly got away with yukking to Jay Leno that his poor bowling scores were like "Special Olympics." (Obama also, deservedly, has gotten high marks for changing the tone of American foreign policy, and other achievements.)

Maybe the explanation is that the president is a fox, and his BCS BS is a diversionary tactic to pacify yahoos like Congressman Barton while Obama hits one out of the park with his nominee to replace retiring Supreme Court Justice David Souter.

Whatever the outcome, this is all about the uses and misuses of kitsch in an epoch of bread and circuses. The brilliant Czech writer Milan Kundera has defined kitsch as "the absolute denial of shit." Kundera added, "Whenever a single political movement corners power, we find ourselves in the realm of *totalitarian kitsch*."

America's saving grace, so far, is that our kitsch is bipartisan.

8 MARCH 2012 — — — — — — — — — — — — — — — — — — —

The President of the United States has spoken on the football concussion crisis. With the utmost unseriousness. I'm thumbing through my thesaurus for the antonym of *gravitas*.

Interviewed last week for Bill Simmons' "B.S. Report" at Grantland. com, Barack Obama made his obligatory pitch for expanded college football playoffs and his obligatory riffs on the Chicago Bulls and March Madness. Asked about concussions, Obama allowed:

Concussions is a tough one. When you see what's happened — I actually knew Dave Duerson and used to see him at the gym sometimes, and [he] couldn't have been a nicer guy. And when you think about the toll that NFL players are taking, it's tough. Now, the problem is, if you talk to NFL players, they're going to tell you that that's the risk I take; this is the game I play. And I don't know whether you can make football, football if there's not some pretty significant risk factors.

Part of the problem is just the speed and the size of these guys now is — you watch the old tapes from the '50s and the '60s — they look like they're going in slow motion. And now, what, they just had the Combine and they're talking about some guy who is like 340, who runs a 4.8 —

In the video, the camera cuts back to Simmons — who has built a superfan persona into a mini-empire — sitting there with a shit-eating grin. No follow-up questions on the Congressional hearings that have analogized the National Football League to Big Tobacco; on the dozens of lawsuits by hundreds of retired players; on the journalistically elemental point that we are talking about the prevalence of traumatic brain injury in this sport because it affects millions of American kids at the feeder levels — in the Pop Warner and in our public high schools, where informed consent and risk are a slippery slope toward material decline of gross national mental health.

B.S. Report, indeed.

And thanks a bunch, Mr. President, for making sure your fellow citizens know that you rubbed shoulders with the great Dave Duerson, and for not wasting a moment of their time reflecting on the meaning of his suicide after years of denying the reality of the long-term brain damage suffered both by himself and by other NFL veterans whose disability claims he had helped reject while serving on the NFL retirement fund board.

In 1962, John F. Kennedy threw out the ceremonial first pitch at baseball's all-star game in Washington. After mugging appropriately for the cameras, he used his broadcast interview to plug the new President's Council on Physical Fitness. His point was to remind us that, while on this day we were all fans and spectators, the next day we would resume acting as participants in our lives and our futures. In the chief of state's expression of interest in professional sports, there was at least the faintest hint of a communal philosophy . . . some care in public presentation . . . a smidgen of intellectual and moral heft.

That was then. Obama — along with all the other cardboard-cutout presidents you and I create — is now. I've written about how I believe those who compare this moment in football history with President Theodore Roosevelt's intervention to spur the banning of the "flying wedge" 100 years ago have it wrong; these critics grossly underestimate the greater influence of football in today's culture, even as they grossly overestimate the solutions that have been proposed to fix the sport. But as Obama's useless preening on the concussion issue shows, there's another reason to be worried. Today, only celebrity-sniffing hand-wringers need apply for the Oval Office.

In the 1980s, Ronald Reagan was criticized for going years without uttering the word "AIDS." But if Obama has just shown us the best he can come up on the public health ramifications of concussions, I'd prefer that he keep his mouth shut, too.

27 JANUARY 2013 ---------------------------

Last March I gave President Obama an "F" for his first, trivial remarks on football's traumatic brain-injury crisis. In a new interview with the *New Republic*, the President does a little better. Perhaps he is emboldened by reelection, as well as more informed and thoughtful:

I'm a big football fan, but I have to tell you if I had a son, I'd have to think long and hard before I let him play football. And I think that those of us who love the sport are going to have to wrestle with the fact that it will probably change gradually to try to reduce some of the violence. In some cases, that may make it a little bit less exciting, but it will be a whole lot better for the players, and those of us who are fans maybe won't have to examine our consciences quite as much.

I tend to be more worried about college players than NFL players in the sense that the NFL players have a union, they're grown men, they can make some of these decisions on their own, and most of them are well compensated for the violence they do to their bodies. You read some of these stories about college players who undergo some of these same problems with concussions and so forth and then have nothing to fall back on. That's something that I'd like to see the NCAA think about.

Let's hope that over time Obama becomes more worried still about public high school and peewee league players, and also disabuses himself of the fantasy that blood sport is fixable for kids by "changing gradually" — or at all.

ABOUT THE AUTHOR

Irvin Muchnick is author of *Wrestling Babylon: Piledriving Tales of Drugs, Sex, Death, and Scandal* (2007) and *Chris & Nancy: The True Story of the Benoit Murder-Suicide and Pro Wrestling's Cocktail of Death* (2009). His writings have spurred Congressional investigations of health and safety in WWE and of sexual abuse and cover-up in USA Swimming. He is named respondent of the 2010 United States Supreme Court freelance writers' rights decision, *Reed Elsevier v. Muchnick*; the case, which *Publishers Weekly* called "the central rights dispute of the digital age," settled in 2014.